James D. Williams
Prov. 3:5-6

Surprised *By Grace*

A Journey to an Unexpected Reconnection

James D. Williams

Surprised by Grace: A Journey toward Unexpected Reconnection
Trilogy Christian Publishers A Wholly Owned Subsidiary of Trinity Broadcasting Network
2442 Michelle Drive, Tustin, CA 92780
Copyright © 2024 by James D. Williams
Scripture quotations marked MSG are taken from THE MESSAGE, copyright © 1993, 2002, 2018 by Eugene H. Peterson. Used by permission of NavPress. All rights reserved. Represented by Tyndale House Publishers, Inc. Scripture quotations marked NASB are taken from the New American Standard Bible® (NASB), Copyright © 1960, 1962, 1963, 1968, 1971, 1972, 1973, 1975, 1977, 1995 by The Lockman Foundation. Used by permission. www.Lockman.org. Scripture quotations marked NIV are taken from the Holy Bible, New International Version®, NIV®. Copyright © 1973, 1978, 1984, 2011 by Biblica, Inc. TM Used by permission of Zondervan. All rights reserved worldwide. www.zondervan.com. The "NIV" and "New International Version" are trademarks registered in the United States Patent and Trademark Office by Biblica, Inc. TM Scripture quotations marked NKJV are taken from the New King James Version®. Copyright © 1982 by Thomas Nelson. Used by permission. All rights reserved. Scripture quotations marked (Phillips) are taken from The New Testament in Modern English by J.B Phillips copyright © 1960, 1972 J. B. Phillips. Administered by The Archbishops' Council of the Church of England. Used by Permission. Scripture quotations marked (TLB) are taken from The Living Bible copyright © 1971. Used by permission of Tyndale House Publishers, Inc., Carol Stream, Illinois 60188. All rights reserved. Scripture quotations marked KJV are taken from the King James Version of the Bible. Public domain.
No part of this book may be reproduced, stored in a retrieval system, or transmitted by any means without written permission from the author. All rights reserved. Printed in the USA.
Rights Department, 2442 Michelle Drive, Tustin, CA 92780.
Trilogy Christian Publishing/TBN and colophon are trademarks of Trinity Broadcasting Network.
Cover design by: JP Staggs
For information about special discounts for bulk purchases, please contact Trilogy Christian Publishing.
Trilogy Disclaimer: The views and content expressed in this book are those of the author and may not necessarily reflect the views and doctrine of Trilogy Christian Publishing or the Trinity Broadcasting Network.
10 9 8 7 6 5 4 3 2 1
Library of Congress Cataloging-in-Publication Data is available.
ISBN: 979-8-89041-513-4
E-ISBN: 979-8-89041-514-1

ADVANCED PRAISE FOR SURPRISED BY GRACE

"Surprised by Grace" is a touching testimony of how God is able to take the most tragic situations and turn them into beautiful stories of His faithfulness. I was thrilled when Dr. Williams accepted our invitation to serve as an adjunct professor at Dallas Baptist University upon his retirement. When I was a seminary student, Dr. Williams was a role model for me and many others as an encouraging servant leader. His reflections and "50-Second Sermons" will now serve as an encouragement to many who are walking through the difficult season of losing a spouse and navigating the challenges that may follow.

—**Dr. Gary Cook**
Chancellor of Dallas Baptist University

My association with Dr. Jim Williams extends back more than forty years to my time at Southwestern Seminary when Dr. Williams was my professor for the Survey of Adult Education in the Church. After that time, our lives and ministries took different paths before reconnecting in recent years. What was a professor-student relationship has evolved into a colleague-friend relationship. The point is that relationships change. This book is a testimony of that reality. I believe you will be engaged and encouraged by Jim Williams' honest, transparent, and humble communication of his own *journey in this book, and perhaps you, too, will encounter surprises as you continue in a faith walk before the Lord.*

—Dr. Wayne Davis
Dean of College of Christian Faith
Dallas Baptist University

The Christian life is an adventure. If you do not believe it, just ask Jim and Grace Williams. C. S. Lewis was surprised by Joy Davidman. Jim Williams was surprised by Grace Atchley. Both were surprised by how their Heavenly Father could bring such purpose and fulfillment into their lives after experiencing loneliness and grief. To meet and know Jim and Grace is to experience graciousness up close and personal. The providential journey that brought them together is both interesting and inspirational. I highly recommend this book to anyone, but especially to those who have lost a beloved spouse and are struggling to find a new normal.

—Tommy Vinson
President of Tommy Vinson Ministries

"Surprised by Grace" is an autobiographic devotional book, but mostly, it is a book about devotion—devotion to God, devotion to ministry, devotion to family, and devotion to service. Dr. James D. Williams is my brother-in-law. He was married to my wife's sister, Jo, for fifty-nine years. Jim has been my professor and my colleague, but mostly, he is my friend. He has been a scholar of Senior Adult Ministry for his entire career, but later, we were ob-

serving his ministry as a devoted caregiver to his beloved wife in the final stages of Parkinson's.

Many would have thought this was the final curtain of the play or the last chapter of his book—but not so. It was only an intermission to the second act of the play and a precursor to the second volume of the book. This is the story of Jim and Grace as they have joined years of ministry together into a new venture of service to a denomination, to the church, and to their families. There is no retirement in the kingdom of God for these two. They are not riding off into the sunset—they are creating new prospects for surprises of God's grace. May we all be surprised by such grace!

—Dr. William A. "Budd" Smith

Founding and Distinguished Senior Fellow of B. H. Carroll Theological Institute

Jim Williams towers over me in physical stature—and over most people who stand beside him. But for me, his spiritual stature of love, warmth, and Christlikeness stands out most. Jim's journey in Christian calling is in many ways like mine. Each time, as God opened a new chapter, it seemed it was for life. But there followed a new "surprise" in God's maze of grace. Our calling, his and mine, resulted in a fulfilling colleagueship and lifetime friendship. Jim's calling and the unexpected connections of his life are detailed in this autobiographic and devotional book. At every turn in his life, I found great joy in the way he kept on saying "yes" to life and to God's calling. You will be blessed and inspired, especially by the way he was led from grief to gratitude. This remarkable story reveals how God's maze of grace brings him a new, unexpected relationship and meaning to his faith journey. He is a fine writer. "Surprised by Grace" demonstrates why I heartily recommend this book to you.

—Dr. Johnnie C. Godwin

Retired President and Director of Broadman-Holman Publishers

ALSO BY JAMES D. WILLIAMS

Guiding Adults

How to Study the Bible

Studies in Hosea

Evangelism in the Church

Leading in Public Worship

In the Company of Others

Coaching Leadership, Building a Winning Ministry Team

Mission Center Leadership, Translating Vision into Reality

Medical Mission Opportunities for Older American

DEDICATION

This book is written to validate the importance of marriage and provide advice and encouragement to those considering a second marriage. The genesis of the book was inspired by my wife, Grace Atchley Williams. To my *surprise*, she had electronically saved all one hundred fifty "50-Second Sermons" I emailed her each night following phone conversations during our engagement year. She was in Memphis, Tennessee, and I was living in Fort Worth, Texas, so to her, I give grateful thanks.

Also, I must recognize the many *surprise* moments I was privileged to experience during nearly sixty years of marriage with my first wife, Jo Clayton Williams. We raised three wonderful children. Jo was a God-sized helpmeet. We shared ministry in churches, academic institutions, and denomination entities, which also provided many global ministry opportunities. To Jo, I owe a great debt of gratitude for helping me fulfill my calling. Life for me was shaped by this wonderful partnership. Much of the professional growth and challenging opportunities that came to me, I owe to her incredible support. Her influence prompted my doctoral dissertation to be dedicated to the four "Js" in my life: Jo, James Gregory, Jami Jo, and Jeff. I forever remain in their debt.

However, I would like to dedicate this book to my parents, Reverend Otho and Blanche Williams, who nurtured me, taught me, and, as a lad, led me to the ultimate *surprise* of the grace of God. No one could have had a more godly parentage. Other than years of training at Southwestern Baptist Seminary, their effective ministry was in churches and state entities of the Illinois Baptist State Association. All that I am is molded from the strong and faithful guidance of my father and mother. From them, I learned about life and, through their influence, was led to receive God's eternal salvation through faith in His Son.

Part One of this book is an autobiography of my own discovery of God's "surprising" grace.

Part Two is all about how those surprises resulted in an unexpected second marriage. The two are intertwined. Each step of the journey has certainly been shaped by the primary influence of my dear parents, to whom I gratefully dedicate this book.

ACKNOWLEDGMENTS

In the years of reading and publishing books, I have never known one person to write a book alone. There are editors, publishers, typists, colleagues, friends, and also wives and children who have provided suggestions and encouragement.

So, I want to give a thank you to the following, all of whom deserve much credit. The dictionary says "appreciation" is "the act of estimating the qualities of people and things." It's gratefulness and gratitude.

Grace and I want to thank several persons who helped prepare *Surprised by Grace* for publication. My deepest appreciation goes to our children, hers and mine, for accepting the changes that a second marriage of parents requires. They are mentioned throughout the book, but certainly worthy of grateful support are Greg, Jami Jo, Jeff Williams, Cindy Forsythe, and Tim Atchley. They have given us, to this date, nine grandchildren and eight "greats."

Dr. William A. "Budd" Smith, my brother-in-law and Founding Senior Fellow of B. H. Carroll Theological Institute, gave excellent assistance with his critique of Part One. He, like me, is an admirer of C. S. Lewis. His suggestions helped clarify and strengthen the use of the Lewis books I reference. Many regard Lewis as the most outstanding Christian apologist of the twentieth century. His seminal writings aided me through my own grief process. His book *Surprised by Joy* was, in part, the inspiration for this book title.

Dr. Johnnie Godwin, retired president and director of Broadman-Holman Publishing, Lifeway Christian Resources, provided editing and publishing assistance. His extensive background in Christian book publishing and high editorial skills was invaluable.

Final editing was done by Steve Barber, who was the coordinator of communications and, in a staff role, did editing and speech writing for the office of the president at the Brotherhood Commission, SBC, during my tenure as president. His last employment was on the communications staff of FedEx.

Endorsers of the book include Dr. Gary Cook, Chancellor of Dallas Baptist University; Dr. Wayne Davis, Dean of College of Christian Faith, DBU; Dr. Tommy Vinson, dear friend and pastor of Baptist churches in Mississippi, Florida, and Tennessee and now president of Tommy Vinson Ministries. Lastly are Dr. William A. "Budd" Smith and Dr. Johnnie Godwin.

No man is an island. These and countless others, some described in the content, have been helpful in evaluating the purpose and structure of the book.

James D. (Jim) Williams

TABLE OF CONTENTS

INTRODUCTION..................................15

PART ONE: 21
Surprised by Grace, A Journey toward
Unexpected Reconnection

PART TWO: 53
50-Second Sermons

CONCLUSION 441

BIBLIOGRAPHY................................449

INTRODUCTION

Surprised by Grace has come about in a unique way. You discover this from a careful reading of the dedication and this introduction. The message of the book is rooted in the Biblical concept of marriage. No married couple has experienced it fully, as God intended. But, it should be a goal for marriage partners. In Scripture, marriage is viewed in a special way; it is a special world of belonging.

In phrases of rare and sensitive beauty, God's written Word sketches the oneness and privacy of marriage. "Therefore, shall a man leave His father and his mother, and shall cleave unto his wife, and they shall be one flesh" (Genesis 2:24, KJV). God had first created the woman from the man when He made Eve. But, then, He commanded them to be joined together again as one flesh. Notice that in this brief counseling session, God established an order for marriage. Before sin and its resulting selfishness entered the human race, three important marriage values were God-ordained:

Value One: When two marry, they should stop being dependent on their parents, seeking to become independent from them and becoming dependent on each mate to satisfy their needs.

Value Two: The man is the one responsible for holding the marriage together by "cleaving to his wife." The best way to say this is each is "mutually submissive" to the other, so each becomes a part of the other.

Value Three: God intended the two joined together in sexual union, to be one flesh.

The ideals of this God-ordained command are blissfully worded, "[T]hey were both naked, the man and the wife, and were not ashamed" (Genesis 2:25, KJV). They are two people seeing each other as they really are, without any shame, disappointment, or frustration. It is wise to note this command for meaningful, fulfilling sexual union producing pure delight was established before the command to bear children was given (Genesis 3:16, KJV).

God's plan for marriage has never changed. The more we accept and practice this eternal reality, the greater understanding we have of truth, as stated by the psalmist who said, "[We are] fearfully and wonderfully made" (Psalm 139:14, KJV). When marriage partners discover the many intricate details of two human bodies brought together for wonderful sensations, they are on the way to understanding God's plan for complete intercourse. Full satisfaction in marriage means physical union but also an intellectual, emotional, social, and spiritual union. Without question, the marriage bed and the union it represents is a holy place in the sight of God. As Paul would later write, "Marriage is honorable in all, and the bed undefiled…" (Hebrews 13:4, KJV).

So, this book stands on tall ground. In it, you will discover how two persons were influenced by these biblical values in their first marriages. Neither does one or the other suggest those first marriages were perfect, but they lasted "till death do us part." James D. (Jim) Williams and Verna Jo Clayton Williams were united in marriage by Jim's father on March 12, 1954, at First Baptist Church, Harrisburg, Illinois. Jo went to the Father's house on June 27, 2013. James LeRoy Atchley was married to Grace Ray Randle Atchley at Highland Heights Baptist Church, Memphis, Tennessee, on August 24, 1956. LeRoy inherited his heavenly home on November 17, 2008.

Two marriages: one lasting nearly sixty years and the other fifty-two years. After marriages of such length, is it possible or practical to even think of a second marriage? That is what *Surprised by Grace* is about. The byline tells the story. We both believe it "was a divine journey to an unexpected reconnection." This journey is highlighted in two parts.

Part One is a brief autobiography of the writer. The descriptions of the narrative reveal the many "grace periods" that shaped life's direction. Without this context, the rest of the story could not or would not have happened. As a reader, pay attention to the various "crescendos" of surprises that may await life's journey.

Part Two contains one hundred and fifty "50-Second Sermons" that embody the details of an unexpected reconnection between Grace Atchley and Jim Williams. You will discover the mystery of the journey. Relationships are reestablished, including families, friends, and the community of faith. The dialogue between Grace and Jim raised many of the questions a second marriage might represent. It is in this dialogue the reader may discover meaningful help for those considering a second marriage or a desire to renew a first marriage.

These "sermons" were written in 2015. Grace was in Memphis, Tennessee, and I was in Fort Worth, Texas. After evenings of telephone conversations, I sent an e-mail with a "50-Second Sermon" and a P.S. that highlighted friendship building in what became an "engagement year." To each were added a hymn text and medication.

After seven years of a fulfilling second marriage, we decided to share this journey with you.

The book lends itself to a devotional guide, allowing the reader to join our journey. It is our heartfelt prayer that the reading of it will be a marriage prompter and, most of all, for the reader to discover anew God's surprising grace in life and marriage.

The book is heavily shaped by many significant persons thoughtfully described throughout its pages. There are too many to list here, but without question, Grace and I owe a great debt to our first spouses, LeRoy and Jo. Without those years of bonding with them, we could not fully value what our marriage now means. We salute them, and in our marriage, we often celebrate many happy memories we each shared with our partners.

A second important influence in my years following Jo's death is C. S. Lewis. Lewis was surprised by Joy (Davidman), and I was surprised by Grace Atchley. In Part One, there is a section called "Renewing Grace." In it, many of the seminal works by Lewis are noted. It goes without saying this great Christian apologist helped me reorder life's purpose. In his book *Surprised by Joy*, he helps the reader discover the events in life that can be the source of joy.

He calls them "stabs of joy." From these and other rich sources, finding joy in grief or loss comes from a "longing" that searches for a new direction.

For Lewis, it ultimately led to Joy Davidman, his second wife. His discovery and my discovery are loaded with surprises. In no way do I pretend to be the scholar of C. S. Lewis, but I prayerfully hope God's surprises of grace will help heighten life's longings and "stabs of joy"!

No matter what may have occurred in past experiences, whether grief, disappointments, failures, or separations, learning how to receive agape love, which God makes available, can renew and transform life in every area, even touching the smallest details. As you read, you will encounter these longings and "stabs of joy." The source is agape love. It is not natural; it is supernatural. It is a love poured out on us in a beautiful abundance, seeking nothing but our highest good. It does not depend on our actions. God longs for our response, but our reaction to Him has no bearing on whether He will love us. That is already decided. He does love us and has made the irrevocable choice to love us. He proved it by giving us His Son. Happiness in life and certainly in marriage depends on this kind of love. It is never practiced perfectly, but it is the amazing way of loving *God's way*, which can become our way of loving by God's power. To Lewis and many others whose works magnify this truth, we give thanks. I hope you will prayerfully read with an understanding that connecting with God's ways of loving produces countless *surprises* and shows the way to regions of joy unending!

PART ONE:

Surprised by Grace,

A Journey toward Unexpected Reconnection

This book you are about to read has a most interesting context. It is formed from parts of a long and varied life journey. Actually, it helps define the chosen title, *Surprised by Grace*.

Your story is more important to you than mine, but I am grateful to each reader for taking the time to follow the reason for this book. This brief autobiographical sketch provides background for the book's intent.

My life has been filled with surprises. It was shaped on the farm and formed by the values of a preacher's kid. Rural Saline County, Illinois, was my birthplace. I lived on my grandfather's farm, but he had gone to the Father's house before I was born. I slept with my grandmother in a feather bed until I was four years old.

My father, until 1938, had served as a school teacher and bi-vocational church pastor. In that year, he took my mother, my two sisters, and me to Fort Worth, Texas, so he could enroll in theological studies at Southwestern Baptist Seminary. Among other things, while he studied, I learned about hot weather, horned toads, tarantula spiders, and grass burs, and I thrived on "cowboys and Indians." I was, in fact, Tom Mix reincarnated.

Those childhood Texas years taught me about both sacrifice and service. Dad worked at Leonard Brothers Department Store (two dollars per shift completed). He supplied in nearby small and rural churches for meager honoraria. He graded for Dr. W. T. Conner, one of Southern Baptist's greatest theologians and a distinguished professor of systematic theology. But, at the time, my favorite thing about Dr. Conner was not his academic stature but his attention to a shy country lad from a distant state. Dad not only graded papers and exams for Dr. Conner but also worked in his garden and tended his cows. When he went to the Conner household, I got to go along. Some of my earliest childhood surprises, now memories, are the Wild West stories and adventures Dr. Conner would voice. He was a big man with big hands, and when he pulled me onto his big lap to unravel a Western yarn, I was spellbound. There was always a new surprise.

Even though times in the late 1930s were tough and economically tight for my family, my early years in Texas taught me about a bigger world. I learned to appreciate the sacrifices required for an education. I learned that God-called persons have a Spirit-filled drive to improve their skills in proclaiming the simple yet incredible surprises of gospel good news. I learned there is a place of permanence in a world of constant transition. I began to learn how a God-life is filled with amazing and surprising graceful acts of giving and receiving. Most of all, I learned that Christ-followers are given fortress-like confidence so that difficult valleys may be crossed because the mountaintops are loaded with unbelievable surprises.

Already, you may have noticed my life has been shaped by surprises. Even though I was convinced Dad's seminary studies would keep us in Texas, God called him back to Southern Illinois and to a church he had pastored before his seminary studies, Dorrisville Baptist Church in Harrisburg. The church was a haven in a troubled world. World War II was upon us. Rationing, war bonds, weapons manufacturing, and daily news accounts of death and destruction surrounded us. Neighborhood conversation included news of young men going off to war. The tough news dealt with funerals for fallen soldiers (including the death of my best friend's father). Would Germany or Japan, as they had done at Pearl Harbor, bomb the cities of America? In the midst of a stress-ridden world at war, the church was a precious commodity for a growing boy. My father was thoughtfully compassionate to a needy congregation and to his son.

Responding to God's Grace

At the close of the war, a spiritual revival exploded in the church. It was spontaneous, starting with a testimony given by an Army Air Corps pilot who was shot down over Germany but survived. He testified that before escaping from a German prisoner-of-war camp, he had read from a pocket-sized New Testament my father had given him when he went away to war. The New Testament contained the plan of salvation, and according to his testimony before the church, given at a New Year's Watch Night Service, he "gave his life to Christ."

That supercharged testimony to the church caused an unplanned revival to break out and lasted for six weeks. My father preached every night for a month, and a neighboring pastor preached for two weeks. More than 200 people came to Christ, and on February 4, 1945, I was one of seventeen persons who responded to the "surprising" grace of God.

At ten, going on eleven, I began to grasp for the first time that being a preacher's boy doesn't save anyone. Salvation is not based on a family tradition, not through the right rituals, not through the right doctrine (faithfully taught by teachers like W. T. Conner), or the right devotionals. It is impossible for any person to save themselves. God's salvation is received upon surrender, not awarded on human effort, and, in a transforming way, God's "surprising" grace is given when there is total surrender to the indescribable, underserved gift of God through faith in His Son!

Max Lucado, in *The Applause of Heaven*, Word Publishing, 1990 (p. 32), eloquently states,

> Mark it down. God does not save us because of what we have done. Only a puny god could be bought with tithes! Only an egotistical god could be impressed with our pain. Only a temperamental god could be satisfied by sacrifices. Only a heathen god would sell salvation to the highest bidders [...] Only a great God does for His children what they can't do for themselves.

God did it for me, too!

Even though there was so much of the surprising grace of God I needed to learn at this stage of my life, salvation came to me, not because I could earn it, but because I reached out in trust and belief and claimed the matchless grace of God.

Growing in Grace

The following years of my life opened new and exciting surprises. My father was called to be pastor of First Baptist Church in Harrisburg, Illinois. It was in that church I met Jo Clayton. Her father, mother, and grandfather were active members. Her parents were fourth-generation owners of a funeral home. They were well-respected in the city and in the church. Their daughter and I were in the same Sunday school department. Soon, Jo and I became our first sweethearts. It was "puppy love" at the time. Little did I know someday, she would become my life partner. Later, after reconnecting with her during our college days at Southern Illinois University, we fell deeply in love. A bit later, I will share a word about how God brought us together in marriage and a call to ministry.

After another Illinois pastorate, my father was selected to be the first director of evangelism for the Illinois Baptist State Association. In those years, the state office was located in Carbondale. It was during those years I grew into manhood. High school days at Carbondale Community and baccalaureate studies at Southern Illinois University provided great years of intellectual and spiritual growth.

Like most "PKs" (preacher's kids), I was active in local church education programs. I gave my first speech in the Youth Education Department for Church Training. I was active in Boy Scouts and especially in a mission program for boys called Royal Ambassadors, rising through the ranks to Ambassador Plenipotentiary. In my late teens, I was selected to be a bugler and lifeguard for state R.A. camps and to be a Page at the 1950 Southern Baptist Convention. Interestingly, it was the first time the Southern Baptist Convention had crossed the Mason-Dixon Line for its annual meeting held in Chicago.

In that same summer, I attended a young men's mission conference at Ridgecrest Baptist Assembly in North Carolina. The featured speaker was Clarence Jordan, one of the early Southern Baptist leaders who focused on social justice. The impact of that great visionary led me to understand the importance of sharing the gospel with the people of every race and culture. Jordan truly embodied an incarnational witness. In a world of deep hostilities and threatening divisions, never has the deed and word of reconciliation been as urgently needed as now. Everybody everywhere has the right and need to discover God's amazing grace.

After graduating from high school, I entered Southern Illinois University as a pre-med student. My preacher dad wanted to be a doctor, but God called him to Christian ministry. Perhaps his interest in medicine prompted him to encourage me to do the same. In those years, there was a shortage of doctors, so medical schools were accepting students from a third-year pre-med curriculum. At the end of my junior year, I was accepted to medical school.

But God had other plans for my life. During my years at SIU, I was active in the Baptist Student Union and took courses at the Southern Illinois College of the Bible, which was housed in the Baptist Foundation located on the university campus. Courses in theology, religious education, and church music were taught, and in those days, up to twelve hours of credits could be applied to university degrees. The Baptist Foundation professors had an enormous influence on my life. Dr. George L. Johnson taught theology. Professor Harrell Hall was the teacher of religious education, and Dr. Eugene Quinn taught church music courses. It was Gene Quinn whom God used to help me examine my gifts and interests and discover how those gifts could be expressed in kingdom service. He enlisted me to lead music in a spring break student-led spiritual emphasis week at First Southern Baptist Church in Peoria. There were not many public decisions during the week, but I began to feel restlessness and a growing conviction that perhaps medicine was my call, not God's.

Also, that spring, the love of my life and my bride-to-be for nearly sixty years, Jo Clayton, said yes to a proposal of marriage. She quietly and purposefully joined me in a quest to verify God's call, either to medicine or a church-related vocation.

The quest for knowing the will of God for my life culminated in one of life's most important connections. Jo and I went with my father and mother to attend youth night at the late Billy Graham's St. Louis crusade. Dr. Graham's powerful sermon was directed toward young people but focused specifically on saying "yes" to God's plan for one's life. As he did frequently, Dr. Graham called persons to claim the graceful gift of salvation through faith in Christ. And he also focused on saying "yes" to God's plan for life rather than one's own. For me, it was a magnetic moment. At the time of the invitation, Jo and I joined the large group that responded. It was a benchmark moment when I realized, finally, that medicine was not His call for me. So, together, we responded to a call from God to serve in the field of Christian education. I can assure you God does call persons to medicine, engineering, and other professions. But it is important to make sure you are in the place of His calling.

I learned at last that saying "yes" to life, to each stage of life, is the responsibility of each person. In the life of faith, there is or can be a single thread that runs through all of it. It requires an affirming "yes" to childhood, "yes" to youth, and "yes" to God's call to salvation, followed by growth for life's journey. It also means saying "yes" to young adulthood, "yes" to adulthood and later adulthood, "yes" to extreme old age, and finally "yes" to death that ushers us into the eternal "yes," "But then shall I know as also I am known" (1 Corinthians 13:12b, KJV).

The main purpose for you, the reader, is to grasp the truth that through God's graceful plan, we are chosen people. The follower of Christ is chosen by God, but in man's freedom, he or she must say "yes" to God. Likewise, one does not choose Christian ministry. It is chosen by God, but the chosen one must say "yes" to such a call and be faithful to its claims to the end of the age. That pathway is packed with amazing surprises.

Maturing Grace

Maturing grace at work in a believer's life often prompts surprising changes and redirection. My pre-med studies at Southern Illinois University included a few of the liberal arts courses that seminaries then required for admission. Most of my previous studies included science and math courses. Having fully committed to a divine call to Christian education ministries, I was aware that seminary training was necessary. Early in my response to God's calling, I felt a strong interest in pursuing a course of study that would prepare me to teach in the field of Christian education.

So, in the fall of 1953, I sought help from university counselors and was referred to the chairman of the Sociology Department, who I learned was an active Methodist layperson. He helped me put together a B.A. degree plan with a sociology-psychology double major and a chemistry minor, salvaged from the pre-med curriculum. One of the elective courses in sociology was a brand-new course taught by the chairman, entitled "Problems in Aging," a study in gerontology. It was to become, in many respects, a life prompter. I relished my studies, and a vision for lifelong growth and development became ever so real. Those last years of study at SIU helped me prepare for graduate theological education.

Later, when I enrolled for studies in the School of Religious Education at Southwestern Seminary, little did I know God would soon open a door for me to have a faculty post. At the time, the school was the largest such school of religious education in the world. And, as with the seminary, it was accredited by the Association of Theological Schools and Southern Association of Colleges and Schools. Dr. J. M. Price founded the school in 1915 and retired the year I enrolled in 1956. Having earlier taught his classic book *Jesus the Teacher*, I was totally impressed with his biblical understanding of the importance of following Jesus's teaching methodologies. Little did I know he would take me under his wing and become both a hero and mentor.

In the Southern Baptist denomination, Dr. Price and Dr. Gaines Dobbins, the founder of a similar school at Southern Baptist Theological Seminary, stand as respected leaders in the formation of schools providing graduate training in Christian education. The touch with Dr. Price is an example of how God's graceful acts of new relationships blossom and mature in the life of His followers.

So it was in the fall of 1956 that my wife, Jo, God's first gift of a life mate, along with our sixteen-month-old son, James Gregory, and a black cocker spaniel puppy, left Southern Illinois for Fort Worth. I was highly anticipating studies at Southwestern, and also, being a second-generation student, I felt at home there. It was Southwestern that was to become the primary influence in our lives. During those first years, I was blessed to serve Ash Creek Baptist Church in Azle, Texas, and then at First Baptist Church, Hurst, Texas, as Minister of Education. During my master's degree studies, I was asked to be a teaching fellow and grader. When Dr. Lee McCoy, a Southwestern teacher, developed an illness, I was asked to teach all his courses for a semester. The churches I served graciously allowed me time from busy staff responsibilities to teach part-time and complete my master's and doctoral studies.

One of life's surprising "grace moments" was a decision by the seminary administration to offer me teaching opportunities, first as a teaching fellow, later as a contract teacher, and then elected to a faculty post as an instructor in adult education. The president of the seminary, Dr. Robert E. Naylor, interviewed me for a position that had been recommended by Dr. Joe Davis Heacock, the dean of the School of Religious Education. I am still amazed that such a wonderful career opportunity was opened to such a young guy. I spent twenty-two years on the faculty, rising through the ranks to full professor and having the opportunity to develop a complete curriculum in adult education for the master's and doctorate levels.

In addition to the thousands of Southwestern Seminary students enrolled in the master's and doctoral levels, large numbers chose courses offered by the Department of Adult Education. It was an honor to see many select specialized training in ministries to and with adults. I was also honored by many highly qualified students majoring with me in adult education for doctoral-level degrees. Joe Eugene Autry, a missionary to Korea, was the first to enroll. Later, he did finish his degree, but because of missionary furlough schedules, he graduated later. Bob Ivan Johnson was the first to complete a major in my field and earn an Ed.D. (Today, he remains one of life's best friends.) He and the other doctoral majors were highly competent and went on following graduation to attain high levels of academic and ministry-centered careers. Also, a highlight of that period was the privilege of serving as Associate Dean for Advanced Studies, directing the Doctor of Education (now Ph.D.) and Doctor of Ministry with a major in religious education degrees.

Supported fully by my wife, Jo, those years brought untold personal and professional development. It was during these years our daughter, Jami Jo, was born (1959), and our second son, Jeffrey Clayton, was born (1961). When I completed the doctoral dissertation, I dedicated it to the "Js" in my life: Jo, James Gregory, Jami Jo, and Jeffrey Clayton. No dad could ever be more blessed with a loving wife and children than me. As has often been said, my Jo was not only a wonderful wife, mother, and supportive ministry helpmeet, but she also had her own ministry in music. Her gifts were expressed as a church organist/pianist and were devoted to the churches we served.

Wonderful, surprising, surpassing grace blessings came to us during those years. Two productive sabbatical years doing post-doctoral studies at Kings College, London University, broadened my world. Dr. Louis Drummond, well-known to the Baptist world, was then a professor at Spurgeon's College, located in London. It was his influence that first directed me to King's College. Likewise, it was his influence that made it possible for me to serve as guest faculty at Spurgeon's College in a fourth-year program in Practical Theology. This program was developed by Spurgeon's College so students completing the three-year Bachelor of Divinity curriculum could add to their preparation for ministry. Dr. George Beasley Murray, the president and principal, led the faculty to add a fourth-year curriculum in Pastoral Theology because the prescribed London Bachelor of Divinity program of study was very logic-centered, without studies in pastoral care skills. Many Spurgeon students stayed for the fourth year of study.

Both in 1970–71 and 1977–78 sabbatical years, the influence of Spurgeon's College and the personal friendships with the faculty and students helped me extend my appreciation for the global Baptist witness. Most notably, the profound influence of George Beasley-Murray and Louis Drummond in shaping and broadening my life story cannot be overstated. I owe much gratitude to Reverend Frank Cooke, at that time pastor of Purley Baptist Church and also chaplain at Spurgeon's. He deserves commendation for shaping my understanding of church growth. Christian ministers from many countries have trained at Spurgeon's College, a remarkable institution. For the benefit of the reader, the biography of Dr. Charles Haddon Spurgeon, written by Louis Drummond, and for whom the college was named, is considered by many to be the very best of many biographies on the life of this great biblical scholar and preacher.

At King's College, London University, my studies in philosophy, church history, and European adult education methodologies advanced my readiness for productive academic endeavors. During a second sabbatical year back at King's College, I was privileged to do a directed study in medical ethics and a student practicum at St. Christopher's Hospice. There, I studied the seminal work of Dr. Cicely Saunders, longtime director of this model hospice institute. It was through this experience I began developing skills in caring for dying patients and learned how hospice settings enabled persons to live fully until physical death. After such a mind-stretching experience, I developed courses in death and dying. At Southwestern Seminary, colleagues from other cooperating universities, healthcare entities, and my own seminary colleagues helped me conduct a national conference on hospice. Also, I was privileged to serve as a consultant in the establishment of the first hospice in Fort Worth at what was then St. Joseph's Hospital (a hospital-based home health model). This, in turn, opened doors of colleagueship with the North Texas State University Center for Studies in Aging and the Baylor University Gerontology Institute. A joint agreement among these three schools provided me with adjunct professorships at Baylor and North Texas. Later, joint degree programs with Southwestern and these schools gave seminary students interested in varied ministries with older persons the opportunity to receive joint degrees from the seminary or one of the other schools.

Maturing, "surprising grace upon grace" doesn't stop! My chief fulfillment was working with Southwestern Seminary students called to Christian ministry. Specialties in adult education were developed, including ministries with college students, single and married adults, and senior adults. Assisting me were colleagues Dr. W. F. Howard and Dr. Brittan Wood. However, other doors of opportunity opened.

Productive writing made it possible to author ten books and numerous professional and academic articles. My role at the seminary opened many doors in Christian education, in and beyond the Southern Baptist Convention. Also, I was blessed to serve as an interim minister of education in seven churches, including a six-year interim at Gambrell Street Baptist Church, where, once again, I am now a happy member. It was in that church I came to love and value a true hero and friend, Dr. Lloyd Elder, a much-beloved former pastor of the church. Later, when he became president of the Sunday School Board of the Southern Baptist Convention (now LifeWay), he asked me to join him as his associate and later to serve as Executive Vice President. The decision to leave Southwestern was one of the most difficult decisions of my life.

Even for someone interested in management, the bureaucracy of a large agency was a challenge, but I reveled in it. It was a great laboratory of learning. All the theories I had proposed in the classroom were tested. During the 1980s, the Baptist Sunday School Board, with its seventeen program assignments from the Southern Baptist Convention, was growing rapidly. Sunday school enrollment in the churches reached an all-time high; all the other programs enjoyed significant growth. My position's influence gave me untold, surprising opportunities in the Baptist world, including leadership and participation in the Baptist World Alliance. It was a happy time of personal and professional growth.

In the midst of a strong sense of fulfillment in ministry, my spiritual roots and clear understanding of God's purpose were tested. Regrettably, changes in my Baptist denomination brought forth an effort to capture control of Southern Baptist Convention agency leadership.

At the Baptist Sunday School Board, this led to the ultimate dismissal of my "Barnabas brother," Lloyd Elder. Over a two-year period, several hundred other Baptist Sunday School Board employees were also terminated.

One of the haunting regrets of my life was to experience the outcome of changes in Southern Baptist Convention life and national entities. Godly persons lost ministry employment and, in my judgment, were sacrificed on the altar of political control. (Others would argue differently.) Nevertheless, the abrupt onset of fragmentation in my beloved Southern Baptist family was a testing time for me and drove me back to my theological roots. Even then, God spoke in powerful ways, reminding me of His sufficient "amazing grace."

In a time of spiritual quest, new doors of opportunity opened. I was offered a post at the Southern Baptist Theological Seminary. Dr. Gary Cook, a beloved former student, discussed with me a post at Dallas Baptist University. I was invited for an interview with the president's search committee at Missouri Baptist College. A dear friend recommended me to the president's search committee at Southwest Baptist College. However, the search committee at the Southern Baptist Convention Brotherhood Commission was convinced I was the person needed to lead this historic agency.

My first thought was they needed someone from the Brotherhood network, but as our conversations and prayers continued, I began to realize my whole life was pointed toward this challenging ministry opportunity. The circle of life had expanded, and the connections made it complete. The trustees wanted to get an executive with a strong management and educational background. God said yes, and so did I.

For me, the seven years at the Brotherhood Commission were a ministry capstone. First of all, the agency was never politicized. In my election dialogue with the trustees, I told them if at any time an adversarial relationship between the trustees and the president developed, they would have my immediate resignation. I pledged if they worked hard to keep convention politics out of the operations of the commission, I would pledge to be a servant leader in shaping the purpose, the character, the programs, trustee-approved policies, and major goals and strategies. To their credit, they freed me to lead, and not one time was the commission troubled by politics. I was empowered by the trustees to be a transactional leader and to model team leadership, create a new vision, lead by example, celebrate victories, and keep on reaching.

Our main focus was lay mission involvement. Working with the Woman's Missionary Union Southern Baptist Convention, we challenged lay people not only to learn about missions but to do missions through "experiential missions' education." This included programs like World Changers and expanded involvement in Disaster Relief and Baptist Builders, seventeen different lay mission fellowship groups, including the Baptist Medical Dental Fellowship. At a high point in a single year, more than 70,000 volunteers served in lay mission endeavors around the world. That was a significant contribution to global missions. By 1996, annual enrollment and participation in all Brotherhood Commission age-graded and volunteer programs reached an all-time high of 750,000.

My years of leadership at the commission were akin to Camelot! At every turn of the corner, we experienced God's surprising grace at work in and through those lay people committed to His service. I had by my side a most competent staff. They included Executive Vice President Mike Day, Vice Presidents Jack Childs and Douglas Beggs, Assistant Vice President Rusty Griffin, and Executive Assistant Grace Atchley, in addition to a host of department heads, editors, artists, human resources officers, and distribution personnel, all of whom served faithfully. It was a very happy time!

1996 was also the year the Southern Baptist Convention Executive Committee received a recommendation from an appointed committee to consider downsizing and restructuring the nineteen Southern Baptist Convention boards and commissions. Several agencies would be eliminated, and others would be merged. The Brotherhood Commission, the Home Mission Board, and the Radio Television Commission were to become a newly proposed North American Mission Board. The top-down decision came as a shock and surprise, not only to those entity presidents but to the trustees of the Brotherhood Commission. Though we worked together to challenge the decision on its program and business merits, the decision to downsize prevailed by a vote of Southern Baptist Convention messengers.

Again, even in the midst of surprising change, God opened new doors of opportunity. I was, at the time, near normal retirement age. The Baptist Medical Dental Fellowship, since its beginning in 1977, had been housed at the Brotherhood Commission headquarters in Memphis. The founding executive director, Henry Love, was retiring, and the search committee determined I was the logical replacement. The BMDF executive board had already decided to keep the headquarters in Memphis rather than move to Atlanta, where the North American Mission Board was to be housed. Baptist Memorial Hospital in Memphis offered free office space, and for eight wonderful years, I was blessed to serve with more than 1800 quality physicians, dentists, and other healthcare professionals who, to this day, provide medical mission service around the world.

Helping to manage the myriad of programs and services of this grand organization was a spiritual blessing I could never have imagined. Having started my university training as a pre-med student and then being called into Christian ministry, it was as if God had brought me full circle. My earlier interest in medicine came to full fruition, serving with the BMDF. The thirteen Memphis years were "amazing grace" years.

In 2004, retirement at age seventy took me back to Fort Worth to be near family and friends, but a primary purpose for the Texas return had to do with health issues with which my wife, Jo, was struggling. In the early 1990s, she was diagnosed with Parkinson's disease. Her symptoms were slight during the first years of her illness, but it was now impossible for her to function without help. She was also losing some of her treasured gifts, including her noted musical gifts. My primary mission changed from a ministry to the masses to a ministry to one. I was to be her hands and feet in a way the two of us could remain as independent as possible for as long as possible. In a very real sense, she had been a prime example of self-giving love, and I will forever marvel at the way she modeled grace and gratitude in the midst of pain and loss.

Eternal Grace

The move back to Fort Worth provided a reconnect with all three of our children who lived there. In fact, our daughter, Jami Jo, and her two children lived with us for some of those years. Almost immediately, I was offered an adjunct professorship at Dallas Baptist University, thanks to Dr. Gary Cook, Dr. Bernie Spooner, and later Dr. Steve Mullen. Also, a teaching opportunity was extended at the newly formed B.H. Carroll Theological Institute, where I am listed as a Distinguished Fellow. The next years of my life deserve much more time than this life overview could and should describe.

In summary, it was a time for us to return to our earlier roots in Christian ministry, including church membership at Gambrell Street Baptist Church. This beloved church was and is for me like the apostle Paul's "Philippian church." He loved all the churches he served, but the church at Philippi was special, and Gambrell Street is like that for me. In those nine years, Jo and I were bolstered in our faith and received spiritual support from a loving congregation and special care from our beloved pastor, Dr. Clyde Glazenor, as well as the rest of the church staff.

I refer to those nine years because they represent the last years of Jo's life. Her memorial service was held at our church on July

3, 2013. Parkinson's had taken its toll, but all of our close family stood at her bedside when she went to the Father's house. To this day, I thank God for a hospice setting that helps dying patients "live" to the very moment of physical death. Also, I thank God for my church family, who surrounded me with compassion. Jo had a good death, and our believing family is grateful we could join with Job in saying. "For I know that my Redeemer lives, And He shall stand at last on the earth; And after my skin is destroyed, this I know, That in my flesh I shall see God" (Job 19:25–26, NKJV). God has promised those who believe in His Son, the Lord Christ, that death is not the end. The exit of physical death is the entrance into the heavenly home prepared for all who believe. This great eternal truth is the result of His eternal grace. No believer should be surprised by this truth because it is the promise of God that "whosoever believeth in him should not perish, but have everlasting life" (John 3:16, KJV).

Renewing Grace

The Grace Journey Continues

The reality of "renewing grace" is the primary reason for writing this book. Jo's death had caused my life to turn shades of gray. Even though there was time to prepare for her homegoing, when it happened, it left me without my primary mission, namely, caring for her. In earlier years, my mission involved the masses, but in the last years, it was to her. There were other outlets. My students and colleagues at Dallas Baptist University, where I have served as an adjunct professor since 2005, were extremely responsive during the initial grief process. I also had family and wonderful friends supporting me. Having taught courses in death and dying, I was academically armed to deal with her death. Busy day activities, church worship with Gambrell Street Baptist Church, and other ministry opportunities, along with social interaction with neighbors, brought encouragement. And most importantly, my three children, who lived within a twenty-minute drive, surrounded me with warmth and devotion.

I was also wonderfully supported by Jo's sister Cloe. Her husband, Dr. William A. (Budd) Smith, was a longtime faculty member at Southwestern Seminary and one of the founding faculty at the B.H. Carroll Theological Institute. Our family has been very close for many years. Their son, Todd, is like our fourth child. And during the years we served in Tennessee, Budd and Cloe were "nearby parents" for our Texas kids. The Smiths could not have been more helpful in providing emotional support for me.

But in spite of such wonderful support from these and others, there was an emptiness in my life. And when evening came, I felt so alone and, at times, lost. I took comfort in reading through the many grief books in my library. It was a help but did not relieve the emptiness of purpose that plagued me. I had a big house and a beautiful lawn, with trees and flower beds that had been my therapy during Jo's illness. There was golf I dearly loved. There were church activities providing ministry opportunities. There were dearest neighbors, like Paul and Nancy Penny, Larry and Ginger Cohen, Aubrey and Susan Stratton, Larry and Paula Larken, and other neighbors I could mention, all of whom spoiled me rotten!

I am forever indebted for all the help given, but it did not take away the emptiness. There were a number of lifelong friends—men and women whom I felt close to, and some of them had shared a similar grief experience. Some were related to us in our ministry years. I was strengthened by their loving friendship and correspondence.

However, nothing took away the emptiness and loneliness that plagued me. Jo and I had been married for nearly sixty years, and since I was not quite twenty when we married, my whole adult life was filled with companionship. My days were filled with activity, but it was in the evening that I felt strongest this sense of loss. One of the most poignant and inspirational books I have read (and reread) was by C. S. Lewis, *Surprised by Joy*. This great British philosopher and teacher, the author of some of the greatest books of the Christian faith, had walked my same pathway. Words are inadequate to describe the enormous contribution of Lewis. Truly, he remains one of the world's best Christian apologists.

I could spend pages recounting some of Lewis's most poignant and inspiring books. (There are volumes of material that analyze the ultimate meaning of his writings.) For any reader treading the same life challenges or struggling with the ultimate meaning of Christian faith, I would point you to C. S. Lewis. His books *Mere Christianity*, *The Problem of Pain*, and *A Grief Observed* are three of his best sellers. I knew from his writings after experiencing the loss of a mate that he was renewed by the life and giftedness of

Joy Davidman, a God-sized person if I could so explain! To read Lewis is to grasp the significance of finding joy in the midst of suffering and grief. For in that emptiness, there is also an intense "longing" (*Sehensucht*) that searches for new direction and fulfillment.

I resonated with Lewis's feelings of emptiness. It seemed much of my own purpose had been lost. I had found escape in other avenues, but much of it left me feeling guilty that I had not been a better husband. I had to look inwardly, but I needed also to look outwardly and accept the reality of a different life experience. Some of what I imagined was good therapy for handling my care for Jo also haunted me because it took time away from her. Every caregiver needs care, I know, but now I was agonizing over what I might have done better. Guilt was eating at me, and I knew this to be self-destructive. This life change was part of an eternal plan. I finally concluded Jo was in God's hands, and in better moments of discernment, I knew it to be true. But grief not processed can end in desolation. That was happening to me. Down deep, I knew I needed to refocus on God's call for my life and was determined to live the rest of my own years as productively as possible.

One of the best examples of processing grief constructively is found in Lewis's book, *The Problem of Pain*, a deeply personal confession of the pain he endured following the death of his first wife. Those who have walked this same pathway can fully identify with his pain. It was the same for me. But his great loss brought new victory for this great Christian apologist! In his book *Surprised by Joy*, he identifies and describes "the events that occur in life which can be the source for discovering true joy." For him, this joy was so good and so high it could not be exclaimed with words, and he indicates he is struck with "stabs of joy" throughout his life. I take this to mean he was able to see the pain or suffering of life as the open door to new joy. That happened to Lewis as it has happened to me.

As it has often been said, "Every exit in life is also an entrance." For the believer, this "entrance" is filled with God-given opportunities to find new sources of joy. It is helpful to see it happening for Lewis and for you and me.

Let me provide an illustration. For example, perhaps you have observed it in the movie *Shadowland*. In the movie, the inference is made to Joy Davidman being a "surprise of joy" for Lewis.

She was later to be his partner in a second marriage for him. Those who look back at his life see her as a part of those "surprises." Later, after their marriage, she edited his final draft of *Surprised by Joy.* She became a new "good" and intensely powerful source of joy for him. I knew it was the kind of joy God wanted for me, regardless of whether I got a second marriage or not.

God never intended for His children to live in emotional pain and agony. There is a questing or longing inside of us to seek and find new joy, especially for those dealing with intense grief, such as the loss of a marriage partner. "Where do I go from here?" is a necessary next step in handling grief.

It goes without saying that God used the writings of C. S. Lewis to reorder my life purpose. I remember vividly saying to God,

"Going forward, everything I have and everything I hope to be is in Your hands!" That moment was like the conversion experience I had as a young child or the time when Jo and I responded to a call to Christian ministry at a Billy Graham crusade. It was a moment filled with certainty. There was a new kind of future waiting. There was "joy" promised. It has been true for millions; it was for C. S. Lewis, and it certainly could be for me. I needed to claim it as part of God's plan for the rest of my life. As Paul Harvey was known to say in his magical and probing news accounts, "Page two for the rest of the story."

All of that brings me to the title of this book. There are others with the title *Surprised by Grace*, but none with the byline I have given. The inspiration for the title comes from C. S. Lewis. His life was surprised by joy, including his second wife, Joy Davidman. The joy that comes from serving the Lord cannot be bought with money. For nearly sixty years, my whole life was energized and filled with joy because of Jo. No one could have had a more helpful, supportive, and loving mate.

For both of us, the twenty-two years she suffered from Parkinson's were extremely challenging. With the help of good treatment, her first twelve years were fairly normal. But the last ten brought increasing physical restrictions. She handled it better than I, even to the moment of her death. In it all, I tried my best to surround her with love and support. No marriage is ever perfect, but ours was a "haven of happiness," rejoicing in all God's blessings to us. Jo loved life and loved me and her family. Add a "y" to her name, and you have *Joy*! She was the prime source of earthly joy.

Down deep, I realized the "joy of the Lord" is my strength. That is an eternal truth, and I needed to reclaim such strength. And, in those innermost moments of longing, I kept asking God to restore my joy. Like Lewis, God brought "new stabs of joy" into my life. He "surprised me with Grace." I never thought I could or would consider remarriage, but God had other plans. It may be true for you, the reader, but it certainly was for me. Let me explain.

It would require pages of introduction to introduce her, but the essence is developed in the content of the one hundred and fifty "50-Second Sermons" contained in this book. So, let me briefly introduce you to Grace Atchley. She is beautiful inside and outside. I discovered her God-sized personality several years ago when she served as my executive assistant during the years I was president of the Brotherhood Commission, Southern Baptist Convention. Later, when I served as Executive Director of the Baptist Medical Dental Fellowship, she served in a similar role. For thirteen years, we worked together. Highly gifted, graced with godly compassion for others, and a brilliant manager of detail, she could not have been a more willing servant to the people she served. Those who served with us in these two entities can verify her skills in managing the details of an executive office. Trustees and board members alike would echo this same praise.

No one is perfect. But everyone can model Grace Atchley for trying to make everything as near to perfect as it could be. During the years after our service together, she handled the illness and later the death of her first husband, LeRoy, and the care of an aged mother with amazing grace and compassion. LeRoy went to the

Father's house in 2008. Her mother lived until age one hundred and two and made her home with Grace after LeRoy's death. She passed away in 2014. For years, Grace served our Lord and the Baptist world with vigor and personal commitment. Her service began as a secretary of a local church, then a state Baptist convention, the Brotherhood Commission, and the Baptist Medical Dental Fellowship, and for ten years at the Mid-South Baptist Association. In all, she completed forty-seven years of faithful service within the Baptist family.

You have learned how we met. Let me take a moment to capture the reconnection of our lives. After my retirement from BMDF in 2004, we were in Texas and did not get to see much of Grace and her family. However, she kept us posted on family news of BC and BMDF personnel. We also exchanged seasonal greetings. Our contacts were business and family-related. When LeRoy died, my wife, Jo, was having back surgery, so we were unable to go to Memphis for his funeral. A scheduling conflict kept me from attending her mother's funeral in 2014. Later that year, my son Jeff and I agreed to be volunteers at the 2014 PGA golf tournament at Valhalla Golf Club in Louisville, Kentucky. I drove to Louisville, but Jeff went by air. On the way to Louisville, I thought it would be a considerate thing to check on Grace, extend my sympathy due to her mother's death, and catch up on Memphis news. We met for dinner at a restaurant near her home. It was a happy time for me to relive wonderful years of Christian service together and share meaningful personal memories.

The following weekend, my daughter Jami flew to Louisville

to visit her daughter and my granddaughter Rebecca and her family. Since I was there by car, Jami bought a one-way ticket to Louisville and drove back to Texas with me. On the way back, we stopped and had lunch with Grace. It was a pleasant visit, and I was reminded again what a beautiful, charming, and godly woman Grace is. From the visit, we promised to keep in better touch, and we did! A pretty regular telephone exchange began, and the rest of the story is told in this book.

Those telephone visits, mostly at night, developed in both of us a desire to know each other in a more personal manner. And by the end of 2014, it was becoming obvious our friendship was taking on a new meaning.

I had been praying for relief from the guilt and burden of not being as helpful to Jo during the last of her days. And yet, those around me were expressively complimentary of the way I served her needs. I had found some relief from a remarkable life friendship. However, the pages of the past needed turning.

I had asked the Lord to give me a fresh start in fulfilling His call in my life. Without question, He did so through reconnection with Grace. Her testimony as a caregiver to her husband and mother made me very aware our experiences were similar. Having worked with her for thirteen years, I was most confident of her "grace gifts." Now, in the midst of my own need, she was filling a void that had produced in me an emptiness and feeling of loss.

Those telephone calls were becoming nightly, and beginning the first of January 2015, I began following up the call with a

"50-Second Sermon" e-mailed to her, and I ended the scriptural message with a P.S. intended to personalize the inspirational theme of the conversation. It was a first step in giving the Lord the right kind of relationship-building and character development with a significant other.

At this point, let me share with you the idea of a "50-Second Sermon." Before my bedtime, I would e-mail Grace a sermon largely based on the evening telephone visit. I typically selected a sermon idea from many I had developed earlier. During my years of teaching classes at Southwestern Seminary, I began my classes with a 50-second devotional thought followed by a prayer. The original idea of these "50-Second Sermons" came to me from Dr. Roger Carstensen, a former president of Atlanta Christian College. I met him from our mutual involvement with the National Interfaith Coalition on Aging. In addition to his years of ministry, he did a local radio program in which he shared 50-second sermons. During my years at Southwestern Seminary, I began my classes with a "50-Second Sermon." Many of them were from Roger and were (and are) used with permission. He sent them to me regularly. A lot of those I reworked, adapted, and reused with my students as a way of highlighting the very profound yet practical truths of the Holy Scripture. Some of those revised sermons I shared with Grace.

I gratefully acknowledge the creative efforts of Dr. Carstensen in providing the source of ideas in many of the sermons. Others are new creations inspired by the telephone conversation of the evening call, and still, others are ideas and themes from respected devotional literature. The hymns chosen for each devotional thought are traditional Christian hymns. I have chosen special verses, not necessarily the entire text. The hymn writer is cited but not the music composer. The meditations reflect the sermon theme. In any event, I am indebted to these and other cited sources for the ideas expressed. Each "sermon" emphasizes a special moment of conversation Grace and I shared in the nightly telephone visits. They could be dated starting the first of January 2015. However, for the purpose of this book, I have chosen to number each one so the reader can use the devotional material at any time.

In summary, the main points of this life history and the introduction of Grace Atchley are to demonstrate how God's abundant grace is offered to each who willingly receives it. I would also hope our experiences will be helpful to those considering a second marriage. Certainly, biblical truths and values are important to any marriage, regardless of the number. The sermons were written during the year of our engagement to show how God brought two lives together.

Our private wedding occurred on January 2, 2016, at First Baptist Church, Nashville. Dr. Lloyd Elder, assisted by his wife Sue, performed the wedding ceremony. Longtime friends Jack and Ann Knox were witnesses. Since the wedding was private, we planned receptions for family and friends in Memphis at Germantown Baptist Church and, for family, friends, and colleagues in Texas, a reception at Gambrell Street Baptist Church in Fort Worth. In the concluding chapter, I provide more details about the ceremony.

From that good hour until the writing of this document, Grace and I have been doubly blessed by a host of family and friends. Without question, we have continued to be surrounded by graceful acts of friendship and support. Some of the dynamics and spiritual influences that brought us together are contained in these brief devotional themes. Hopefully, as a resource, the reader will discover insights and pathways onto a higher plane for life and living. Whether a first or other marriage, they are best fulfilled in a commitment to God's design for marriage.

Most of all, my prayer is the reader will allow God's Spirit to challenge his or her own personal devotion to the Creator of all things. It is the Creator and Father God who is the ultimate Giver of grace. Like the healing grace described by C. S. Lewis, it is eternally enshrined in Holy Scripture, His highest expression of such grace. It is exemplified by the gift of His own Son, whose sacrifice, death, and resurrection are the ground and source of all redemption and are the pathway to eternal life. I hope you have or will claim this reality. And, as you read these devotional thoughts, be open to this matchless grace God makes available to you.

PART TWO:

50-Second Sermons

An Introduction to the "Sermons" along with Reasons for Sharing Them with Readers

The year 2015 is the time frame for this book. The "50-Second Sermons" start next in sequence.

They provide the conversations from nightly telephone visits. The interaction with Grace Atchley leading to a proposal of marriage is the primary reason these "50-Second Sermons" (devotional thoughts) were written.

Nearly every night of the year, we talked on the telephone, especially when we were separated, her in Memphis, Tennessee, and me in Fort Worth, Texas. During the year, we had brief visits with each other. On three occasions, we met in Arkansas, a halfway point for the two of us. Some weekends, I would drive to Memphis, and on special holiday weekends, she would fly to DFW. Until December of that year, she was still working as the executive assistant to the director of the Mid-South Baptist Association. Her work schedule limited real time together, so the telephone became our world. The calls were late at night, and I must confess there were nights when I deprived her of valuable sleep time. After our calls, I would e-mail her a "50-Second Sermon," followed by a postscript. Grace, as is her organized manner, kept an electronic file of each "sermon." So we had in an electronic storehouse one hundred and fifty of these devotional moments shared within the context of getting to know one another in a more personal way.

After these years of being bonded as husband and wife, we decided to share our story with others. Because of the fragility of marriage in the current cultural environment, our intention is to share our story with those who long for marriage to be built on a strong God-like foundation.

No marriage is ever perfect, but marriage can become increasingly perfect when based on mutual submission from one to the other. The biblical view of "till death do us part" is the thread and theme for a lasting marriage. It is never within the perfect will of God for marriage to be broken for any other reason. Sometimes, in His permissive will, circumstances inevitably lead to separation and divorce. Often, marriage breakup is the result of infiltration and intrusions from the outside world battering down the private kingdom of marriage.

This kingdom is not to be taken lightly. If the gates of marriage are left wide open, intruders will walk right in. Enemies of the important relationship of marriage are selfishness, lust, pride, self-pity, resentment, anger, bitterness, and jealousy. When the gates are open wide, temptations of all kinds tempt one or both marriage partners to leave the kingdom. Marriage is on a solid rock when both partners safely trust in each other.

Such is a God-like marriage. Two people should long to start right or start right over again, with mistakes of the past put aside and wrong ways of doing things shattered in an instant. A first marriage or a next marriage can be shaped nearer to the heart's desire if both partners truly commit to following God's perfect design for the union.

There is a great book written by Ed and Gayle Wheat entitled *Intended for Pleasure*, Fleming H. Revell Company, 1977. I have used this book in premarital counseling. In the last chapter, they echo the realities of a God-sized marriage. The writers say, "You can change the world of your marriage should it not now be the private kingdom of God's design." It can be the intimate, precious relationship of total commitment it was meant to be.

> The resources for this change come from the power of God as made available in the Lord Jesus Christ. He can enable you to love and give, to forgive and ask forgiveness, to forget yourself in your caring for your loved one. He can cause you to be sensitive to each other's needs, always on the other's team, always seeing what is admirable in the other, and never focusing on faults and failures. He will make marriage ever more intimate and harmonious and full of delights" (*Intended for Pleasure*, p. 208).

This is the kind of marriage Grace and I have tried to build. It is based on our own past experiences. We both had happy first marriages. There were obvious mistakes, but each of us had determined to keep the vows made at the marriage altar. Learning from the experiences of the past, we now have the intention and spiritual commitment to build a second marriage based on God's pattern.

The rest of the book represents the thoughts and feelings energized by this purpose. Or, as C. S. Lewis says, "Be strengthened and empowered by those 'stabs of joy' which inspire new directions." So come join us in the conversations of our engagement year and the devotional aspects, which we hope will inspire you to fulfill your own destiny.

As you read through each "sermon," let the theme, the scripture source, the hymn text, and the meditation challenge and inspire your own thoughts and commitments. Hopefully, you will find this a helpful guide for daily devotional time. The sermons are approximately fifty seconds long. Reading the P.S., the hymn text, and the meditation adds a minute or two. If you are married or considering a second marriage, our prayer for each reader or partner is to be guided into a more mature understanding of love and marriage. As a well-known song reminds the hearer, "the two go together." That's what being *surprised by grace* is all about!

Devotional One:

Telephone Conversation

I did not include a sermon, but you can read what I said to Grace in our first serious telephone conversation:

I am sure the flutes we purchased in Little Rock are truly beautiful in your china cabinet. But even more beautiful is the thought of toasting in what I truly want to be "our friendship-building year." Whatever 2015 brings, it will be sweeter, brighter, and now more complete because we have committed to "journey through it" together. I can only imagine the excitement and fulfillment that will be ours as the year unfolds. My thoughts run deep when I think about the awesome interconnectedness of our lives to realize what we are to be in the future we are now becoming. Our past is not as remote and unrelated as it may have appeared. For us, right now, it is a significant part of a mosaic in the process of two separate lives being completed. Like the flutes, it is beautiful to behold. So, as we talked on the phone tonight and as we toast the New Year, let us, with imagination, envision the pieces of our lives being shaped and placed. Looking back and going forward, I am giving grateful praise to our great God for His guiding hand in creating the mosaic of our lives. For in the final analysis, it is what God has made of us, not what we have made of ourselves, that makes all the difference. That will be in my grateful heart as we ask God to bring us together in friendship, whatever the outcome.

Devotional Two:

"Broken, It Is to Begin"

There is something final about a broken vase. Recently, my housekeeper dropped a vase given to me by students at Hong Kong Baptist Seminary in 1983. She was mortified, but I insisted that accidents happen. Try as you will; you could not glue it back together as it was. Cloisonné is difficult to repair. The vase is like Humpty Dumpty, "All of the king's horses and all the king's men [can't undo the damage]." Ecclesiastes describes the finality of death as a pitcher broken at the fountain. The death of Jo still plays heavily in my mind and heart as a reminder of this reality. You experienced the same thing with the loss of your first mate, LeRoy (has it been eight years)? The death of a mate is high on the stress chart. We have managed to survive the assault of grief as pieces of our lives were shattered. They were broken but not destroyed. A huge chunk of life has been defined by the lovely vases that represent, for us, the beauty of first marriages. What is to become of those broken pieces? There is a purpose for them, one can imagine, but what?

On the other hand, the shortage of writing material in the old days led scribes to write on clay shards. So, a vase could become a tablet and be a grocery list, a calendar, a poem, or a letter to a cherished friend. Psalm 51 tells us the sacrifice acceptable to God is a broken and contrite heart. Before God, to be broken is to begin.

Where better could redemption be written than on the fragments of a broken heart?

P.S.: Grace, I am glad our great God is always in the "mending business." I thank Him most gratefully for the way He seems to be putting the pieces of our lives together. In our case, it is a mosaic of color, forms, shapes, past relationships, and the hope we have for an anticipated, joyful future. We are being pieced together, not by Humpty Dumpty, nor all of the king's horses and men, but by God's creative potter's hand!

Hymn: "Spirit of the living God, fall fresh on me […] Break me, melt me, mold me, fill me. / Spirit of the living God, fall fresh on me" (Daniel Iverson, "Spirit of the Living God").

Meditation: Father, You are forever in the mending business! Even though, at times, life's circumstances bring change, You place broken pieces of fragments into a recreated, beautiful work of art. Renew us by the power of Your Spirit and by the eternal sacrifice of Your Son. Amen.

Devotional Three:

The Heaviest Burden

One of life's best friends stopped by to see me soon after Jo passed away. He wanted to make sure I was okay. But as is always the case when he visits, we ended up chatting about many things. Before he concluded his visit, he said, "I have an insight to share."

"I used to hear we are supposed to leave our burdens at the foot of the cross, and Christ would take care of them," he told me. "That's not enough. We need to get on the cross with Him."

My friend went on to explain he had no interest in suffering for its own sake. He felt to be crucified meant to give it all, whatever the cost. "To choose the cross sounds strange," he added. "But it works." We shared Paul's cry in Galatians 2:20 (KJV), "I am crucified with Christ; nevertheless I live; yet not I but Christ liveth in me."

My friend had discovered the cross is not meant to lift occasional burdens. I am the biggest burden. The cross is meant to lift me.

P.S.: Grace, there are mistakes in our lives we might want to forget. How glad I am that in confession, God's amazing grace has covered them all. On the human side, the memory of those mistakes may linger, but the pain is taken away when we truly deposit them in the redemptive forgiveness of God's grace. One of the empowering things about our relationship with God is He allows us to participate with Him in bringing purpose, order, achievement, and fulfillment to our lives. Learning from the mistakes of the past allows us to work with God in shaping a better future. As we move forward, sharing a growing relationship, let us resolve to let the cross of Christ's sacrifice be the ground of our relationship. How good it is that the "foot of the cross is wonderfully level"!

Hymn: "But drops of grief can ne'er repay, the debt of love I owe, Here Lord I give myself away, "Tis all that I can do. / At the cross, at the cross where / I first saw the light, and the burden of my heart rolled away. / It was there by faith I received my sight, / and now I am happy all the day" (Isaac Watts, Ralph Hudson, "At the Cross").

Meditation: Dear God, past experiences we might change, like the death of spouses. We rejoice; we do not have to carry those burdens alone. That is true because Your Son paid the price for man's salvation. Thankfully, all of life's sorrows and difficulties can be deposited in the empty tomb of Christ's bodily resurrection. Because He lives, we, too, may live joyfully now and forever. Amen.

Devotional Four:

Stain, Go Away

Robert and I were friends in high school, largely because we were in the same boat. He was an eccentric made to be pushed around. I was shy but also took up for the underdog. Bob lived with his grandma. Unfortunately, she was an odd recluse considered half crazy.

Early one morning, when we met in the hall at adjoining lockers, Bob said, "Grandma wants you over for dinner sometime. When can you come?" I told him Friday.

Friday morning, my new friend Gary said to me, "The folks told me I could invite you out to our farm for the weekend!" Remembering what I had heard about all the exciting things happening on their farm, I went to a phone, called my folks, and arranged to go home with Gary right after school. Then I saw Robert. "Hey, something came up. I can't go to your place tonight." His face fell, and I knew he was hurt. "But Grandma wants to meet you! She's been getting ready all week!"

"Sorry," I said. "Tell her something came up."

Why, after all these years, does this haunt me? In 1 John 4, we learn if anyone does not love, he walks in the shadow of murder. Did I kill something that Friday morning?

P.S.: There are some experiences in life that last forever. That is one. We talked about mutual friends who have dealt with self-image issues and have often been ignored by people who could have been helping friends. I hope your day is filled with opportunities to befriend the "Roberts" in your world. Our lives have experienced similar mistakes, some based on careless, selfish choices. How good it is to be open with each other. In building a relationship, it is so important to be mutually inclusive of one another's feelings. It is so easy to look past your own faults and focus on another's. May we determine to help each other be true and steadfast in every aspect of behavior.

Hymn: "Savior, teach me day by day, / love's sweet lesson to obey; / Sweeter lesson cannot be, / Loving Him who first loved me […] Teach me thus thy steps to trace, / Strong to follow in thy grace, / Learning how to love from Thee, / loving Him, who first loved me" (Jane E. Leeson, "Savior, Teach Me Day by Day").

Meditation: Dear Lord, remove the guilt of selfish choice and give us the wisdom and courage to love ourselves and others in the same selfless way You love us. Amen.

Devotional Five:

Belief and Test Tubes

Pierre Curie said to his wife, Marie, "I can't believe it. There's got to be something there." In the night, they walked to the drafty shed they used as a laboratory.

Pierre and Marie Curie believed there was an undiscovered element, one giving off energy. They secured a freight car of pitchblende from Bohemia. Shovel by shovel through bitter winter and summer, the Curies reduced their ore. When they finished, they found that nothing, nothing at all, remained on the dish of wax that was to hold the substance of their dreams. As they neared the laboratory, Pierre complained to Marie, "You left the light on!"

"I didn't. I never do." They opened the door. Out of revealing darkness, a tiny film of radium pulsed and glowed.

Hebrews 11 tells us faith is the substance of things not seen. The Curies found an unseen substance, but belief got there before the test tubes did.

P.S.: Grace, this has a message for all, but especially for us. It grows out of a message from Roger Carstensen. In essence, for us, it means that faith and belief in the "rightness" of our reconnection precedes the light and life we know is there. You have been instrumental in helping me find a new purpose. Thankfully, already, there is light to brighten the journey and also a beacon of light that marks the destination. I do believe that!

Hymn: "Creator God, we give You thanks for all the glories You have made, Help us to see You in Your work, the Artist in the art displayed. / What You have given us in trust is only ours to rightly use. Deliver us from thoughtless deeds that plunder, pillage, and abuse. / Help us to see Your draftsman's hand in every blade of grass, each flower, that we may stand in awe before the work of Your creative power" (Betty Anne J. Arner, "Creator God, We Give You Thanks").

Meditation: Masterful Creator, as new horizons develop, may we, like the Curies, not give up until You, the source of all truth, lead us on till our work is complete in Thee. Amen.

Devotional Six:

Upstaged by a Conversion

I was told of an incident when the brothers at a Midwestern college fraternity decided to stage a revival for the spring talent show and dance. It was intended to be a "farce and spoof." A sophomore with a flair for the dramatic was the preacher. A honky-tonk pianist and a few good voices rounded out the choir and cast. Practice for the "big night" was scheduled in the fraternity basement.

The service began. The basement rocked with "Amazing Grace" and "On Jordan's Stormy Banks." The preacher really got into the act. The boys grinned. They had it made and were sure the act was a winner.

"Just as I Am" was the invitation hymn, and the janitor, who had been watching and listening in the shadows, came forward and accepted Christ. The act never recovered. The boys could handle anything but God's saving power. One who had gone to Sunday School recalled Philippians 1, where Paul said even those who preach Christ insincerely are cause for rejoicing. When this story was related to me some years ago, it caused me to say, "The news of Christ is greater than any tongue that can propose it."

P.S.: Regardless of where life takes us, may our highest devotion be the power and truth of the gospel, however and wherever it is proclaimed. I am so glad we share common values. Though we are vastly different personalities, we share a common mission. We also lived and learned together in the corporate responsibilities required of us at the Brotherhood Commission, Southern Baptist Convention, and the Baptist Medical Dental Fellowship. That relationship required mutual trust, cooperation, and commitment to advance the work of God's kingdom. Through those thirteen years, we developed a common trust in each other, and quite frankly, if there ever was a major disruption or anger toward each other's performance, I do not remember it. It was a sweet time of fellowship in doing God's work. That spirit of togetherness was enhanced by the very best kind of people within the organizations we were privileged to lead. Well over 1,800 physicians, dentists, and other health care providers stand as proof.

Hymn: "God moves in a mysterious way, / His wonders to perform, / He plants His footsteps in the sea / and rides upon the storm [...] Blind unbelief is sure to err / and scan His work in vain; / God is His own interpreter, / and He will make it plain" (William Cowper, "God Moves in a Mysterious Way").

Meditation: Saving Lord, we thank You that the truths of the gospel are forever powerful and complete, however they are presented. Give us a willing spirit to share them with everybody, everywhere. Amen.

Devotional Seven:

The Gift of a Discord

I have a former colleague and dear friend, Dr. C. L. Bass, who is an accomplished musician and composer. As a matter of fact, he is brilliant, and his compositions are award-winning. C. L., a retired professor of music theory and composition at Southwestern Baptist Seminary, told me he often gets his finest compositions by hitting discords. He views discord as an opportunity. He says, "If you get the right notes before and after a discord and maybe rearrange it a little, it isn't a discord anymore."

First, it becomes interesting, then beautiful, then fantastic.

In Jeremiah, God is compared to a potter who, making a clay vessel, takes any flaw that shows up in the clay and uses it to make a new vessel. God improvises with human weakness and makes it interesting and unique, something the angel helpers could never have thought.

Praise the sweet genius of a God who takes the discords of my life and even my rebellion, shapes a lamp to light the world, and writes a song that brings harmony back into my life. Thanks for the beauty and strength of divine life that evokes from me such a symphony of emotions, including praise and gratitude for the gift of your friendship and support. What could possibly blossom from this kind of friendship? What new song could be written from within the strings of the heart?

P.S.: I do not want to get ahead of the subject. But I have strange and wonderful feelings that our relationship has the promise of a tighter friendship. I am not saying it may go as far as marriage. Because you and I have both said, "I would never consider remarriage as a realistic option." But it is becoming obvious we do need some time to consider what is to become of this friendship. The writer of the proverbs says, "A friend loveth at all times" (Proverbs 17:17, KJV). One thing is for sure: there is reason for our friendship to grow in strength regardless of the next steps it takes.

Hymn: "Savior, Thy dying love Thou gavest me, / Nor should I aught withhold, Dear Lord, from Thee: / In love my soul would bow, / my heart fulfill its vow, / Some offering bring Thee now, Something for Thee. / Give me a faithful heart, Likeness to Thee, / That each departing day Henceforth may see / Some work of love begun, / Some deed of kindness done, / Some wand'rer sought and won, Something for Thee. / All that I am and have, Thy gifts so free, / In joy, in grief, thro' life, Dear Lord, for Thee! / And when Thy face I see, / My ranson'd soul shall be, / Thro' all eternity, Something for Thee" (Sylvanus D. Phelps, "Something for Thee").

Meditation: Thank You, Eternal Composer of Creation, for always bringing harmony from disharmony. Though our carelessness and the result of sin cause discord, Your hand holds the eternal baton. May Your song of salvation and deliverance be our song all day long. It is in the name of our conductor, the Lord Christ, we pray. Amen.

Devotional Eight:

Albert Einstein Goes to School

We have been told that when Albert Einstein was a child, his teacher considered him a moron. The classes were too advanced for him.

He was supposed to add numbers, but he could not figure out what "one" was. He was supposed to learn to read the face of the clock, but Albert couldn't fathom time. His teachers wanted him to measure his desk, but Albert couldn't understand space. He had trouble with the alphabet, but he saw mysteries written everywhere. So Albert educated himself as seemed appropriate.

God tells Moses that for a special project, he is to seek out those who have appropriate skills. The writer of Hebrews says, "For the word of God is living and active. Sharper than any double edged sword" (Hebrews 4:12a, NIV). Do you have an able mind? Ask the simplest questions you know, and you'll be right where Albert Einstein started.

P.S.: Grace, going forward, I would like us to experience concomitant growth, resulting in generativity and a sense of mutual fulfillment. There are no points beyond that striving and growth are not called for. So, like Einstein, let us keep asking the simple questions about faith, hope, and love and let God surprise us with the unimaginable. The sense of friendship we are experiencing is a mystery worth a lifetime of exploration and is built on the faith and hope we have in each other, growing from years of working together. We truly can say God, in His providence, has brought us back together.

Hymn: "Set our feet on lofty places; / Gird our lives that they may be; / armored with all Christ-like graces, / in the fight to set men free. / Grant us wisdom, grant us courage, / that we fail neither man nor Thee! / That we fail neither man nor Thee!" (Harry Emerson Fosdick, "God of Grace and Glory").

Meditation: Dear Lord, remind us You are the source of all truth. Likewise, may we realize wisdom comes from learning how to apply knowledge. There is always so much more to learn. So, may intellectual and spiritual humility bloom in our lives, producing a lifetime desire to keep asking the simple questions. We ask this in the name of the author of all truth, the Lord God. Amen.

Devotional Nine:

The Logic of a Whetstone

Jo and I were married during spring break of my junior and her senior year at Southern Illinois University. Our first abode was a mobile home. We parked it on a vacant lot next door to Mr. Thompson, a lifelong deacon in our college church. He prepared the site with new gas lines and sewer connections just for us. Behind the site was a very large garden area that our new landlord maintained every year. I admired his gardening skills and noticed he spent an inordinate amount of time keeping his tools sharp as a razor. "Makes hoeing and digging like a vacation," he confided.

So it seemed like half the time, he was sharpening hoes, clippers, shovels, axes, etc. He honed with tender, loving care. Then, he loosened the soil and sliced through weeds in a relaxed, rhythmic way.

I have often thought since those days, Mr. Thompson would have enjoyed a talk with the wise man of Ecclesiastes, who said, "If the iron be blunt, and he do not whet the edge, then must he put to more strength" (Ecclesiastes 10:10, KJV). The Lord Himself likes sharp tools. Hebrews 4:12a (NIV) says, "The word of the Lord is sharper than any double-edged sword."

Ever notice that the man who is really sharp grins a lot as he works?

P.S.: Grace, I will use this "sermon" early in the new semester with students at Dallas Baptist University. The idea for it came from Roger Carstensen. The experience is mine. I will never forget Mr. Thompson. In addition to his generosity, he taught me discipline and industry. I will do so to remind us all that a lazy mind, like dull tools, makes endeavor much harder. When I count my blessings in having you not only as a friend but as a fellow co-worker, I am also very grateful you have kept your skills sharpened, and because of it, your work has not been drudgery but a joy! It's just one of a multitude of things that have not gone unnoticed by this grateful admirer and friend.

Hymn: "To the work! To the work! We are servants of God, / Let us follow the path that our Master has trod; / With the balm of His counsel our strength to renew, / Let us do with our might what our hands find to do. / To the work! To the work! In the strength of the Lord, / And a robe and a crown shall our labor reward, / When the home of the faithful our dwelling shall be, / And we shout with the ransomed, / Salvation is free!" (Fanny J. Crosby, "To the Work").

Meditation: Dear Father, forgive us when laziness and indifference keep us from being productive. Sharpen our tools so we can labor in Your vineyard and, therefore, produce quality fruits of righteousness. In the name of Jesus, who prayed in the garden, "Not my will, but Thine be done." Amen.

Devotional Ten:

Flat Feet but a Caring Cinderella

It had been a rough evening. At a prayer meeting on a Wednesday night before Thanksgiving Day, November 25, 1959, my wife Jo, the mother of our three wonderful children and also our church organist, signaled to me from the organ bench that her "labor pains" had started. We rushed home after church and headed for the hospital. Few people understand what an expectant father goes through when his wife is in labor. Trying to stay awake, wondering whether it is a boy or a girl. Of course, I'd have been happy with another boy. We already had one, and I'd come to love him as a father should love a son. I never figured I was the kind of egotist who had to have a girl to show off a boy and a girl. Before the days of sonograms, I had already said to Jo we would have a little girl on Thanksgiving. I had prophesized that our first son, Greg, would be born on Father's Day. Sure enough, he was. So I was convinced that, as predicted, the second was a girl.

The nurse's aide shuffled down the hall. Life had been hard, and her feet hurt. They should have, as she asked a good deal of them in a hospital setting. From hard use, those feet were flat as boards and sounded her approach as she walked down the hall of the waiting room.

I heard her plod up and saw those flat feet near my chair. At

4:40, Thanksgiving morning, I looked up. She was smiling. "Congratulations! You have an eight-pound, six-ounce baby girl." We named her Jamie Jo, after her father and mother.

Paul said in Romans 10:15 (NIV), "How beautiful are the feet of those who bring good news." Paul was right. She brought good news, and her feet were the prettiest I ever saw!

P.S.: Now, adding up my three and your two makes five. Between us, we have a basketball team. Some of life's best news moments were the announcements of the birth of our children. I love mine dearly, and I know from many conversations you love and adore yours. And, I will never forget, when you were serving as an executive assistant in my office, the excited scream you released when you learned your daughter Cindy was pregnant with Nicole. Your two and my six grandchildren make eight "grands." (And since this writing, I have been blessed with six great-grandchildren.) I want to give praise and thanksgiving for each one of our flesh and thank God for the feet of those who delivered the good news of their birth. But thanks also to our first spouses who teamed with us to nurture them through their formative years.

One thing is sure: I want to be the kind of father who mirrors the love of God for each one of them.

Hymn: "O perfect Love, all human thought transcending, / Lowly we kneel in prayer before Thy throne, / That theirs may be the love which knows no ending, / Whom Thou forevermore dost join in one. / O perfect life, be Thou their full assurance of tender charity and steadfast faith, / of patient hope and quiet, brave endurance, / with child-like trust that fears no pain nor death" (Dorothy B. Gurney, "O Perfect Love").

Meditation: Help us, dear Lord, to thank You for extending life through the flesh of our flesh. We rejoice in the mystery of physical birth but also celebrate the birth of Your own Son, who forever brings "new birth" to everyone who believes in Him. Let our feet go everywhere proclaiming the way of Your eternal life through Jesus Christ. Amen.

Devotional Eleven:

Higher than Ararat Is God's Redemptive Plan

In Matthew's Gospel, we read that John the Baptist sent disciples from prison to ask Jesus whether He was the Christ. Jesus replied, "Go back and report to John what you hear and see" (Matthew 11:4, NIV).

I read some time back about another expedition headed for Mount Ararat to find remnants of Noah's Ark still rumored to be on the peak. Success, it was believed, would initiate a worldwide revival through proof that the Bible is indeed true.

As my friend Roger Carstensen opined, "The trouble is that the central message of the Bible is too big to be proved by a piece of an old ship, an apple from Eden, or a feather from an angel's wing." The Bible teaches us God loves you, me, and every creature and changes sinful men by the power of the gospel through repentance and faith in His Son, the Lord Jesus.

One sinful human life, cleansed and reborn, is bigger news of God than the seas that once dashed the sides of Ararat.

P.S.: For all of us who believe, there is no greater proof of redemption than the joy that comes from seeing someone come to believe. Whether gifted as an evangelist or not, nothing is more rewarding for the believer. The two of us have been blessed to be a part of a global witnessing network of churches, associations, state conventions, and denominational entities that worked together to proclaim the grandest news of all. My prayer is our Baptist family will return to a more cooperative global response to evangelism and missions. Billy Graham taught us how to cooperate with other Christian bodies so committed to sharing the gospel. In the meantime, thanks for the common love we share in the Lord's redemptive mission.

Hymn: "If you will only let God guide you, / and hope in him through all your ways, / whatever comes, He'll stand beside you, / to bear you through the evil days; / who trusts in God's unchanging love / builds on the Rock that cannot move. / Sing, pray, and swerve not from His ways, / but do your part in conscience true; / trust His rich promises of grace, so shall they be fulfilled in you; / God hears the call of those in need, / the souls that trust in Him indeed" (Georg Neumark, Catherine Winkwort, "If You Will Only Let God Guide You").

Meditation: Father, You have produced countless miracles through the ages. When everything else fails, let our faith be in You. Noah's Ark reminds us that You intended for Your world to be free from evil and hate. When it so became, it was destroyed at Your hand, save for Noah, his progeny, and the living things of earth. Your rainbow of promise is expressed in the eternal plan of redemption embodied in the gift of Your Son, the Savior of the world. Let everyone believe that good news. Amen.

Devotional Twelve:

Childhood Glimpses of the Morning

My maternal grandparents lived in the country in Pope County, Southern Illinois. It was great fun visiting them, especially in the summertime. In addition to a huge garden, there were wooded acres of pastures with horses, cows, and goats, eliminating the need for a weed eater. There were always new ventures to fascinate this curious grandson. Was it especially true when I could visit by myself without interference from my two nosy sisters, Phyllis and Sandra! Early one morning, I got up earlier than usual to look for a lost toy; my bare feet were dew-drenched and cold in the grass of a June morning.

Then God turned up the rheostat of the morning. Diamond drops of moisture on the grapevine at my grandpaw's back porch flamed into the jewelry of the sun. A tiny cup of dew shimmered on a grape leaf. I drank it, savoring with my tongue a flavor unlike anything I ever tasted.

In Psalm 110:3b (NIV), we read, "From the womb of the dawn you will receive the dew of your youth."

Poor Ponce de Leon! He hunted in vain for the fountain of youth. It takes a child to drink dew or admire diamonds strung on a spider web. If the old explorer had tried dew on a crystal morning, he'd have been young for that moment at least.

Be a child of the morning, and you'll be young all day.

P.S.: We have teased about our age and laughed about exploring a new relationship in the so-called "later years of life." To be quite candid, it has been like the morning dew, not that we need to be children again. But drinking from the fountain of fresh, meaningful friendship has put the fires of youth in my veins. So there, Ponce de Leon!

Hymn: "Morning has broken / like the first morning, / blackbird has spoken / like the first bird. / Praise for the singing! / Praise for the morning! / Praise for them springing fresh from the Word! / Mine is the sunlight! / Mine is the morning / born of the one light Eden saw play! / Praise with elation, / praise ev'ry morning, / God's recreation of the new day!" (Eleanor Farjeon, "Morning Has Broken").

Meditation: Creator and Redeemer, everywhere one turns in nature's grandeur, there are constant reminders You made it all. How could anyone, on beholding the design, not believe in a great and powerful designer of creation? Thank You for speaking to us, not only in nature but also in the redemptive price You paid for man's sin by the shed blood of Your Son. Amen.

Devotional Thirteen:

The Shared Prescription

Sunday dinners were family occasions when I was a kid. One Sunday, nostrils twitching with the flavors teasing the air, we kids gathered around Mom's feast. How can you improve on fried chicken, mashed potatoes, cream gravy, fresh green beans, creamed corn, and hot rolls? There was one empty chair. Five-year-old Sandra, my youngest sister, was missing.

A quick hunt of the premises located her. Attired in her Sunday dress, she was sitting in a pool of mud, waving a soup bone and talking to herself. Mom was horrified. "What are you doing," she screamed. "Creating woman," Sandra replied.

My father's sermon that morning had cited Genesis 2, where God formed Eve from a rib of Adam, who himself had been put together out of the dirt. Sandra made a good try at applying Dad's sermon, but a woman had already created her in the womb from a fertilized egg from Dad's male sperm, in keeping with God's procreative laws.

Deep in our bones, men and women are the same. Whatever makes a man a real man or a woman a real woman comes from the same prescription.

P.S.: Isn't it time our society and our world regarded men and women as equals? Obviously, they are different in function, but they are the same flesh. Their procreative tasks are different, but in that process, like love and marriage, you can't have one without the other. It takes a man and a woman to make a man or a woman. The prospect for happiness in marriage is based not on male dominance but rather on the beautiful metaphor in Ephesians 5, where the Greek word translated "submission" literally means "mutual submission one to the other as unto the Lord." The presence of Christ relativizes all earthly relationships.

I am so glad that I am a man and you are a woman, but in the eyes of God, we are equal in His sight. Going forward, we should relate to each other through this eternal truth in all things.

Hymn: "In Christ there is no east or west, / in Him no south or north; / but one great fellowship of love / throughout the whole wide earth. / In Him shall true hearts everywhere / their high communion find; / His service is the golden cord, / close binding all mankind. / Join hands, then, children of the faith, / Whate'er your race may be; / who serves my Father as a child is surely kin to me. / In Christ now meet both east and west, / in Him meet south and north: / all Christly souls are one in Him / throughout the whole wide earth" (John Oxenham, "In Christ There Is No East or West").

Meditation: Dear Father, help Your created order to recognize each person is uniquely made and, therefore, equally precious in Your sight. May the love and compassion of our lives replicate the unlimited favor of Your gift of forgiveness and boundless grace. Amen.

Devotional Fourteen:

Words are Deeds

You have to admire the American mind. For example, take the ability to forget sermons. That is why, prompted by the influence of Roger Carstensen, I do the 50-second variety. I have successfully forgotten thousands of long sermons, but occasionally, I have a problem. Some of the longer ones grip me. For example, I remember a sermon a student preached in a homiletics class at Southwestern Seminary. He said his high school class motto was "Deed, not words." He has wised up since. "Words are deeds," he said. I never forgot that insight.

In Isaiah 50:4 (NIV), we read, "The Sovereign Lord has given me an instructed tongue, to know the word that sustains the weary." There is a weariness for which words from a friend are the sole refreshment.

Such words are a gift. They breathe the energy of the Creator, who said, "Let there be light." And there was light.

P.S.: Grace, there is a destiny that makes us brothers and sisters. None goes his way alone. And all we send into the lives of others comes back into our own. So, it is incumbent upon the believer to be careful with the use of the tongue. I can honestly say one of the attractive things about you has nothing to do with the physical. That special trait is a gift of compassion for others. I have marveled at your sense of acceptance and forgiveness. No wonder you have been sought after by others. People are naturally drawn to those characterized not by the "me" but the "we." God has chosen us to be proclaimers of His new creation of love and acceptance of all people.

Meditation: Great Healer and Friend of Man, empower us by Your eternal Spirit to let our words become actions of love and kindness to everyone, not that they belong to us, necessarily, but because each person is a child of God and worthy of respect. May our tongues speak praise, always! Amen.

Devotional Fifteen:

Sailing in the Desert

Isaiah 43:14–21 tells of a God who specializes in the unexpected. He makes a path of dry land through the sea. He puts rivers in the desert.

Isaiah's was not ho-hum theology. You took notice. You found out that armies would march through breakers and that ships could sail the desert. When God's people were on the move, freeways appeared under their feet.

Never count God out. When you deal with the Creator, you're up against the unpredictable. He'll make a roadbed in the ocean. He'll brew water out of the sand.

People who have a place to go find a way to get there even without a GPS, which I am just now learning to use. Guess what may be the greatest test of God's imagination…to make heaven more fascinating than the trip there.

P.S.: It is obvious our friendship has taken on new meaning. Even though we have not determined marriage as a viable option, we have been discussing what marriage might require. In light of all the questions that remain, separation from each other, selling a house, a family wedding, decisions to make, family to tell, writing pre-nuptials, choosing a venue, just to name a few… In all of it,

God will give us the wisdom and confidence to trust His hand in creating a river through the desert in preparation for an anticipated heaven. If we truly trust Him, the trip there will be a taste of the heaven we long for. I am *sailing*!

Hymn: "My God, how wonderful You are, / Your majesty, how bright; / how beautiful Your mercy seat, / in depths of burning light! / How wonderful, how beautiful, / the sight of You must be; / Your endless wisdom, boundless pow'r, / and glorious purity! / O how I fear You, living God, / with deep and tender fear and worship / You with trembling hope, / and penitential tears! / Yet, I may love you, too, / O Lord, almighty as You are; / for You have stooped to ask of me / the love of my poor heart!" (Frederick W. Faber, "My God, How Wonderful You Are").

Meditation: Father, it is becoming obvious that the relationship between Grace and me is leading toward a permanent connection. May we take the time to decide our future, knowing that we can and need to be guided by divine wisdom. We pray for that discernment and understanding. Amen.

Devotional Sixteen:

Exploring the Gifts of Grace

God has given me a very special person named Grace. Having served as my executive assistant for thirteen years, she has shown herself to me to be a godly person. Her life is the inspiration for these thoughts. None of us could ever perfectly reflect God's grace gifts, but she radiates the goodness of God in a remarkable way.

In Paul's Roman letter, he writes, "We have different gifts, according to the grace given us. Let him use it in proportion to his faith" (Romans 12:6, NIV). By that statement, Paul means that we need to use gifts that differ from one another and according to the grace given to us. When I receive the gift of a toolkit, what I get is not simply a toolkit; what I get is not simply the tools. Rather, it is what I make with them. To be given a useful gift is to receive something priceless. How valuable it is depends on how I use it. If the tools are kept in the gift box and never touch my hands, their value is greatly diminished.

Believe it or not, this untrained carpenter built a dining room onto a house Jo and I purchased in 1962. It included a brick compartment for displaying silver, beautiful drapes, and a traditional chandelier. It also featured brand-new furniture. Made us proud!

When I finish a project like that, my gift is more than something packaged. It is something of me. And it's just the beginning.

Next time, after my skills with the tools had developed, I could boast of a grandfather clock made from a kit that required carpentry skills. My son Greg has it now. That gift of mine is full of surprises!

The gifts of the grace of God are tools of Christian craftsmanship. When I, like my very special friend Grace, practice the arts of service, giving, forgiving, trust, and understanding, I broadcast the goodness of God. I furnish my house with gifts. And the very best gift is love. I hope every room of the house is full of it.

P.S.: This sermon inspired by Roger Carstensen and adapted to my own "carpentry endeavor" is dedicated to you. You epitomize the above-mentioned "grace gifts" and more. And, the more I come to know you, the greater my capacity to love and appreciate the way you practice the art of Christian service. As we build our friendship together, I want every room of our lives and our houses to be full of love. Obviously, that very best "grace gift of love" happens because we are using the tools of service for each other, for family, friends, and others who need to experience God's love.

Hymn: "Marvelous grace of our loving Lord, / Grace that exceeds our sin and our guilt, / yonder on Calvary's mount outpoured, / there where the blood of the Lamb was spilt. / Marvelous, infinite, matchless grace, / freely bestowed on all who believe; / all who are longing to see His face, / will you this moment His grace receive? / Grace, grace, God's grace, / grace that pardon and cleanse within; / grace, grace, God's grace; / grace that is greater than all our sin" (Julia H. Johnston, "Grace Greater than Our Sin").

Meditation: Dear Father, the hymn inspired at Your hand through Julia Johnston is one my own earthly father sang frequently. It was one of his favorites! As Grace and I anticipate the blooming of a life partnership, may Your abundant grace flow in and through us, giving us grace upon grace. Amen.

Devotional Seventeen:

Light a Flame

In Hebrews 10:25, Christians are urged not to forsake the assembling of ourselves.

I was at a Royal Ambassador Camp roasting wieners in the woods of Lake Sallateska in Southern Illinois. It was the permanent campsite for churches associated with the Illinois Baptist State Association. I attended these camp weeks each summer and, in later years, served as a bugler and lifeguard.

Do you like roasted wieners over a campfire? Want a unique taste experience? Try wieners and tar. The boys loved it. Night fell. A problem! You guessed it. Thirteen Royal Ambassadors and no flashlight! We made torches and formed a smoky, noisy procession.

Then, a shout, "Hey! Mine's out!"

"Let's get together." Thirteen torches made a new bonfire. After three marches and three assemblies, we saw the lights of home.

It reminded me of Sunday worship. We bring our smoldering torches together in the presence of God; a light will flame among us. Turn over the fresh leaf of just one Sunday worship experience to find the autograph of God!

P.S.: It was just a week ago that we were at Germantown Baptist Church for worship. It was a great day, and as we move forward, I will likewise anticipate worshiping with you again. Corporate worship is such a blessing. We meet God there! But he is with us 24/7! Still, it is always good to meet Him at His house. One of the marks of a believer is he or she has a longing to worship with others who believe. In that regard, we are on common ground. To miss worship is to create a blank space on the calendar.

Since we spent the weekend together in Memphis, we were able to be back at Germantown Baptist, the place where Jo and I, too, were members from 1991–2004. It was refreshing to recall some very high moments in worship in that church. Both of our families were blessed by Dr. Ken Story's productive ministry. Often, you, LeRoy, Jo, and I would go to lunch after church. A highlight for me was to share in the Friday men's prayer breakfast together, which LeRoy helped lead. He was always extremely helpful in the church kitchen. He was quite the chef at home and at public functions, like the men's prayer breakfast. In a special way, he "lighted a flame." So, LeRoy, thanks for your special gifts.

Hymn: "From all that dwell below the skies, / let the Creator's praise arise; / let the redeemer's name be sung, / thro' ev'ry land by ev'ry tongue. / Eternal are Thy mercies, Lord; / eternal truth attends Thy word; / Thy praise shall sound from shore to shore / till suns shall rise and set no more" (Isaac Watts, "From All That Dwell Below the Skies").

Meditation: Father, You asked Your children not to "forsake assembling themselves with one another." Corporate and individual worship are avenues of praise and worship of You, our great God. How glad we are to be identified with churches that are houses of worship. Bless them and us as needy worshipers. Amen.

Devotional Eighteen:

The Whole Cup

Things are getting scarce in the world's marketplace, including such things as silver, sometimes oranges, and, for a while, coffee. A really scarce commodity is love. Love is given away, and yet it's hard to find. Wealthy people and poor people are famished for love.

When things get scarce, we think of rationing. I remember World War II. Ration books were secured, and purchases were based on ration tickets.

Regrettably, water is being rationed all over this country. Sometime, maybe sooner than we think, we are going to have water bootleggers. My father once remarked, "Son, soon a gallon of water may be as expensive as a gallon of gas." But love is hard to ration. Dole it out, and you don't have love at all. You can't ration love any more than you can make it rain one drop at a time. Or take a somewhat trip to the South Sea Islands.

Jesus said, "Having loved his own which were in the world, he loved them to the end" (John 13:1b, KJV). God's love is scarce, but not because it is rationed. Christ went all the way for His followers. Unless we drink the full cup, there's not a drop to be had.

P.S.: I have thought a lot about our friendship in recent days. It is the "full thing, not as perfect as Christ's love for all mankind, but it is full and "very real." We are learning how to drink from it. Each day adds to the blessing it is. Forgive me if it isn't always given in full measure. For sure, it can't be doled out. Who would ever want to ration what we have discovered in each other?

Hymn: "What wondrous love is this, O my soul, O my soul! / What wondrous love is this, O my soul! / What wondrous love is this that caused the Lord of bliss / to bear the dreadful curse for my soul, for my soul, / to bear the dreadful curse for my soul" (Anonymous, "What Wondrous Love Is This").

Meditation: Great Giver of Life, how we adore You because of the price You paid for our redemption. It was an incredible and unimaginable sacrifice that Your Son suffered for the salvation of fallen humanity. Just as Jesus gladly went all the way to the cross to purchase our redemption, may we always love and care for others and ourselves in the same selfless way. In His name. Amen.

Devotional Nineteen:

The Vision and the Dream

Tonight was the first time we seriously considered putting our two lives together. I confess I was being more than a dreamer but a visionary. Not unlike God's prophet Joel, I was dreaming dreams of a possible future for us. After telling of days to come when the drought in Israel would be over, Joel says, "And it shall come to pass afterward, that I will pour out my spirit on all flesh; and your sons and your daughters shall prophesy, your old men shall dream dreams and your young men shall see visions" (Joel 2:28, KJV).

Israel had known spiritual drought before. It seems evident, in those days, that the Word of the Lord was rare.

How will we know when the famine of the Spirit is about to be broken? Take a tip from Joel. Watch the very young and the very old. When we get back the vision and the dreams, the drought's over.

P.S.: Too late to have much to say, except I have nothing but dreams about our future. So, please don't fret it! It will happen faster than we think! Nothing will change my mind unless you tell me "no." *I am dreaming dreams!* I certainly do not want to get ahead of your decision-making. It is that time when decisions are being forged. I will wait patiently as you process your own choice. It will be difficult for you to leave your current work role. It would not be necessary, but we could envision freedom from the responsibility of work but, in a sense, not denied the privilege of being of service in God's kingdom.

Hymn: "Be thou my vision, O Lord of my heart; / naught be all else to me, save that Thou art; / Thou my best thought, by day or by night. / Waking or sleeping Thy presence my light?" (Translation of the Old Irish hymn "Bí Thusa 'mo Shúile" by Mary E. Byrne; versified by Eleanor H. Hull, "Be Thou My Vision").

Meditation: Father, Grace is still pondering the marriage question. We are both right on the edge of a decision. Let Your holy and penetrating light give us sureness and mutual purpose. Whether it is to be "yes" or "no," help us keep dreaming dreams. Close any door that keeps us from making a mistake. Amen.

Devotional Twenty:

The Fragrance of Prayer

Our telephone call tonight related to the consequences of a marriage decision. We must prayerfully seek God's wisdom. In Revelation 5, we read, "[L]iving creatures and twenty-four elders fell down before the lamb. Each one had a harp and they were holding golden bowls filled with incense, which are the prayers of the saints" (Revelation 5:8, NIV). The prayers of saints are incense in heaven.

You would not think any human product would suit the requirements of heaven's throne room. The golden harps are in perfect pitch. The temperature is always like a spring morning in Virginia. The choir never goes flat.

When angels looked for incense to provide fragrance for the scene, why did they import, from way down here, the prayers of human beings?

Jesus taught us there is joy in heaven over one sinner who repents. Let's face it: God has always been partial to humanity. When people reach out of darkness and grasp His presence, a fragrance makes the angels pause.

Looks like heaven is one place we can get to faster on our knees than on our feet.

P.S.: Moving our friendship together, we need to be ever mindful that we are dealing with ourselves but also seeking to find and do God's will. The two are not separate if we really want to walk in His way. He does direct, but only if there is a willingness to follow His lead. The two are inclusively one, and it is never my way, your way, but Yahweh. I thank Him daily for bringing us together and for holding us together in the palm of His hand. Let's make the angels sing!

Meditation: Father, obviously, our prayers for Your wisdom get us to Your throne room. Lead us lest we stray from Your will rather than the bidding of human pleasure. Keep our spirit free and clean. Let the fervent prayers flow from righteous hearts open to divine direction. In Christ's name. Amen.

Devotional Twenty-One:

Pinched Hearts and Empty Pockets

Tonight, we talked about how our families would handle a second marriage. We don't know for sure, but it may be easier for our sons than daughters. It is hard to know. I am very anxious how they might react. I sure do know I do not want to cause any sense of estrangement with them. My kids dearly loved their mother, and yours felt the same way about their father. The love of God, if practiced, is big enough to handle a new family structure. It is a reminder from the Old Testament that the wonder-worker Elisha was walking down a lonely road, minding his own business. Suddenly, a haggard, weeping woman stood before him. "Help me!" she begged him. "My husband, the prophet, is dead, and my creditors are coming to take my two children as slaves."

The prophet inquired what the woman's assets were. One jar of oil was all she could raise any money on. He instructed her to borrow empty vessels from her neighbors and, with her boys' help, empty her oil in them.

A miracle! The golden oil flowed in a steady stream till all the jars were full. As the last one filled to the brim, she called for another. "Ma! There ain't no more!" said her son, and the oil stopped. She paid her debts and lived on the rest.

Why didn't the widow have more? God didn't run out of oil;

she ran out of a place to put it. In 2 Corinthians 6, Paul challenges his readers to widen their hearts. The love of God was everywhere, but the Corinthians weren't big enough to handle it.

P.S.: If marriage is an option for us, we are about to take on more "family"! They will have to widen their hearts. That may take some time and special love and consideration. I am really glad we talked about it. We will need to widen our capacity to care more and love more. And, the more we love each other, the greater our capacity to widen our hearts to include them all. I want to be big enough to handle it.

Hymn: "There's a wideness in God's mercy, / Like the wideness of the sea; / There's a kindness in His justice, / which is more than liberty. / But we make His love too narrow / by false limits of our own; / and we magnify His strictness / with a zeal He will not own. / If our love were but more simple, / we could take Him at His word; / and our lives would be more loving / in the likeness of our Lord" (Frederick W. Faber, "There's a Wideness in God's Mercy").

Meditation: Lord, forgive us when selfish desire and personal gain become more important than compassion for family and friends. Give us the kind of faith that is large enough to hold Your full measure of compassion and grace gifts. May that same spirit of mutual compassion and understanding flow freely to each member of our two families. Amen.

Devotional Twenty-Two:

Free as a Bird

In Psalm 98:4 (KJV), the singer exclaims, "Make a joyful noise unto the Lord, all the earth."

We talked tonight about your need for sleep and the fact you arise at 5:30 each day to prepare for the workday. You mentioned you heard the birds sing yesterday morning. I, too, was in my office early, checking e-mails and getting ready to drink coffee with Paul Penny, my close friend and next-door neighbor. Shortly after dawn, a bird outside my window tuned up with a morning cadenza. I thought about a "50-Second Sermon" from Roger Carstensen. As he said, in that bit of pondering, "Wish I were free as that bird!" I grumbled to myself. Then, I remembered the studies of the naturalist Konrad Lorenz. He says birds sing because their little genes and chromosomes make them sing. They literally have to sing.

Birds have to sing? We do, too.

Some moment of song, some moment of daily joy, is a part of being a person. The voice that will not laugh in time becomes inhuman. Praise is not a Sunday luxury. It is a daily necessity. When I refuse to praise, I throw dirt on my coffin.

P.S.: I knew I had this sermon from Roger. Found it almost in nothing flat. It is personalized to my own experience. It also mirrors tonight's conversation. Our love has elevated my praise and thanksgiving exponentially. I have had some down days, but the growth of our love has given me such happy days. The past six to eight months have brought double-duty praise for *you* and the gift of *you*. With apologies to David Cory, the poet, "When not with you, miss you, miss you. / Everything I do echoes with the laughter / and the voice of *you*. / You're on every corner, / every turn and twist, / every old familiar spot / whispers how you are missed." So, remember, I love you, not only for what you have made of yourself but for what you are making of me. Lorenz was right; I can't help but sing!

Hymn: "Praise to the Lord, who o'er all things so wondrously reigneth, / Shelters thee under His wings, yea, so gently sustaineth! / Hast thou not seen how thy desires e'er have been granted in what He ordaineth?" (Translator Catherine Winkworth; Author Joachim Neander, "Praise to the Lord, the Almighty").

Meditation: When the day seems weary, remember the singing of birds. It is the constancy of their very existence. Great Creator, You made them to sing. May it ever be so with us. Amen.

Devotional Twenty-Three:

The Lord Sets Prisoners Free

One of the great promises of the Old Testament is found in the Psalms: "The Lord, who remains faithful forever, He upholds the causes of the oppressed, and gives food for the hungry, The Lord sets prisoners free" (Psalm 146:6–7, NIV). That truth is true for many prisoners bound by faulty charges. Today, the world needs to get back in touch with Aleksandr Solzhenitsyn. He was imprisoned in Stalin's concentration camps in Siberia called the Gulag Archipelago. In his words, it was an arctic hell. He suffered imprisonment for eight years in cells full of rats because he had spoken slightingly of Stalin in a private letter. Near the end of his eight years, he was diagnosed with terminal cancer.

Instead of raging against such misfortune, he gave his heart to Christ. As affirmation, he wrote a prayer, circulated in secret until it was finally published in *Vogue* magazine in January 1971. It is a historic prayer, one of the most moving ever written. The opening lines are, "How simple for me to live with You, O Lord! How easy to believe in You!" The rest of the prayer is filled with poetic validations of his conversion. From being an atheistic socialist mathematician and Soviet artillery captain imprisoned for a flimsy charge, he came after eight years of raw punishment to find "freedom in Christ." The world knows the rest of the story.

In prison, there was not enough light, and with no pen or paper, he could not write his thoughts but wrote volumes in his mind. He did write and, in 1970, received the Nobel Prize for literature. For years, many people read his books. It is time for citizens in our nation to read them again.

Through his masterful pen, today's world can know once again the truth about Marxism, radical socialism, and the evils possible when nations are under the control of an authoritarian leader. Freedom is possible when people are not under the bondage of groupthink and government control of individuals and their property. And most certainly, it more likely occurs when a nation has little respect for its "Founding Fathers" desire for religious liberty. "In God We Trust," not government. That is the best environment for religious decisions and the best environment for blooming faith in God's Son, whose belief in sets prisoners free. Thank God for freedom.

P.S.: Grace, we know creeping socialism is invading the nation. Particularly, is it becoming more evident in academics, Hollywood, and a liberal press? Going forward, may we resolve to help our children and their offspring understand the need for freedom. Likewise, it is enhanced when they understand the great price others have paid to make freedom possible. Hope none of them have to go to war to protect that freedom or be persecuted like Solzhenitsyn. Our nation is not yet a perfect union, but working together to make it so for every race and kind should be our "stretch goal." As we have the opportunity, may we champion the protection of religious liberty. Most of all, let us stand up and challenge those who seek to destroy it.

Hymn: "My country, 'tis of thee, / sweet land of liberty, of thee I sing: / land where my fathers died, / land of the pilgrims' pride, / from every mountainside, / let freedom ring! / My native country, thee, / land of the noble free, / thy name I love; / I love thy rocks and rills, / thy woods and templed hills; / my heart with rapture thrills / like that above. / Our sovereign God, / to Thee, Author of liberty, / to Thee we sing: / long may our land be bright / with freedom's holy light; / protect us by Thy might, / great God our King!" (Samuel R. Smith, "My Country, 'Tis of Thee").

Meditation: Father God and Creator of people and nations, we earnestly pray for protection and freedom for each of Your children. We know, even in places of deepest despair—a bombed-out Syria, a deadly war in Afghanistan, a Pearl Harbor, a 9/11 tragedy, a dreaded Soviet gulag, and certainly the desolation of Golgotha—You are there with a message of hope and salvation for everyone who believes in You for it. In all things, we know all things do work together for good, even when we can't see it. Amen.

Devotional Twenty-Four:

The Principle of Obedience

In Psalm 40:8 (KJV), the writer says, "I delight to do thy will. O my God, thy law is within my heart."

When we deal with the law, "delight" is not always commonplace. Imagine: "Making out my income tax was a delightful experience," in quadruplicate? Delighted? Or a delightful conversation with a policeman: "When do I have the privilege to appear in court?"

But suppose Aunt Penelope left you her fortune, and the lawyer requested your receipt in quadruplicate. You might handle that red tape with a smile.

If we had magic spectacles to see the consequences of doing God's will, we would line up at 5 a.m. for applications. And, if we lived up to our own best hopes, St. Francis would ask for each other's autograph.

P.S.: I have told you this before, but one of the reasons God brought us together again has to do with the way your life demonstrated servanthood. In the thirteen years of our work together at the Brotherhood Commission, Southern Baptist Convention, and the Baptist Medical Dental Fellowship, not one time did I ever note in you an arbitrary spirit. You always demonstrated a "second-mile" attitude. Your trust, patience, understanding, and sincere desire to serve the Lord helped me be the leader God called me to be—how I thank Him for knitting our lives together once more. May we always seek to be obedient to God's calling.

Hymn: "Teach me, O Lord, I pray, / Your precious truth divine; / Lead me to understand Your Word / and make its precepts mine. / Impart Your wisdom Lord, / shed light upon my way, / that I may know Your boundless love; / teach me, O Lord, I pray" (G. Kearnie Keegan, "Teach Me, O Lord, I Pray").

Meditation: Dear Father, sometimes, in selfish pride, we want to boast of our uprightness. Remind us that our righteousness is as filthy rags in Your sight. Teach us to be servants in attitude and action, recognizing that every person deserves understanding and service. May we render that service, not for claim but for Your glory. Amen.

Devotional Twenty-Five:

The Nearness and Wonder of Sacred Delight

Max Lucado is one of my favorite authors. His writing style is filled with faith and creativity. I was first captivated by his earlier book, *No Wonder They Call Him the Savior*. The inspiration for this "sermon" comes from *The Applause of Heaven*, a graphic introduction to the Sermon on the Mount (Matthew 5–7). The first chapter is called "Sacred Delight." In it, he helps the reader grasp the wonder and surprise of God applauding His children with blessings.

Long in my memory is an account Lucado gives of the life of Beverly Sills, acclaimed opera singer and retired director of the New York City Opera. In the midst of international acclaim, she experienced personal setbacks. She was not immediately accepted by American critics. It was only after stunning successes with European audiences she found professional acceptance in her homeland. Personally, she dealt with mothering two handicapped children. Instead of allowing bitterness and rejection to swallow her, her friends called her "Bubbles." She had learned how to be cheerful in the overwhelming wonder of God-sized blessings.

The eyes of her heart stretched as far as needed. I truly believe that is "sacred delight."

P.S.: Tonight, we talked at length about how far love reaches. To realize we are blessed (applauded) by God is an eternal wonder. On both sides of our families, there have been moments when the "eyes of the heart stretched as far as needed." Going forward, we will experience our love for each other being used by God to help us deal with mistakes we make or the mistakes of those we love most dear. With true love, a mistake or feelings of rejection can be a first step to success if we are willing to learn from it. It is hard not to respond in anger or righteous indignation when an obvious injustice is done. When God writes His law of love and blessing on our hearts, it is amazing how much His blessing to us and others is experienced. May those who know us call us "Bubbles," as did the friends of Beverly Sills.

Hymn: "Christian heats, in love united, / seek alone in Jesus rest; / has He not your love excited? / Then let love inspire each breast. / Members on our Head/ depending light reflecting Him, our Sun. / Christians, His commands attending, / we in Him our Lord, are one. / Grant Lord, that with Thy direction, / 'Love each other,' we comply, / aiming with unfeigned affection Thy love to exemplify; / let our mutual love be glowing, / so that all will plainly see that we, / as on one stem growing, / living branches are in Thee. / O that such may be our union as Thine with the Father is, / and not one of our communion e'er forsake the path of bliss; / may our light shine forth with brightness, / from Thy light reflected, shine' thus the world will bear us witness, / that we, Lord are truly Thine" (Nicholas L. von Zinzendorf, Frederick W. Foster, "Christian Hearts, In Love United").

Meditation: May the words of our mouths be Your words, dear Lord. We do want to hold the light of Christ for each other and all those who are flesh of our flesh. Let us always be found faithful in our devotion to deeply loved family and, beyond that, certainly to those more difficult to love. Amen.

Devotional Twenty-Six:

The Source and Wonder of Joy

As I previously mentioned, I love Max Lucado and his incredible gift of painting word pictures. One of the stories he tells in *The Applause of Heaven* is about Robert Reed. According to Max, Robert's hands are twisted, and his feet are useless. He has cerebral palsy. Though he can't feed himself and his shirts are held together by strips of Velcro, those infirmities did not keep him from earning a degree with a major in Latin and teaching at a St. Louis Junior College. Later, he moved to Lisbon, studied Portuguese, and followed his call from God to be a missionary in Portugal.

According to the story, he stations himself in a park, where he distributes brochures about Christ. Within six years, he had led seventy people to the Lord, one of whom became his wife. Max Lucado tells about hearing him speak. Others carried him to the platform, and another laid a Bible on his lap. At the end of his message from a hushed and tear-stained audience, he concluded by saying, "I have everything I need for joy!"

"Wow!" Is your life held together by joy? The words of Nehemiah ring so true, "The joy of the Lord is your strength" (Nehemiah 8:10, NIV).

P.S.: Joy has to be received before it can be given away. I am so sorry to hear about your daughter Cindy's surgery; please tell her, in her struggles, I want her to know my love for her is not just because I have come to love her mother. It is in part, but it is also because of her mother's love for her and also because I am convinced that life is destiny and in all things—the bitter and the sweet—God is at work for good, and "joy comes in the morning." Each day, we are more convinced that God has brought our lives together, and because of it, we are becoming family. So, remind her I will continue to pray for her throughout the day of the surgery and through her rehabilitation. Hope soon she is enjoying happy, pain-free days. God bless your dear one with the joy of a Robert Reed.

Hymn: "Teach me Your way, O Lord, teach me Your way! / Your guiding grace afford, teach me Your way! / Help me to walk aright, more by faith less by sight; / lead me with heavenly light, teach me Your way! / When I am sad at heart, teach me Your way! / When earthly joys depart, teach me Your way! In hours of loneliness, in times of dire distress, / in failure or success, teach me Your way! / Long as my life shall last, teach me Your way! / Wher-e'er my lot is cast, teach me Your way! / Until the race is run, until the journey's done, / until the crown is won, teach me Your way!" (B. Mansell Ramsey, "Teach Me Your Way").

Meditation: Father, we rejoice in the assurance that "all things work together to produce good for those that love the Lord and call on His name." May the lyrics of Esther Burroughs be ours because we do want love, joy, and hope to be sheltered in our homes and in our relationships with others. Amen.

Devotional Twenty-Seven:

Honoring the Eternal

In the Holy Scripture, we read God's dwelling place shall be with His people. I don't know about your neighborhood, but we have some huge houses, yet not big enough for God to live in. Does your neighborhood have a house big enough for God to dwell in? When dedicating his temple, King Solomon said, "But will God really dwell on earth? The heavens, even the highest heaven, cannot contain you. How much less this temple I have built!" (1 Kings 8:27, NIV).

The other day, a friend said to me, "Your neighbor Paul Penny has a heart as big as all outdoors!" Maybe Paul's heart would hold God. He would modestly say, "Not good enough." But he was more than the beautiful home he lived in. He loved his Irish setter and his cat. He loved nature and the beauty of creation. He loved a morning fire in the outdoor fire pit. He talked to the squirrels and the birds. For sure, he would say, "Bricks and mortar won't get it done."

The God who holds the heavens in the hollow of His hand cannot be penned up in any fancy corral. The apostle Paul says that people are God's real temple. Are there any big hearts and open minds in your neighborhood?

Only a heart without borders can house the Eternal.

P.S.: This one goes without saying. Whether where you now live or my abode, wherever we are, your neighbors or mine, may our hearts be without boundaries. May it be true for you and me, our families, but most of all, for the God we love and seek to serve.

Hymn: "O for a closer walk with God, a calm and heavenly frame, / a light to shine upon the road that leads me to the Lamb! / The dearest idol I have known, what e'er that idol be, / help me to tear it from Thy throne, and worship only Thee. / So shall my walk be close with God, serene and calm my frame; / so purer light shall mark the road that leads me to the Lamb" (William Cowper, "O For a Closer Walk with God").

Meditation: Dear Lord, give us redeeming and forgiving capacity in order we may be "friend to man and thee." In the name of Him whose very heart was given in sacrifice for the sins of the world. Amen.

Devotional Twenty-Eight:

Turn Back the Clock

Grieving Judah asks God to "renew our days as of old" (Lamentations 5:21, KJV).

One of my favorite TV shows in another era was *All in the Family*. Every show began with a horrendous rendition by Archie and Edith singing, "Those Were the Days."

How's your imagination? Would you like to turn the clock back? There went my sore ankle. Hey—my four absent teeth are back, and the bridge was removed. I don't need reading glasses when the light is dim. The river's clear, and the trout are jumping. I shot par golf! Smell the sweetness of the spring air. There's my old friend Clyde coming up the walk with the same lopsided grin and, doubtless, one of his lousy jokes. What a guy!

God, take me back! Take us all back.

Well, Thomas Wolfe was right. You can't go home again. But God, could You do me this favor? Put some yesterday in tomorrow, and we'll give You today. And let my tomorrow be filled with unadulterated happiness so later we can sing with Archie and Edith, "Those Were the Days."

P.S.: Grace, I promise we won't try to sing like Archie and Edith but will sing because we have put "newness and creativity" today and our tomorrows. Don't need to go home again. The only reason to turn back the clock is to remember the good things that will make tomorrow better. Come on today, and can't wait for tomorrow! Gobs and heaps of love and support for you!

Hymn: "O God, our help in ages past, / our hope for years to come, / our shelter from the stormy blast, / and our eternal home! / Under the shadow of Thy throne, / Thy saints have dwelt secure; / sufficient is Thine arm alone, / and our defense is sure" (Isaac Watts, "O God, Our Help in Ages Past").

Meditation: Father, memories are not to be worshiped, but they do remind us of rich heritage and life blessings. Let the empowering Eternal Spirit guard and guide our hearts. Teach us to learn from life experiences. May the memories of the "bad and good" of life challenge and inform decisions for today and tomorrow. Amen.

Devotional Twenty-Nine:

The Scariest Skeleton

Ezekiel 37:1–10 tells of the vision of a mystic valley filled with millions of hollow-eyed, grinning skeletons. Those skeletons were dry as dust. In the vision, the four winds of God summoned across those dry bones, turning them into a host of healthy warriors.

God told Ezekiel those dry bones were hopeless people, not yet in the graveyards. Embalmed before they died, they had shriveled in despair. There's something about dry bones rattling around inside living folks more upsetting than skeletons piled in a pasture. Talk to a hopeless person, and you feel you've been to his funeral.

You may even hear the rattle of dry bones.

The vision's bones sprang to life under four winds blowing at once. Feeling hopeless lately? I pray that across your weariness may develop the sweetest wind of spring—the quiet breathing of the Presence who made man a living soul.

P.S.: In Texas, today, with 82 degrees and no wind, it felt like a spring day. The grass is just beginning to turn green. It won't be much longer till the leaves match the trees. Valentine's Day approaches, and you will be here, God willing. The want of you is like no other thing. It smites my soul like Ezekiel's experience with dry bones. It binds my being with a wreath of me, this "want of you." You have spent a lot of time wanting things "just right." Just having you here will be enough to bring alive the joys of our growing friendship and developing love for each other.

Hymn: "Praise the Lord who reigns above, / and keeps His court below; / praise the holy God of love, / and all His greatness show; / Praise Him for His noble deeds, / Praise Him for His matchless pow'r; / Him from whom all good proceeds / let earth and heav'n adore. / Him, in whom they move and live, / let ev'ry creature sing. / Glory to their Maker give, / and homage to their King. / Hallowed be His name beneath, / as in heav'n on earth adored; / praise the Lord in ev'ry breath, / let all things praise the Lord." (Charles Wesley, "Praise the Lord Who Reigns Above").

Meditation: Father, the budding of love for a significant other is both mystical and magical. It brings heightened emotions and a sense of new life to emotions deadened by grief and separation. Thank You for this weaker brother; You have introduced new reasons for valuing worthy companionship and friendship. Thanks for Grace and the grace of God that brought her back into my life. Amen.

Devotional Thirty:

The Peril of Answered Prayer

One of the stories I loved as a child was King Midas, at whose touch everything turned to gold. The king was punished by getting what he asked for.

A host of people are concerned their prayers are not answered—if anyone prays as selfishly as Midas, God's kindness may turn the request down.

The people of Israel, newly released from slavery, longed for the fleshpots of Egypt. Manna from heaven was not good enough for them. God granted their request by sending acres of quail all over their camp. It appears that a bunch of folk ate themselves to death. Numbers 11 tells how they dug a graveyard called *Kibroth-hattaavah* for all those "who had the craving."

The first thing to ask God for is the grace to pray right so we don't self-destruct on our knees.

P.S.: This sermon is so relevant for us. After such a great day yesterday, growing and going deeper in understanding our past and how those experiences relate to us, all of it makes me more aware of the importance of praying right. I can be so very selfish and forget that the journey toward our destination is filled with challenges and change. My wish is we do not have to wait. But I, too, am convinced there are some necessary hurdles that must be crossed before a longed-for destination. So, both of us need to look beyond the "craving" and let God's supply lead us safely home. And in the meantime, I am doing everything in my power to make the destination happen as quickly as possible, in His way, not mine. For people of faith, God is the horizon under distant skies. He is the air we breathe. His smile is our weather, and His intelligence is our geography. We are walking by both flesh and faith. The two are inseparable, and I am glad that we want to exercise both. It is easy to let one be stronger than the other. One of a million reasons I love you so is because you are a person of faith and flesh. Life is never perfect, but we both have a longing desire to let God's sure path be ours. So my prayer is, "God help us with the details, but don't let us wait too long!" (That gets it out in the open.)

Hymn: "My God, how wonderful You are, / Your majesty, how bright; / how beautiful Your mercy seat, / in depths of burning light!" (Frederick W. Faber, "My God, How Wonderful You Are").

Meditation: Father, Your living Word provides clear instruction for daily living. As Grace and I fathom the surprises of a growing relationship, remind us that everything is right except what the Word of God says is wrong. May the days of our yearning for each other be tempered by Your standards, not ours. Amen.

Devotional Thirty-One:

Can Love Be like an Olive Tree?

The olive tree is a parable of the tree of life. It grows in rocky soil with little water. It is tough and persistent. The fruit is fine for eating. The oil works for cooking and lubrication. The wood is used for fuel, lumber, and finished works of art.

The olive need not die. When an old stock becomes rotten, shoots appear from deep roots and start a brand-new tree. Isaiah 1 speaks of the Messiah as a branch from the roots of Jesse.

When I first stood in the garden of Gethsemane, I saw a shoot springing up between the cloven halves of an old olive trunk. We were with a large group of fellow pilgrims. Bill Pinson, a former colleague at Southwestern Seminary and retired executive director of the Baptist General Convention of Texas, joined me as a tour leader.

We were privileged to guide large groups of schoolteachers and many single adults on a Mediterranean cruise during the summers of 1972–73. We were in Israel for five days. One older lady had gone with us both years. The reason she went the second summer was because she got sick and missed Gethsemane on her first trip. She had dreamed all her life about the olive trees in that special garden. Some of those trees were there at the time of Jesus's crucifixion. For her, the old olive tree was a reminder of Jesus in that garden the night of His betrayal. He prayed to the Father to let His cup pass, but nevertheless, He prayed, "[T]ake away this cup from me; nevertheless not what I will, but what thou wilt" (Mark 14:36, KJV). In that instance, His disciples drowsed, but the trees around Him spoke of a resurrection lost to the dreams of men. In all of life, resurrection love is forever being renewed and made strong. It can be preserved like those trees 2,000 years old.

P.S.: In today's conversations, we talked at length about the connection and then the reconnection of our lives. Both of us seem amazed at how our friendship has grown. In tonight's telephone visit, we lived, laughed, and loved because we have, in a sense, blended our personalities. That does not mean we lose our own identities. As I came back to prepare for bedtime, my mind was thinking about how totally rooted we are to each other, and the thought made me think about the olive tree and a 50-second sermon sent to me by my friend Roger and adapted based on my own visit to Jerusalem in 1972 and again in 1973. It does not stretch the imagination too far to see that our love has blossomed from the roots of yesteryears. Now, however, we have experienced not only the birth of genuine, eternal love, but we are learning how to prune it, shape it, and value the many "products" it generates. It could and can have timeless value.

Hymn: "Immortal love, forever full, / forever flowing free, / forever shared, forever whole, / a never ebbing sea! / O Lord and Master of us all, / whate're our name or sign, / we own Thy sway, / we hear Thy call, / we test our lives by Thine" (John Greenleaf Whittier, "Immortal Love, Forever Full").

Meditation: Dear Father, may the surprising fruits of friendship with Grace be a resurrection kind of love; like the resurrection love of Jesus, may it be forever renewed and made strong. The standards of the world leave you unfulfilled at best. May the agape love that Jesus modeled characterize our wants, desires, and behavior. Amen.

Devotional Thirty-Two:

For This One Night:
"How About a Poem?"

I Love You

    I love your lips when they're wet with wine

    And red with a wild desire.

    I love your eyes when the love light lies,

    Lit with a passionate fire.

    I love your arms when the warm white flesh

    Touches mine in a fond embrace.

    I love your hair when the strands enmesh,

    Your kisses against my face.

    Not for me the cold, calm kiss

    Of a virgin's bloodless love.

    Nor for me the saint's white bliss,

    Nor the heart of a spotless dove.

    But give me the love that so freely gives

    And laughs at the whole world's blame,

With your body so tender and warm in my arms.

It sets my poor heart aflame.

So kiss me sweet with your warm, wet mouth,

Still fragrant with moist, wet wine,

And say with a flavor born in the South

That your body and soul are mine.

Clasp me close in your warm, smooth arms

While the pale stars shine above.

And we'll live the rest of our lives away

In the joys of a living love.

—Ella Wheeler Wilcox

P.S.: I thought this night was a good time to share a poem rather than a "50-Second Sermon."

In the past sermon, I had been enmeshed in your visit here, hating to see you return home, and then, because of Memphis weather conditions and your office closed, we were able to talk long hours via the phone. So, in the theme of "faith and flesh," I thought it wise to share a poem of "flesh," which summarizes where our love has taken us. We are at home and so in love with each other. We patiently wait for the complete fulfillment, whatever or whenever it may occur. Summarizing the night's conversation, we are happy in the joys of a living love.

Hymn: "For all the love that from our earliest days / has gladdened life and guarded all our ways, / we bring You, Lord, our song of grateful praise: / Alleluia! Alleluia! / For all the joy that childhood's days have brought, / for healthful lives and purity of thought, / for life's deep meaning to our spirits taught: / Alleluia! Alleluia!" (L. J. Edgerton Smith, "For All the Love").

Meditation: Loving God, in the midst of celebrating a newfound relationship, remind us that we are likewise bound by faith in Your redemptive relationship with us. We glorify Your name! Amen.

Devotional Thirty-Three:

Prophecy and Digestion

In Jeremiah 28:3, the prophet Hananiah predicted Judah's captivity would be over in two years. Jeremiah insisted that seventy years would elapse before God delivered His people.

There used to be a newspaper that ran a syndicated column called "Good and Bad News about the Cold War." As a child, I was frightened about the onslaughts of World War II, afraid we would be bombed again following Pearl Harbor. Reading those reports, I found out something about myself. That is, I am a good news specialist. I caught myself believing the good report, disbelieving the extent of the bad ones. That is still true today as we observe our beloved nation so politicized. Each day brings reminders of deep division. I keep hoping the gloom of bad news will go away and welcome immediate good news like it was "Grandma's apple pie."

Really, the best way to read the "Good News, Bad News" column was to leave the bad news out.

So, I can understand why Hananiah's kind of prophet is so popular. But Jeremiah knew it was best to know the truth, pleasant or unpleasant. If you look twice at a collection of unvarnished truth, you'll have all the prophecies you can say grace over.

P.S.: Tonight was a fabulous "telephone time." We shared experiences of the past, which prompted a greater understanding of how life has shaped us. I marvel at the way you were able to handle all the challenges that, at times, were "dumped" on you! You were remarkable with the way you were able to sort things out and make sense of them. I do admire your tenacity and resolve. It makes me love you more and more. You were remarkable in keeping life together during the last three years of LeRoy's bedfast condition while also doing your work in such a professional way. Even though we both have met many challenges due to spouse illnesses, even the worst things can never go badly wrong if the heart is true and the love is strong. Oh, how you have demonstrated that fact. Let us resolve to keep ourselves renewed and ready for the changes that take place over time.

Hymn: "Children of the heav'nly Father, / safely in His bosom gather; / nestling bird nor star in heaven, / such a refuge e'er was given. / Neither life nor death shall ever / from the Lord His children sever; / unto them His grace He showeth, / and their sorrows all He knoweth" (Caroline V. Sandell-Berg, "Children of the Heavenly Father").

Meditation: Father, down deep, we know life cannot always be a bed of roses. Give us the grace and fortitude to handle all of life's challenges, good or bad, and even those we would like to change. As Grace and I continue to explore knitting our lives together, let it be according to Your way and will. Amen.

Devotional Thirty-Four:

Human Lamps

I'm so glad today was a good day for worship in your church and mine. In Ezekiel 18:25 (NIV), we read, "Hear, O House of Israel: is my way unjust? Is it not your ways that are unjust?"

God loves us far more than we love ourselves. His name reaches others through us. He keeps us on our feet and holds us together not just for our welfare but for those who read our lives.

The only way some people can sense the light of God is through our human lamps, flickering and smoky though they are. The Lord brushes past our stupidity, and He shines with a light brighter than we can see.

If God didn't love more people than us, He might not love us at all.

P.S.: Jim Spivey, my pastor at Gambrell Street Baptist Church, continued a series of messages on "sharing Christ." And as you recalled, in your church, baptisms, the Lord's Supper, good music, and a good sermon made such a difference for you. As our love has developed, we have learned many things about ourselves. We do hold much in common. We are different in some ways but, in most, the same. It is incredible how we have a common love for Christian values but also for others to know and love the Lord as we do. Going forward, may God use our lives to bless others, including family, friends, and strangers we know not but are loved by the Creator.

Hymn: "When Christ was lifted from the earth, / His arms stretched out above / thro' every culture, ev'ry birth, / to draw an answering love. / Still east and west His love extends / and always near or far, / He calls and claims us as His friends / and loves us as we are. / Where generation, class, or race / divides us to our shame, / He sees not labels but a face, / a person, and a name. / Thus freely loved, tho' fully known, / may I in Christ be free, / to welcome and accept / His own as Christ accepted me" (Brian Wren, "When Christ Was Lifted from the Earth").

Meditation: Dear Father, it is so easy to love those who are lovely and so tough to touch and care for the unlovely. Give us Your kind of love that knows no bounds. In the name of Him who was a "friend to sinners," the Lord Jesus. Amen.

Devotional Thirty-Five:

The Glitter of Getting "Unlost"

In the Psalms, we read, "I do not hide your righteousness in my heart; I speak of your faithfulness and salvation (Psalm 40:10a, NIV).

Something about a rescue is bigger than what the salvage would bring on the market. When the woman in Luke's parable found her memorial coin, she may have spent more celebrating her good luck than the coin itself would have paid for.

To lose something hurts more than never having it at all. There is a shine in what is rescued brighter than when it was new. The coin was not just found. It was the shine of rescue. The coin was unlost.

Maybe the shine of rescue is the luster added by the touch of caring. This light we dare not hide under a bushel. God's light speaks of rescue. This rescue is the brightness of the love of God, a caring that, across a sea of human lostness, illuminates the earth.

P.S.: To lose something is tough at best. In our case, we have found something. That something is the infinite love to which our lives are committed. It certainly means we have an unending mission on earth. It means that for as long as life lasts, we have purpose and meaning. It does mean caring for one another, but it also means letting the "unlostness" of our lives be open to shining gospel light wherever we are. Maybe that's why Jesus said in Matthew, "Let your light so shine before men that they may see your good works, and glorify your father which is in heaven" (Matthew 5:16, KJV). We can do the works all right, at our time and pace. But when something shines, that's more than us. We just let it go. And praise the Lord right along with the spectators. I am reminded of a hymn written by a longtime friend, Bill Reynolds, a colleague at Southwestern Seminary and, for a number of years, head of the Church Music Department of the Baptist Sunday School Board, now LifeWay.

Hymn: "Come, all Christians, be committed / to the service of the Lord. / Make your lives for Him more fitted, / tune your hearts with one accord. / Come into His courts with gladness, / each your sacred vows renew, / turn away from sin and sadness, / be transformed with life anew. / God's command to love each other is required of every-one. / Showing mercy to another, / mirrors His redeeming Son. / In compassion He has given of His love that is divine; / on the cross sins were forgiven; / joy and peace now fully thine" (Eva B. Lloyd, "Come, All Christians, Be Committed").

Meditation: Father, remind us this day and always that it does not take a doctorate in theology to know that we are to love as You loved. Teach us authenticity and obedience. Instill a spirit of compassion that moves us beyond selfish pleasure. May our love indeed be "broader than earth's vast expanse." Amen.

Devotional Thirty-Six:

Prophecy and Grace

"Mark my word," I said to Jo, "those boys are headed for the penitentiary." We had just witnessed another teenage squabble in the Wedgewood neighbor's backyard. It ended with Mark and Jody cursing their mother again at the top of their teenage lungs.

So I imagined those young savages in jail, beating on rocks, wearing stripes, repenting of their crimes. Repenting, they never gave the neighborhood any peace.

Well, that was more than forty years ago. Grace, you and I were in my old neighborhood recently to visit my "across the street neighbor," whose wife was also a longtime friend of yours from Vaiden, Mississippi. Jo and I lived in that neighborhood for eleven years and, in recent years, had not fully kept up with neighborhood news. So, guess what? I was wrong with my prophecies about the neighborhood boys. We learned from your friend those boys made a liar of me. Mark is a school principal, and Jody is a recreation director for the city. Furthermore, news from the neighbor indicated that each of those boys is raising a brace of "housebroken kids."

If you read 1 Corinthians 1, you learn how God made an apostle out of Saul of Tarsus, a persecutor of Christians. That does it. I'm turning in my prophet's license and giving some thought to the grace of God.

P.S.: We never know how life turns out. I have written to you several times about the marvelous gift of grace. Though other exceptions could certainly be noted, isn't it wonderful to know you can't always predict a book by its cover or know how kids will turn out from the way they behaved as teenagers? As imperfect creatures, we are each open to the majestic ways of the Father God, who, through His Son, is in the business of "making all things new," including Mark and Jody. And don't forget the apostle Paul. God turned a persecutor of Christians into a first-century Christian missionary. That goes for you and me too! God, in His wisdom, created us all. So, why was I surprised by how these neighborhood boys turned out? Yes, and I am, more than ever, *surprised by grace*.

Hymn: "All thing bright and beautiful, / all creatures great and small, / all things wise and wonderful, / the Lord God made them all. / Each little flower that opens, / each little bird that sings, / He make their glowing colors, / He made their tiny wings. / The purple-headed mountain, / the river running by, / the sunset and the morning that brightens up the sky. / He gave us eyes to see them, and lips that we might tell how great is God Almighty, / who has made all things well" (Cecil F. Alexander, "All Things Bright and Beautiful").

Meditation: Dear Lord, when we judge other people, remind us that if our sins were judged according to Christ's standards rather than man's, we would all deserve to be in jail. May the grace and forgiveness of the Savior be reflected in our moral judgments of one another. Amen.

Devotional Thirty-Seven:

"Fasting and Full Refrigerators"

In Mark 2:19–20, Jesus was criticized because His disciples did not fast. He insisted that just as people do not fast at weddings, His disciples do not fast in His presence. When He is gone, Jesus suggests, His disciples will fast.

People fast for many reasons. *Diet. Poverty. Meditation. Suicide. "Brownie points."* Sometimes, they lose their appetites and do not eat because they simply cannot eat.

There is another kind of fast. When life is empty and without meaning, you can eat and never be full. "I will send a famine in the land, not a famine of bread, nor a thirst for water, but of hearing the words of the Lord" (Amos 8:11b, KJV).

To those who know Him, the absence of Christ is the fast of famine, whether we have breakfast or not.

P.S.: We talked quite a lot about food today—your liquid lunch, my supper menu, what you should get for the refrigerator while I am there. However, life for us is not empty and without meaning. We are feasting on incredible, mysterious, indescribable, and powerful love. *Our love refrigerator is full.* Doubt it will ever be empty because our presence with each other ignites a fiery flame. Also, I do want to thank God there is within us a desire for feasting on His Word and allowing the bride of Christ to keep our hearts fully trusting in Him. Without question, this eternal reality gives sustenance and direction for each day He provides. The love refrigerator and the Lord's refrigerator are running over.

Hymn: "Christian hearts, in love united, / seek alone in Jesus rest; / has He not your love excited? / Then let love inspire each breast. / Members on our Head depending, / lights reflecting Him, our Sun, / Christians, His commands attending, / we in Him, our Lord, are one. / O that such may be our union / as Thine with the Father is, / and not one of our communion / e'er forsake the path of bliss; / may our light shine forth with brightness, / from Thy light reflected, shine; / thus the world will bear us witness, / that we, Lord are truly Thine" (Nicholaus L. von Zinzendorf, "Christians Hearts, in Love United").

Meditation: Dear Lord, help us keep our spiritual pantry and refrigerator full of Your living Word. Forgive us when we feast from less worthy supply. Amen.

Devotional Thirty-Eight:

An Appearance of Wisdom

In Colossians Chapter 2, the writer describes how we find freedom from human regulations through the life of Christ. In verse 23, Paul says, "Such regulation indeed have an appearance of wisdom, with their self-imposed worship, their false humility and their harsh treatment of the body, but they lack any value in restraining central indulgence" (Colossians 2:23, NIV). And Luke states, "And he said unto them, Ye are they which justify yourselves before men; but God knoweth your hears: for that which is highly esteemed among men is abomination in the sight of God" (Luke 16:15, KJV).

Self-made religion or self-imposed humility gives the appearance of wisdom, but it is the self that is magnified. Such false religions cannot do anything with the flesh. The flesh can only have its needs met by obeying God. Once a law of God is broken, the flesh jumps into action. *Where do I go for help?*

This becomes something I cannot do on my own but a work of God in my life, producing the fruit of righteousness. Charles Spurgeon said, "The only difference between a very wise man and a very great fool is the wise man knows he is a fool, and the other does not."

So, pray the prayer of Augustine, who pled, "Deliver me, O

Lord, from that evil man—myself!"

P.S.: Grace, how easy it is, given the years of academic endeavor and accumulation of material resources, to elevate the self rather than God, the Giver of Life. It is so easy to be carried away into the realm of self-righteousness. It is a constant challenge for me. Early in my academic training, I was asked to read essays about Abraham Lincoln's leadership style. It is clearly evident he trusted in God's wisdom. On one occasion, he stated, "I have been driven many times upon my knees by the overwhelming conviction that I had nowhere else to go. My own wisdom and that of all about me seemed insufficient for the day." One of the "surprised by grace" revelations for me is to discover, once again, one's humble spirit. You have confidence in yourself, but it is a confidence grown out of your trust in God's counsel. Let us pledge to walk together in trusting God's direction when human wisdom is weak and afraid (and academic degrees fail). I promise to work on it!

Hymn: "I love the Lord; He heard my cries/ and pitied every groan. / Long as I live, and troubles rise, / I'll hasten to His throne. / I love the Lord; He heard my cries / and chased my grief away. / O let my heart no more despair / while I have breath to pray" (Isaac Watts, "I Love the Lord; He Heard My Cries"/"Psalm 116 Part 1").

Meditation: Dear God, Your servant Henry Ward Beecher once confessed, "It is not well for a man to pray cream and live skim milk." Remind us daily that our greatest moments in life are walking in Your wisdom. May it be so for us. Amen.

Devotional Thirty-Nine:

God's Fellow Workers

In 1 Corinthians 3:9 (NIV), we read, "For we are God's fellow workers; you are God's field, God's building." In describing his ministry in Corinth, the apostle changes his illustration from agricultural to architectural. Later, in verse 10, he considers his whole ministry a gift of grace from a loving father. It was a free gift Paul did not earn.

Paul continues that as a wise builder, he laid a foundation, and another was building upon it. In his agricultural illustration, he considered his ministry as one of planting and Apollos's ministry as one of watering. In the architectural illustration, he has the role of architect or a "wise builder." Apollos and others to follow are seen as those who "water."

What a legacy he left for believers. So he says to Apollos and to us who follow, "Let each man be taking heed how he is building upon it" (the redemptive foundation of God's redemptive plan). How much water have you poured lately?

Jesus taught us there is joy in heaven over one sinner who repents. Let's face it. God has always been partial to humanity. When people reach out of darkness to find His presence and share the gospel story, a fragrance makes the angels pause.

P.S.: Tonight, a part of the conversation dealt with the existence of angels and your gratitude for a gifted African-American pastor of a church in Memphis. Among many gifts of ministry, he is most faithful to share the gospel. It reminded me that many of heaven's citizens are there because of prayer and the pointed message of a faithful witness. Thank God for those willing to get their hands dirty and spend time with people some of us may not be comfortable communicating with on a regular basis. But we can all pray for and support those who do. And, in the course of our own community pathways, we can live out and bear witness to those searching for eternal truth. We also talked tonight about God's call. In fact, each of us is called to be a minister, and beyond any special calling to His work, may our lives be found as "gospel partners."

Hymn: Menno Simons, Esther Bergen, "We Are People of God's Peace." This hymn, originally written in 1552, highlights the reality that we are people of God, and in daily living, we are to be God's peacemakers.

Meditation: Dear God, in the smugness of prideful arrogance, show us how hypocritical we sometimes are. May intellectual and spiritual humility emerge in us through recognizing that in Your sight, our righteousness is as filthy rags. Amen.

Devotional Forty:

Confirm Your Reservation

Guess what triggered tonight's thoughts. You guessed it: it was the thought of an airline ticket to see you. Airline travel has changed considerably, but I do remember, especially in the tourist season, you made the mistake of assuming that a ticket meant a seat on the plane. Confirming reservations was simple. You called the ticket desk and let the clerk know, strange as it was, you were really going to leave on a particular flight at a particular time. And how I do remember your handling my busy travel schedules during the years we worked together. As a matter of fact, you always provided an itinerary for me and mailed a copy to Jo, giving her details of the trip. I must say, travel was much easier in those days.

"Therefore, my brothers, be the more eager to make your calling and election sure. For if you do these things, you will never fall" (2 Peter 2:10a, NIV). Reading through Chapter One of that text, the reader discovers the telephone won't do it. You supplement faith with virtue, knowledge, self-control, steadfastness, godliness, brotherly affection, and love. Sounds like you're already flying before you get on the plane.

P.S.: That is how I feel about us. Though the moment of marriage is still a question for us, I feel like we are already flying, not just to Alaska, Hawaii, Austria, or Vaiden (your hometown), but into the utterly amazing and mysteriousness of oneness. Coming together with you will take a moment of time when we are really ready to travel on and able to experience the keenest ecstasy known to human beings. It will be a miracle of God's provision to us. And no one else can tell us just how to share this life with each other. It is ours to plan and complete. The trip will include spontaneity of life, freedom of expression, sensitivity in caring, and yielding, leading to completion. I have confirmed my reservation for the journey. Let us promise to experience the journey as it was intended to be. Committed to God's plan for marriage, then free, enjoyable, renewing, and more filled with meaning than words can tell.

Hymn: "Blest be the tie that binds our hearts in Christian love; / the fellowship of kindred minds is like to that above. / Before our Father's throne we pour our ardent prayers; / our fears, our hopes, our aims are one, our comforts and our cares. / We share our mutual woes, our mutual burdens bear; / and often for each other flows the sympathizing tear" (John Fawcett, "Blest Be the Tie").

Meditation: Father, continue to guide us in this marvelous journey. May Your divine wisdom be the compass for each step of the way. In the name of Him, who said, "I am the way, the truth, and the life." Amen.

Devotional Forty-One:

The Art of Loving Self

In Matthew 19:19 (KJV), Jesus makes it very clear that we are to "Thou salt love thy neighbor as thyself."

To love a neighbor as oneself has a catch in it. I must love myself, big feet, big ears and all.

In an old Jewish tale, a group of passengers boarded a ship. Each was assigned a seat below the waterline. One passenger pulled a brace and bit from his luggage and began to bore a hole in his bench. His fellow passengers protested.

"It's my seat!" he responded. "I paid for it. I can do as I like." His companions answered, "But if you sink, we all sink."

So, take care of yourself. Brush your teeth three times a day. Watch when you cross the street. Look to your health and your heart. Do the right thing. Watch where you punch holes! If you do well, you've begun to love God, yourself, and your traveling partner.

P.S.: The greater you can love yourself, the more you can love your mate. Spouses are meant to love each other's bodies as if they were their own possessions, not as mechanisms that can be used for satisfaction and discarded at will, but as treasures of great and lasting value. As one realizes how infinitely we are appreciated by a mate, we develop the assurance of our own self-worth. C. S. Lewis observed that even his body "had such a different importance" because it was the body his wife loved! This caring and responsibility extends out to other details of life, but it best begins with the sensitive appreciation of the other partner in the love relationship. It continues to be nurtured there because each one's self-worth is being renewed by the other. That is when love, true and total love, becomes mysterious. It is the only way I can describe the essence of our love. It's like a piece of Mozart's music that a listener once asked him to explain the meaning of. Mozart replied, "If I could explain it in words, I wouldn't need music." I do think it has happened because we are mature enough to love God, ourselves, and then each other.

Hymn: "While passing through this world of sin, / and others your life shall view, / be clean and pure without, within, / let others see Jesus in you. / Let others see Jesus in you, / Let others see Jesus in you; / keep telling the story, / be faithful and true, / let others see Jesus in you" (B. B. McKinney, "Let Others See Jesus in You").

Meditation: Father, Grace has brought a newness of life to me and, in a real sense, helped me to rediscover the person I really am. It is remarkable how love of self can lead to love of others. You have commanded us to love others as we love ourselves. May that capacity grow in us day by day. Amen.

Devotional Forty-Two:

The Color of Music

In Matthew 13:31, we have Jesus's parable of the mustard seed.

After describing how great a tree grows from a tiny seed, Jesus concludes that birds come and build their nests in the branches.

Why not bird's nests? They may have planted the tree in the first place. Loren Eiseley, in his book, *The Immense Journey*, tells how, in the distant past, flowers bloomed, and birds began to sing at the same period of time. Why? Flowers made possible the protein in seeds. Birds needed protein to live. So birds would eat seeds and carry the crumbs of their banquet wherever they flew. Now flowers and birds—girdle the earth with color and song.

The next time you see a bright bird singing on a berry bush, pray to God that you, too, be given, in the fields of your sowing, a song and a nest for the night.

P.S.: You have heard all about using the phrase "the birds and the bees" as a metaphor for telling young ones about sex. Tonight, in our phone conversation, we, as we usually do, dwelt at length on the openness and freedom we have with each other. We pointedly spoke about how it will later impact love in marriage. So, rather than the birds and bees, let me just say a word about "the birds and trees." Just as the two are mutually involved in nature's recycling, we already know a wonderful security in each other's love. We also have talked about how pride, self-pity, resentment, anger, bitterness, and jealousy too often slip in when least expected and bring desolation whenever those infiltrations operate unchecked. And a part of the promise we are making to each other is the security that comes from a cooperative commitment with each other. Meeting each other's needs through sharing, understanding, and satisfying the other in the safety of a committed love brings security. Already developed in our relationship is a sense of security—safely trusting in each other. Physical love, when it happens, is a walled garden, the inner courtyard of our kingdom, and it is a sacred place awaiting marriage vows. It makes me want to sing. As Gloria Perkins penned, "To understand and be understood, to know, really know what another is thinking, to say what you will and be sure it is accepted as of value or sifted through without reproof to be you, really *you* and know you are loved—*this is near heaven!*" That is "the color of our music," and it is beautiful. The birds are singing.

Hymn: "Spirit of God, descend upon my heart; / wean it from earth; through all its pulses move; / stoop to my weakness, mighty as Thou art, / and make me love Thee as I ought to love. / Teach me to love Thee as Thine angels love, / one holy passion filling all my frame; / the kindling of the heaven descended Dove, / my heart an altar, and Thy love the flame" (George Croly, "Spirit of God, Descend upon My Heart").

Meditation: Father, teach us that quality of life is greater than quantity of life, especially with Your presence. May the indwelling power of Your Spirit prompt every word we utter and every action we take. Let our lives be worthy of Your creative intent. Would You raise up within us anthems of praise for the gift of eternal life out of our faith in Him who said, "I am the resurrection and the life"? Amen.

Devotional Forty-Three:

The Case of the Platinum Handcuffs

Did you ever read reports of gangsters imprisoned in luxury? They had good furniture, TVs, gourmet food, telephones, visiting privileges, and, by now, computers. A whole lot of us free people never had it so good. But few lined up to apply for those apartments.

Show a prisoner in a dungeon that his handcuffs are platinum, his ball and chain gold, and he'll not brighten much. He'd rather have tin cuff links and be free. Still, there are people so poor they apply to stay in jail. There are rich folk chained by gold. "Free will" is not in their dictionary. In 1 Chronicles 29:9 (KJV), we read that Solomon's temple was funded by free-will offerings. Verse 9 says, "With a perfect heart they offered willingly to the Lord" (1 Chronicles 29:9, KJV). That is the only place the term "free will" is used in the Bible, and it has to do with giving.

If you can't give it, you don't have it. It has you.

P.S.: We did not talk much tonight, so I am kind of following up on last night's theme. We talked in response to your question, "Can what we feel just now continue on?" And I said "yes" because I really do believe we will first trust in God and then in each other, to love and give, to forgive and ask forgiveness, to forget oneself in caring for the other, and, in turn, to receive joyfully from the other. As we each act on the basis of our responsibilities rather than clinging to "my rights," tensions or stress will resolve themselves with an even stronger welding of the two of us together.

Hymn: "Joys are flowing like a river, / since the Comforter has come; / He abides with us forever, / makes the trusting heart His home. / Bringing life and health and gladness, / all around this heavenly Guest, / banished unbelief and sadness, / changed our weariness to rest" (Manie Payne Ferguson, "Blessed Quietness").

Meditation: Dear Father, at times, we complain about life's challenges and difficulties. When we are at times tempted to complain, let us remember, first, to help each other and be a friend to those whose needs are greater than our own. Amen.

Devotional Forty-Four:

Flattening the Geography

They are redoing the road from Weatherford to Mineral Wells, Texas. Highway 80 still carries the traffic alongside the new road. Traveling the old highway is like riding a rollercoaster. First, you look up to the new road, then you peer down, and when you get near Mineral Wells, there is quite a high hill, at least for this part of Texas, and the old road still trails up that hill while the new road will curve alongside it.

The engineers are leveling everything out. If you want to get places, you have to flatten out the geography.

The prophet Isaiah teaches that God is on His way into the world. "Every valley shall be exalted, and every mountain and hill be made low" (Isaiah 40:4, KJV), and John the Baptist preached repentance to prepare the way of the Lord.

Remember the parable of the man who, upon choosing the lowest seat at a feast, was told to come up higher? Unafraid of the mighty respecter of the lowly, John leveled out the ups and downs of the human wilderness. He engineered a highway for the Christ who loved all of us the same.

P.S.: You said yes! God's agape love in giving us His Son to flatten the geography of the human race is a beautiful metaphor. In both Testaments, there are many reminders God is forever seeking to redeem and renew His creation. I am thrilled you said "yes" to my proposal. And, on my mind and heart is the scripture revealing the truth agape love in marriage must involve total commitment. Just as God is totally committed to us, His command to Adam is to "cleave" to Eve. When I proposed to you last Sunday, it was based on the statement in Genesis, "Therefore shall a man leave his father and his mother and shall cleave unto his wife. And they shall be one flesh" (Genesis 2:24, KJV). It was good to read from Scripture and in Germantown Baptist Church, where you are a longtime member and where Jo and I were members during our Memphis years. It is a special place. It is a place where new roads of life are built. In a sense, marriage is like building a new road. Neither partner loses his/her identity, but the emotional and psychological aspects of each other's lives are leveled out, not from feelings, but from commitment through every changing circumstance. Commitment is the bond; the feeling of love is the result. The feeling comes because of the reality of commitment. I am so glad you said "yes"! There is much to be worked out. Moving forward, our growing commitment to each other will produce greater and more powerful feelings. So, Lord, flatten our geography as we come to love each other more and more. Our love for each other is truly "surprising and amazing grace."

Hymn: "Eternal Father, strong to save, / Whose arm does bind the restless wave, / who bids the mighty ocean deep / its own appointed limits keep; / O hear us when we cry to Thee / for those in peril on the sea. / O Trinity of love and pow'r, / Your children shield in danger's hour; / From rock and tempest, fire, and foe, /

Protect them wheresoe'er they go; / Thus, evermore shall rise to Thee / glad hymns of praise from land and sea" (William Whiting, "Eternal Father, Strong to Save").

Meditation: Father of the Universe, a proposal for marriage should not be taken lightly. May the intent to become one with another in marriage represent the same kind of commitment of Christ to His church. May the eternal arm of God bind us into one, strong and true! Amen.

Devotional Forty-Five:

The Flavor of Oxygen

Isaiah 42:5 reports that God gives breath to those who walk the face of the earth.

What is the flavor of oxygen? Sweet? Sour? Try a deep breath on a fragrant spring morning or winter air after a quiet Memphis snow that kept you in for two days.

To the drowning, the hunger for air is the cry of starving blood. Every time I breathe, my nostrils taste the flavor of life.

Some say grace over food three times a day. But who says grace over breathing? The winds of God in our nostrils speak softly to us even while we are asleep. For when He made man, God breathed into his nostrils the breath of life…and we became a living soul.

P.S.: With you almost losing your voice and breath, tonight's conversation reminded me of how very much I am glad God has kept us alive for each other. And, because of it, we will be good stewards of each second, minute, hour, day, month, year, and the years of our time together. The love we share is always the fertile soil for joy and fulfillment. Let me praise the Lord for extending life to each of us. May the breath that He gives us be offered in gratitude and thanksgiving for each other, breath by breath. (Hope by morning your voice is normal, and please, *keep on breathing!*)

How I do give thanks for every breath you take. Most of all, for the breath-supported words that speak of our love. And even then, as we have said many times, language does not convey the fullest meaning of love. What is the flavor of oxygen? It is you; it is me; it is us alive.

Hymn: "Breathe on me, breath of God, / fill me with life anew, / that I may love what Thou dost love, / and do what Thou wouldst do. / Breathe on me, breath of God, / until my heart is pure, / until with Thee I will Thy will, / to do and to endure. / Breathe on me, breath of God, / till I am wholly Thine, / till all this earthly part of me glows / with Thy fire divine. / Breathe on me, breath of God, / so shall I never die, / but live with Thee / the perfect life / of Thine eternally" (Edwin Hatch, "Breathe on Me, Breath of God").

Meditation: Great Breath of God, thank You for the gift of life and each new day given to us to enjoy the fruits of Your creation. In His name, we pray. Amen.

Devotional Forty-Six:

Lined up with Bedrock and Stars

Not long ago, I had a conversation with a bricklayer helping put up the new building at Dallas Baptist University. He was waiting for a plumber to rough in a plumbing pipe through the wall where he was laying brick. I told him as we talked that I'd read a sermon on the plumb line of the prophet Amos. As we talked, he said that a leveled-up foundation was key to a good building and that he wanted the pipe right where it was supposed to be, and then he waited until the foundation was permanently leveled and cured before he started the wall.

Furthermore, he said, "Most folks who build these days lay a rough foundation and expect the bricklayer to cover it up. Makes all the difference in the world if the foundation's true."

In 1 Corinthians 3, we read that Jesus Christ is the only foundation for a lasting Christian life. He was on the level with men and women under God. A good foundation lines you up with the whole wide world—stars above and bedrock beneath. Who would dare build a shack on such true masonry?

P.S.: Tonight's conversation reminded me so much of the bedrock foundation of our lives. Though admittedly not perfect, we are seeking to build our marriage on a rich Christian foundation, which has provided us with unique opportunities to serve the Lord and His people through Southern Baptist churches and denomination entities. Even though we lived through denomination conflict and change, the pattern and commitment of our lives have been shaped by a period of Baptist life that represented the best of God's design and desire for cooperation and Christian union. Oh, how I wish that cooperative global mission commitment uniting believers would once again flourish.

It was a golden time for each of us. We put a lot of ourselves into the structures of the denomination. Of course, many others did as well, and we are a part of a rich heritage. Much disciplined work formed the basis for that era in SBC life.

I thought about it. There is something to be learned here about building a marriage. It takes genuine effort and persistence to establish an intimate relationship. We are certainly on the way. But neither good marriages nor, for that matter, even deep friendships are made in heaven. They may be designed there, as ours surely was, but the work of constructing them is done on earth, and only those who are willing to stay with the long-range task of faithful and constant relationship-building will avoid the loneliness or conflict that destroys denominations and marriages. Yes, we are definitely on the way, and I am "out of my mind" excited about the privilege of building an abiding and life-long partnership with you.

Hymn: "The church's one foundation / is Jesus Christ her Lord; / She is His new creation, / by Spirit and the Word: /from heav'n He came and sought her / to be His holy bride, / with His own blood He bought her, / and for her life He died. / Elect from ev'ry nation, / yet one o'er all the earth, / her charter of salvation, / one Lord, one faith, one birth; / one holy name she blesses, / partakes one holy food, / and to one hope she presses, / with ev'ry grace endued. / Mid toil and tribulation, / and tumult of her war, / she waits the consummation / of peace forever more; / till with the vision glorious, / her longing eyes are blessed, / and the great church victorious / shall be the church at rest" (Samuel J. Stone, "The Church's One Foundation").

Meditation: For every beat of the drum and every sound of the trumpet, we thank You, dear God, that we are marching together in building a lasting relationship in the institution of marriage. Amen.

Devotional Forty-Seven:

Nearsighted Enough to See

In Ephesians, Paul speaks these words: "I pray also that the eyes of your heart may be enlightened, in order that you my know the hope to which he has called you" (Ephesians 1:18a, NIV). The eyes of the heart? Even a child knows that a heart cannot have eyes. The heart loves; love, we know, is blind.

The story of the prodigal son helps us understand. Luke says that when the prodigal son came home, his aged father "saw him afar off." Only the blindness of love could see that far. Only caring could recognize the cadence of that familiar stride.

The old man was so nearsighted he took family disgrace and put shoes on his son's feet, a ring on his hand, and a T-bone steak on his plate. Lord God, if You must look upon us, look with the eyes of Your heart.

P.S.: Our evening conversations, of late, have focused on building our relationship and moving it toward marriage. Each exchanged word and each conversation prompts talk about the unexplainable attraction we feel for one another. Tonight, the main emphasis was on "being," not just "doing." How satisfying it is to know one's worth comes from the love the Father has for us rather than what we do, have, or can earn. Such reality contributes to the kind of perspective that rightly can be called providence. It is the belief that life is destiny and not just a process of blind chance. This means coming to believe in all things God has been at work for good.

I said to you tonight that I am a changed person because of the providential aspects of how we were brought together. Neither of us could know what the death of our beloved first spouses would mean. Now that we understand, it has produced a positive and hopeful perspective about us, our past, and the longed-for bounty of the future. Let me summarize my grateful heart by saying, Grace, because of you, we can say three things about us. First, "By the grace of God, we are who we are." Second, "For all that has been, thank You, Lord." And, third, "For all that will be, *yes*." Wish we could know what it will be, but I am confident we will be receiving each new "surprise" with the "eyes of the heart."

Hymn: "Glorious things of thee are spoken, / Zion, city of our God! / He whose word cannot be broken / formed thee for His own abode; / on the Rock of Ages founded, / what can shake thy sure repose? / With salvation's walls surrounded, / thou mayest smile at all thy foes. / See, the streams of living waters, / springing from eternal love, / well supply thy sons and daughters, / and all fear of want remove: / who can faint while such a river / ever does their thirst assuage? / Grace which, like the Lord, / the giver, never fails from age to age. / Round each habitation hovering, / see the cloud and fire appear / for a glory and a covering, / showing that the Lord is near! / Thus deriving from their banner light / by night and shade by day, / safe they feed upon the manna / which God gives them on their way" (John Newton, "Glorious Things of Thee Are Spoken").

Meditation: Dear Father, may we always seek to be led by the light of Your powerful and creative work. Forgive us when we try to be God and put human desires above divine direction. So, give us "the eyes of the heart" that desire to discover and follow Your will. Amen.

Devotional Forty-Eight:

From Rubbish to Ruin

In Amos 9:14, we read the prophecy that someday, God's people will rebuild ruined cities and inhabit them.

The book of Ezra does not tell how much time it took for the people to lay the foundation for the rebuilding of Solomon's temple, where the old one once stood. When completed, the people gathered to celebrate and raised a great shout. Some people were crying over what had been lost, and others were rejoicing over what had been gained.

True, the Temple of Solomon was much more splendid than the new temple. But Hiram of Tyre built that. This one, the Jews, themselves, were building out of ruin and failure with their own hands and at their own risk. They were lucky. They couldn't build a temple big enough to bankrupt the future.

The Jews made space for God out of the rubble of past failures. Indeed, it was not a mighty temple like Solomon's, but it was a place where God could be at home.

P.S.: Yesterday's "50-Second Sermon" had to do with the basic virtues of building a life foundation, including marriage. Let me share a further word about this foundation. In a sense, we are starting over from bottom to top. Unlike Israel's history, we do not have the ruin and destruction of their temple nor the dispersion that took them from their homeland. But we do have experiences from the past that should challenge and inform the way we put marriage together. I would call them growing pains. I do know I am much more aware of who I am, aware of my strengths and weaknesses, and aware of your needs. It is called maturity, and maturity produces understanding, trust, and a spirit of being a "problem solver" rather than being a "problem producer." We are building a new temple of anticipated marriage. It won't look like the previous ones. Our first marriages produced flesh from our flesh, and we are thrilled God gave you two wonderful children and three for me. Jo and LeRoy made it possible for such wonderful fruitage. But my prayer is the new marriage we are building will be a place not unlike with Jo and Leroy. It must be new, and now ours. May it ever be where God could be at home and where our children and their offspring benefit from an "earthly heaven." That is indeed the essence of an "extended family."

Hymn: "I'm pressing on the upward way, / new heights I'm gaining every day; / still praying as I onward bound, / "Lord, plant my feet on higher ground." / My heart has no desire to stray / where doubts arise and fears dismay; / through some may dwell where these abound, / My prayer, my aim is higher ground. / I want to scale the utmost height / and catch a gleam of glory bright; / but still I'll pray till heaven I've found, / "Lord, lead me on to higher ground" (Johnson Oatman, Jr., "Higher Ground").

Meditation: We give thanks the heavenly Father's arms never tire of holding His children. I am so glad we are a part of the family of God. May His blessing fall on us as we build an extended earthly family. Amen.

Devotional Forty-Nine:

Architect of Time

In 2 Peter 3:8, we are reminded that with the Lord, a day is as a thousand years, and a thousand years is a day. The passage highlights the patience of God.

Patience is the art of using time. To God, time and patience are the way He creates. He is the Architect of time. He is forever making all things new, and in His creative powers, He is bringing about growth. For spring to blossom, there must be a time of winter. For mountains to rise and fall, God rations eons of geologic time.

If God were impatient, He would make all things spring into being with a flip of His finger. But God is patient. He grows us. Since time was put in us, we can say, "Yesterday." We can say, "Tomorrow." We can say, "Now."

P.S.: Tonight, we talked about schedules for a wedding and receptions in Germantown and Fort Worth. I loved it because it brought the reality of our union close to the surface. It also made me aware God has been growing us as persons and as a couple. We are learning so much about each other and each other's needs. We each have had work roles demanding the best of servant leadership. It is not always done perfectly, but it always reaches the desired goal. Now, going forward, I want to be a servant to you, to care for and guide both of us in continued growth and happiness, and to grow a blended family that models godly love for each other.

At the moment, geographical distance makes it a challenge, but quality time and effort in nurturing respect and love will be one of the responsibilities we must share. Also, I am convinced it will best be communicated by the way we love and care for each other and let our union be a model for the rest of the family. Psychologists call this generativity. It happens when parents, in some way, somehow, through their concomitant love and growth, contribute value and unselfish love to the stream of family history. Of course, all of this takes time and patience. It has to begin with us. Following God's pattern, let us resolve to take the ideal of concomitant growth seriously and keep on working at it all our days.

Hymn: "Breathe on me, Breath of God, / fill me with life anew, that I may love / what Thou dost love, and do what Thou wouldst do. / Breathe on me, Breath of God, / until my heart is pure, until with Thee I will Thy will, to do and to endure. / Breathe on me, Breath of God, / till I am wholly Thine, / till all this earthly part of me glows with Thy fire divine. / Breathe on me, Breath of God, / so shall I never die, but live with Thee / the perfect life of Thine eternity" (Edwin Hatch, "Breathe on Me, Breath of God").

Meditation: We thank You, Great Creator; You are the evaluator and also Healer of spiritual health. All health is directly tied to spiritual health. The good news about finding what may be wrong with us is the Great Physician can make us well, not only through modern medical technology but also through the blessing of divine intervention. So make us clean and well. Amen.

Devotional Fifty:

A Six-Year-Old in College

My first year of school was a college education in some ways. I remember it so well. My father was the principal of West Ledford School in Harrisburg, Illinois, and before he completed theological training at Southwestern Baptist Seminary, he was also pastor of Ledford Baptist Church. I was very proud of my dad, and I thought since he was the principal of the school, I was privileged. So, on the first day of school in my first-grade class, I thought I would make a hit with everybody. West Ledford School had three rooms, and I was in the first-third room. I was convinced I would be the most popular student. And why not? My dad was the principal!

Non-academic learning took place on that first day. My parents had a small hoard of pennies and small change they kept in a big jar in their bedroom. Before class, and without their knowledge, I filled my pockets with pennies and, when I got to school, gave them to my school chums. Among others, a favorite buddy got 16 cents. His mother called my mother. Other calls were made. In the first days of September, the school grounds became as cold as December.

Later in life, I read in Proverbs 19 that everyone is a friend to a man who gives gifts while his friends flee the poor man. And remember, the prodigal son described in Luke 15 went to a far country to find out what you can't buy. I learned that in West Ledford School, a mile and a half from home. I also learned you never take something that is not yours!

P.S.: I am so glad our love for each other is "not for sale," nor can it be bought. Friendship cannot be purchased. It may work for a moment, but lasting friendship is based on shared values and commitments. Nor does the possession of certain things make for lasting friendship. I started learning that in first grade. Like in yesterday's sermon, our intangible worth is based not on what we do but rather on the extent to which we allow God's "waters of grace" to lift us upward. I am convinced God is at work for good in our lives. I can't wait for the next chapter. I am glad we have chosen each other out of free will and a love that desires to give and receive.

Hymn: "Gracious Spirit, dwell with me, / I would gracious be; / help me now Thy grace to see, / I would be like Thee; / and with words that help and heal, / Thy life would mine reveal; / and, with actions bold and meek, / for Christ my Savior speak. / Truthful Spirit, dwell with me, / I would truthful be; / help me now Thy truth to see, / I would be like Thee; / and, with wisdom kind and clear, / Thy life in mine appear; / and with actions, lovingly, speak Christ's sincerity. / Holy Spirit, dwell with me, / I would holy be; / show Thy mercy tenderly, / make me more like Thee / separate from sin I would / and cherish all things good, / and whatever I can be give / Him who gave me Thee. / Mighty Spirit, dwell with me, / I would mighty be; / help me now Thy power to see, / I would be like Thee; 'gainst / all weapons hell can wield, / be Thou my strength and shield; / let Thy word my weapon be, / Lord, Thine the victory" (Thomas Toke Lynch, "Gracious Spirit, Dwell with Me").

Meditation: Dear God, help us learn friendship cannot be bought. It is earned by the selfless giving and receiving of shared values and commitments. Forgive us when our actions are selfish, motivated by exaggerated ego and prideful ambition. Most of all, teach us to trust in Your sure forgiveness and grace. Amen.

Devotional Fifty-One:

Ask Your Husband at Home

The lady who cleaned our house in Fort Worth back in the '70s was a beautiful African-American lady who became like family to us. One evening, she missed her bus schedule, so I took her to her home in East Fort Worth. She was then nearly seventy, and she had seen a lot of life. She sketched her story as I drove her home. Back in World War II days, she had married. The union lasted two years after the war was over. She moved back home with her mother. When her mother died, she lived alone.

"You never remarried," I observed. "Why not?" I got the answer my presumption deserved. "Why should I? Men are all alike. Turn the sack over, and they all fall out at the same time!"

I knew Gertie revered her Bible and attended church, so I tried a sly question. The writer of Corinthians 14 says, "If they will learn anything, let them ask their husbands at home" (1 Corinthians 14:35a, KJV).

"Without a husband, how can you do that?"

"Huh!" she snorted. "That husband of mine, always wavin' that bottle! Only question I'd ask him is, 'Are you drunk'?"

Gertie was right. If I want a man's privileges, first of I'll have to be a man.

P.S.: Tonight, after our phone conversation, I really wanted to hug you. You were sleepy and tired, and all I could think about was how hard you work and the fact you hardly have quality time for yourself. For a long time now, I have been impressed with your duty and devotion. I feel unworthy to have you as my own choice friend and soon-to-be wife. Without question, I want the privilege of loving you forever and being the kind of man worthy of you to call "husband." Grace, I thank God that He, in His providential care, brought connection to our lives and now has reconnected us to become one. Yes, I am privileged and always want to be a true man!

Hymn: "We walk by faith and not by sight. / No gracious words we hear from Him / who spoke as none e'er spoke; / but we believe Him near. / We may not touch His hands and side, / nor follow where He trod; / but in His promise we rejoice, / and cry, "My Lord and God! / And when our life of faith is done / in realms of clearer light / we may behold You as You are, / with full and endless sight. / We walk by faith and not by sight, / led by God's pure and holy Light! Prepare us for the journey, / Lord, and may we know Your power / and might as we walk by faith and not by sight" (Henry Alford, "We Walk by Faith").

Meditation: Dear Father, I am so glad that Your hand is in all things. The next time we are tempted to take credit for the blessings of life, help us remember You are the Author of it all. Amen.

Devotional Fifty-Two:

Mountain Turned into a Molehill

In Mark 11:22–25, Jesus talks about the power of faith. He says you can believe a mountain right into the sea. Prayer plus belief gets results.

Jesus never suggests His disciples try this. Instead, He says, "When you stand praying, if you hold anything against anyone, forgive him, so that your Father in heaven may forgive you your sins" (Mark 11:25, NIV).

Imagine a flint mountain in an arctic sea. The home of monsters that giggle by day and scream by night, it breeds foul weather over the face of the earth. This mountain is resentment. Higher than Everest, its universe is the heart. More foul than Everest's monsters, it makes the soul a demon. It shuts off the heart's weather.

But when God comes real in faith, the mountain Resentment dives into the waiting sea. Behind is a quiet valley, bright with the greenness of spring.

P.S.: This "sermon" given to me by Roger Carstensen was shared with my class at Dallas Baptist University. It was right after Jo's death, and I was dealing with issues of resentment, grief, and self-pity. Forget my own emotional needs at the time; I thought about the kind of evening you had last night and intended to send this to you but went to sleep. Right now, you and I are enjoying a plethora of "highs" and "can't waits." And, certainly, we never want the "downs" and "why did this have to happen" events to occur. I really hated you had to deal with a "bruised" scratch on your new car. You were very weary of it, I could tell. I tried to empathize and remind you some "good" could/would usher forth. Please don't think I was ignoring your pain. Your pain is my pain. I always want to be there for you when disappointments come. We will have some pains in our lives, but with each other "holding the fort," mountains become molehills. The important thing now is we have each other as a constant force of faith and fidelity. Beyond all the material matters, nothing else matters as long as we are together. For me, a marriage commitment is for life. It was that with Jo, bless her dear heart, and now I want it for us.

Hymn: "Lift every voice and sing, / till earth and heaven ring, / ring with the harmonies of liberty; / let our rejoicing rise, / high as the listening skies, / let it resound loud as the rolling sea. / Sing a song full of faith / that the dark past has taught us, / sing a song full of the hope / that the present has brought us; / facing the rising sun / of our new day begun, let us march on / till victory is won" (James Weldon Johnson, "Lift Every Voice and Sing").

Meditation: Caring Father, remind us always that pain and struggle will happen in the contours of life. Teach us how to learn from failure caused by our own mistakes and the unwelcome disruptions caused by others. Let our anchor point in life be complete confidence in Your source of wisdom and strength. Amen.

Devotional Fifty-Three:

The Startled Eye of Space

In his speech to Agrippa, Paul asks, "Why should it be thought a thing incredible with you that God should raise the dead?" (Acts 26:8, KJV).

Imagine being on a planet in the galaxy Andromeda and encountering a being with a computer head.

Suppose this being got a radio message describing humans. Can you imagine humans with blood and flesh, heart and lungs; humans with tears and laughter, dreams and work; humans with stupidity and genius; humans living with polar bears, alligators, mosquitoes, flowers, and poison ivy; humans driving cars and peering through telescopes; humans shopping at stores, making love, discussing politics, listening to a symphony, watching television, sending a computer e-mail, talking with their most treasured fiancés and soon-to-be-wives on a cell phone.

What do you mean God can't raise the dead?

P.S.: Tonight, having hosted at my house the "42" group (a domino game) of retired seminary faculty, friends, and their spouses made me aware God is powerfully good in providing social support groups. It is an amazing group, brilliant and variously talented. I have been doubly blessed by this group and the privilege of friendship with each one. I thought about how God raised up this "plain old guy" and gave me untold opportunity. I am forever blessed by students, faculty, friends, travel opportunities all over the planet, leadership in significant organizations, and treasured family dearer than life itself. This group has helped me with the grief of losing Jo, my first love. Indeed, I have been blessed.

And on top of that, He has "surprised me with Grace." The reconnection with you has helped me rise above grief and distress. This amazing love raised up by God has brought new life and a new sense of purpose. Language does not convey all God has prepared for us. This sense of oneness and completeness somehow cannot be explained to anyone not having experienced it. Also, the connection with you in these later years has given me a reason to love my first love, Jo, even more each day. The only persons who know how to love are persons who have been loved and who have experienced love. We each have that benefit. Because of it, there is for us the promise of a transformed marriage. Most of all, the blessings of tonight's visit with friends made me ever more grateful to you. What a gift you are for me now in the later years of life. The mystery of our love and the promise of a "heaven on earth" make me believe *we are a miracle right now*!

Hymn: "Faith of our fathers! Living still / in spite of dungeon, fire, and sword: / oh, how our hearts beat high with joy / when-e'er we hear that glorious word! / Faith of our fathers, holy faith! / We will be true to thee till death! / Faith of our fathers! We will strive to win all nations unto thee, / and through the truth that comes from God, / the world shall then be truly free: / faith of our fathers, holy faith! / We will be true to thee till death! / Faith of our fathers! We will love / both friend and foe in all our strife, / and preach thee, too, as love knows how, / by kindly words and virtuous life: / faith of our fathers, holy faith! / We will be true to thee till death!" (Frederick W. Faber, "Faith of Our Fathers").

Meditation: Dear Father, gratitude flows from grace. When we are reminded so vividly of another's compassion, it raises our sense of gratitude for their commitment to care. Ultimately, we are made aware that compassion is the capacity to put Christlike love into action. Be it ever so! Amen.

Devotional Fifty-Four:

The Informal Reception

Did you ever wonder why God did not see fit to give us the precise schedule of the return of our Lord to the world? What a reception we could arrange: choirs, bands, speeches, banquets; the biggest names in politics, the best entertainers of film and TV.

If God had made His schedule perfectly clear, we could have done much better when Jesus came the first time. The sights and smells of the stable, no reservation at the inn, those were downright embarrassing.

But Jesus, speaking of His second coming, insisted that we take heed and watch, "You do not know when the time will come" (Mark 13:33, NIV). Whoever says he knows is bound to be wrong. I guess that means we have to be ready all the time, to be ready any time. He takes us as we always are to become what we shall forever be.

P.S.: Tonight, we talked about a number of things, but the most memorable was the laughable and yet pensive talk about how many years are left for us. Will there be five, ten, fifteen, or even dare to think we could reach age one hundred? Obviously, we can't answer those questions. And I am glad we can't. I would rather define our intended future in the way I feel and think right now.

Furthermore, I want to believe that every new day, month, year, decade, or generation will be just like today. That in no way is denial. I know fully that age may bring some infirmities. But given how our love has grown each day, I can only begin to imagine how magnificently our love will be by the time we reach one hundred! Regardless of what may happen to either of us, I want to be sensitive to each other's needs, always be "on the same team, always seeing all that is admirable in the other, and never focusing on faults and failures."

Hymn: "Guide me, O Thou great Jehovah, / pilgrim through this barren land; / I am weak, but Thou art mighty hold me / with Thy pow'rful hand; / Bread of heaven, Bread of heaven, / feed me till I want no more, / feed me till I want no more. / Open now the crystal fountain / whence the healing stream doth flow; / let the fire and cloudy pillar / lead me all my journey through; / strong deliverer strong deliverer, / be Thou still my strength and shield. / Be thou still my strength and shield. / When I tread the verge of Jordan, / bid my anxious fears subside; / bear me thro' the swelling current, / land me safe on Canaan's side; / songs of praises, songs of praises / I will ever give to Thee; / I will ever give to Thee" (William Williams, "Guide Me").

Meditation: Dear Father of the Universal Family, remind us always life is either a choice of carnality or moral commitment. You have ordained physical pleasure and renewal of mind, body, and spirit. Let those happy pursuits be directed by Your ultimate intention for all human nature, namely to love You and our neighbors as ourselves. Amen.

Devotional Fifty-Five:

A Texas Royalty

In Proverbs, we read, "Children's children are the crown of the aged" (Proverbs 17:6, NIV). Now that I find grandchildren are the crown of the declining years, I'll have to share a comment or two. Sorry, I can't show you my pictures.

Here are the current stars in the crown. Greg's two girls, Gini and Geri; Jami's two, Rebecca and Michael; Jeff's two, Lauren and Wills; and don't forget eight "great-grands" who occurred after this writing. They are Matthew, Mark, Faith and Blake, Hazel and Vivian, and Oliver and Posy.

Why are they royalty? I don't have to get up at night with our grandkids. Or take them to get shots. Or nurse them through tonsillitis. I spoil them and avoid the consequences.

I really knew I was royalty when Michael ate three bowls of All-Bran because PaPaw liked it. And I will never forget when Lauren stood on her knee and said, "I love you, Pepaw." Wearing my crown, I feel companion to the scribe to whom Jesus said, "You are not far from the kingdom of God."

P.S.: Tonight, we spent a bit of time talking about your disappointment in not having Tucker tomorrow and then some more time scrolling on the web to find cocktail dresses. Talking about our grandchildren made me more pointedly aware we will be referring to our Texas and Tennessee royalty. I want to love your grandchildren like I love mine. Nicole is a beautiful, talented, and loving girl, and Tucker is mature beyond his years. I have been impressed with both of them. And, though I know your children, Cindy and Tim, are not mine by blood, my desire is to love them. That means, first of all, because they are yours, but also because I want to love what you love. I can't be their flesh and blood dad, but I would like to be the kind of husband to you and friend to them that evokes respect and great love for me. That will be earned over time as we have the opportunity to share the gift of family!

It was Kahil Gibran who wisely said,

> You may give your children love, but not your thoughts, / for they have their own thoughts. / You may house their bodies while in your home, but not their souls, / for their souls dwell in the house of tomorrow, / which you cannot visit, not even in your dreams. / You may even strive to be like them, but seek not to make them like you, / for life goes not backwards, nor tarries with yesterday. / You are the bow from which your children and grandchildren are living arrows. / The archer sees the mark upon the path of the infinite, / and He bends you with His might that the arrows may go swift and far. / Let your bending in the archer's hand be for gladness, / for even as He loves the arrow that flies, / so He loves the bow that is stable.

Grace, we can be *stable bows* for our offspring and take joy in the way their arrows fly. History is never a treadmill, nor is one individual a carbon copy of another. We can give them a certain feel for life, a sense of what is right and wrong, pointing them in the right direction, but when it comes to the specific armor they will need, it is not our sacred responsibility, but theirs, to fit themselves out with it. Let us resolve to be to them a constant source of family love and devotion and spend the rest of our lives enjoying the trappings of our *Texas-Tennessee royalty*.

Hymn: "Happy the home when God is there / And love fills everyone, / When with united work and pray'r / the Master's will is done. / Happy the home where / God's strong love is starting to appear, / Where all the children hear / His fame And parents hold Him dear. / Happy the home where pray'r is heard / And praise is ev'rywhere, / Where parents love the sacred Word / And its true wisdom share. / Lord, let us in our homes agree / This blessed peace to gain; / Unite our hearts in love to Thee, / And love to all will reign" (Henry Ware, Jr., Bryan Jeffery Leech, "Happy the Home When God Is There").

Meditation: Dear Eternal God, help us to be devoted parents worthy to be examples for our children. Thank You for the gift of "flesh from our flesh." May their posterity likewise empower those who are touched and influenced by their own influences as well as ours. Amen.

Devotional Fifty-Six:

The Vision and the Dream

Texas has been in a drought, but spring rains have eased the tension. It reminds me after telling of days to come when the drought in Israel would be over, Joel said, "And it shall come to pass afterward I will pour out my spirit on all flesh; your sons and your daughters shall prophecy, your old men shall dream dreams, your young men shall see visions" (Joel 2:28, KJV).

Israel had known spiritual drought before. In the time of Eli, the priest of doddering good intentions, we read that the word of the Lord was rare in those days; there was no frequent vision.

How will we know when the famine of the Spirit is about to be broken? Take a tip from Joel. Watch the very young and the very old. When we get back the vision and the dream, the drought is over.

P.S.: Tonight, we mainly talked about plans and schedules for the wedding and receptions. Also, we talked about Nicole's surgery and plans you now need to make about a "Granny trip." In addition, we spent a jaundiced moment on the state of the nation and the kind of leader this country needs to bring some order and sense to society. It was quite a mixture of conversation. Mostly, however, the exchange had to do with us, our generation, and the new one coming on. It brought my thoughts to the above scriptural truths. Especially is that true at 1:30 a.m. Like on several nights, as soon as our nightly visit was over, I watched the evening news and fell asleep in my chair. I was awakened by loud thunder and lightning. By the time I got to the bedroom, it was gushing rain. So maybe the Texas drought is about over. I hope so.

And, just maybe, the dreams of the older, which would include Grace and Jim, will combine with the young like Lauren, Rebecca, Gini, Geri, Michael, and Wills, along with your grandkids, Nicole and Tucker, and any grands. Hopefully, they will be the mix and magic to bring some order and sense back to our nation. Right now, the main focus of our minds is the happiness and joy awaiting an intended marriage. But just suppose that our dreams and the visions of the young could be cause for a revival of patriotism, freedom, and justice for all. Those are inalienable rights we must hold to. Let us do our part in "dreaming dreams for ourselves and our nation." And challenge our young to have "visions for a better tomorrow."

Hymn: "O God, our help in ages past, / our hope for years to come, / our shelter from the stormy blast, / and our eternal home! / Before the hills in order stood, / or earth received her frame, / from everlasting Thou art God, / to endless years the same. / A thousand ages in Thy sight / are like an evening gone; / short as the watch that ends / the night before the rising sun" (Isaac Watts, "O, God, Our Help in Ages Past").

Meditation: Dear Father, grant us wisdom for the living of each day. Teach us how to apply new knowledge into godly wis-

dom so that we live like You. Renew this nation through the dreams and visions of the young and help each of us to rise above party politics and prejudices in order that we truly may be "one nation under God." Amen.

Devotional Fifty-Seven:

Judgment and the Monday Wash

Tonight, after I finished my lecture for Monday, I washed my sheets and underwear, but it was Friday, not Monday. But I thought about my grandmother. She was a notable housekeeper. Windows always sparkled, floors shone, and walls were spotless. The Monday wash looked great. You could be sure that the sheets and pillowcases had been washed, tumbled, and rinsed to be white as snow.

My grandfather made a mistake. He brought home a pair of sheets he had found on sale. The next Monday wash was a disaster. Those new sheets dazzled the old ones a greyish white. Grandpaw had to buy four more pairs of sheets.

In Isaiah 6:3a (KJV), Isaiah sees the Lord on a high throne, hears a winged seraphim cry, "Holy, Holy, Holy," and feels an earthquake growl at his feet. He cries that he is an unclean man of unclean lips.

Isaiah bathed and brushed his teeth that morning. Why did he feel unclean? He sensed the holiness of God before whom there is none righteous, "no, not one."

P.S.: Two nights in a row, we have not talked, except I thought about a wash on Friday, not Monday, and it made me think of my maternal grandmother. Washing sheets also reminded me that you were sleeping on what I am sure were clean sheets. Knowing your love for cleanliness, I am sure your bed is snowy white. My thoughts were focused primarily on you and how you were feeling, and then, when we talked briefly, I found out that you had been asleep since 5:00 or so. Certainly hope by morning, you are feeling better and that the allergies have quieted down. I have missed our evening conversation.

Thinking of my paternal grandmother made me aware she died at age seventy-four, younger than we are. It also reminded me there is an awesome interconnectedness to the various stages of life. What we are to be in the future, we are now becoming. It also made me feel very glad to have you for my and our future. I love your tidiness, your organizational skills, your creativity, your discipline to get things done, and most of all, I love your compassion and fervor. Cleanliness and neatness are next to godliness, and the thought of having you as my life partner gives me a sense of peace and satisfaction about my own worth. When I stop and think about it, are not those wonderful qualities you demonstrate so beautifully the mirror opposites of despair? Usually, people who don't care about duty and discipline are people who frequently despair from procrastination and regret. Let that not be true of us.

Hymn: "Built on the Rock the church doth stand, / Even when steeples are falling; / Crumbled have spires in ev'ry land, / Bells still are chiming and calling; / Calling the young and old to rest, / Calling the souls of men distressed, / Longing for life everlasting. / Not in our temples made with hands God, / the Almighty is dwelling; / High in the heav'ns His temple stands, / All earthly temples excelling; / Yet He who dwells in heav'n above / Deigns to abide with us in love, / Making our bodies His temple" (Nicolai F. S. Grudtvig, Carl Doving, Fred C. M. Hansen, "Built on the Rock").

Meditation: Remind us, gracious God, that You delight in cleanliness and order. Duty and discipline make it possible to meet our own needs and have time to help others do the same. So, teach us how to order our lives in a way that honors Your commandments "to be clean and pure without and within." Amen.

Devotional Fifty-Eight:

The Autograph of God

In Jeremiah 31:33, we read that the day will come when God will write His law upon the hearts of people. When was the last time you saw a squirrel run across the lawn? A hawk soar? A dragonfly hover? These things are done by instinct.

Jesus insisted that human beings couldn't really live right unless instructed from the inside. Since we are free to choose, we decide whether to trust God for the day's agenda.

Ever hear somebody say about a good deed, "That's just like John," or "That's just the way Mary is?" When God signs His name on your heart, you're real and good, interesting and decent, saved and one of His own, all at the same time.

Want to explore the best there is? Turn over the fresh leaf of just one day for the autograph of God!

P.S.: Tonight was one of the sweetest times we have shared. It was a time of reflection that caused our hearts to leap with joy because of the way God brought us together. It was our common calling that led us to serve at the Brotherhood Commission, SBC. Without that connection, we might never have met. And now, through God's providential care and grace, we have been fully reconnected. It is part of my being *surprised by Grace*.

Furthermore, the nature of our conversation tonight made us infinitely aware we want our lives and the decisions we make to reflect our personal needs but always in keeping with what is best within the perceived will of God. The mutual sharing, including the need for divine insight through "putting out the fleece," helped clarify how to make wise decisions. It made me aware we want the autograph of God to be evident in our walk together. He is the God of our past, present, and future and will help us know what is best when we strive to know it. He gives us insight and wisdom. In most of life's decisions, there is a way that seems right and best. He expects us to use human instrumentality given to us in order to handle life's agenda items. Sometimes, personal will and preferences rob us of objectivity. In those situations, let us resolve to allow the circumstances of the "fleece" to give insight. That may not be the only reason to wait till January for the wedding. At least, right now, it seems best as part of God's plan.

Hymn: "Lord Jesus, I long to be perfectly whole; / I want Thee forever to ransom my soul; / break down ev'ry idol, cast out ev'ry foe: / Now wash me, and I shall be whiter than snow. / Whiter than snow, yes, whiter than snow; / now wash me, and I shall be whiter than snow" (James Nicholson, "Whiter than Snow").

Meditation: Dear Director of the Eternal, how glad we are we may trust You, all-knowing God, for the unseen future. You give us intuitive insight and direction by the power of the Spirit. May we seek to follow Your path as it is revealed to us. Amen.

Devotional Fifty-Nine:

The Gathering of the Clan

There is a lost tribe scattered throughout the world. It has no common language, no sacred family tree, and no specific color of skin or hair. This tribe includes every kind of nose God ever invented.

What are the markings of this tribe? They deal with truth as a necessity. Gentleness is instinct. They cannot eat without sharing or sleep without a prayer. These clansmen feel the pain of others as keenly as their own. Their word is their signature. Where they have walked, there is the singing of brooks and the scent of roses. They are the wanderers of heaven.

I think Isaiah really meant this alien scattering of God's seed when he said, "I will say to the north, 'give them up; and to the south, 'do not hold them back.' Bring my sons from afar and my daughters from the ends of the earth" (Isaiah 43:6, NIV).

P.S.: The idea of this sermon came to me from one of my friend Roger's highly poignant sermons. Tonight, we talked about a lot of things. A favorite of the conversation for me was comments about your beauty, the color and smoothness of your skin, and your high cheekbones. We also talked about the many different persons you suggested nominating for association leadership positions, including the possibility that some of your newest African-American pastors could serve as the next moderator. I hope that happens. A lot of the conversation involved a look at different personalities and types of people we know or have known in the past. Most of the time, we were thanking God that in His gracious and divine providence, He connected us in a work and friendship relationship and now reconnected us in a love relationship, which soon makes us one in marriage.

Giving thanks to God, as I try to do each day, I could not help but express gratitude that the Creator has been working across the sea of time since creation to bring His sons and daughters to fulfillment. How blessed we are to be a part of His kin and to be the receivers of His special blessings. It may be age, life circumstances that we have endured, or trials that found us being caregivers, but without question, I am now deliriously happy because of you and the freedom of love and friendship that is pointing us to that special moment when "our new clan will be gathered together!" It is a beautiful world, as the old song says, "Red and yellow, black and white, they are precious in His sight." And how privileged we are to be a part of God's clan, "wanderers of heaven."

Hymn: "Sing the wondrous love of Jesus, sing His mercy and His grace: in the mansions bright and blessed, He'll prepare for us a place. When we all get to heaven, what a day of rejoicing that will be! When we all see Jesus, we'll sing and shout the victory" (Eliza E. Hewitt, "When We All Get to Heaven").

Meditation: Creator and Redeemer, You have chosen us from the beginning of time and, in Your eternal plan, ordered our lives from the legacy of our ancestors. Teach us how to be responsible and good stewards of what was given to us by those whose choices now give us the freedom of choice. May each decision we make be pleasing in Your sight. Amen.

Devotional Sixty:

The Predicament of an Honest Mind

Billy Ewell was peculiar. Some people in our high school thought he had mental trouble. Billy would not cheat. He refused to help or receive help during exams and never carried a crib sheet.

Billy's honesty aroused a faint suspicion among the ranks of faithful cribbers that something might be wrong with them. They didn't care for that sensation. "You think you're better than the rest of us," Chris said. That hit Billy pretty hard, especially hard since Chris was the homecoming queen and thought by many to be the prettiest girl in our class. So he made an honest effort to cheat on one math exam but never made it.

"Jesus replied: "'Love the Lord your God with all your heart, and with all your soul, and with all your mind'" (Matthew 22:37, NIV). To be sure, Billy loved God with "all of his mind." It seems reasonable to suppose that the Architect of the Universe did His everlasting work without a crib sheet.

P.S.: I don't need a crib sheet to pass the "I love Grace 'exam.'" Furthermore, the card you sent me that came today is the sweetest and most poignant statement. It helps in handling the geographical distance between Memphis and Fort Worth. Thank God for USPS and AT&T. The words of the card and your beautiful closure said it all. I was overwhelmed by the thoughtfulness. *I love you very much*, and that's the absolute honest truth! Don't need a crib sheet to pass that exam. For months now, it is clearly evident our love has grown, blossomed, and exploded. No fakery, no selfish pleasures that are an end to themselves. The proof of our love is best expressed by some beautiful lines from the poet Ivan Wright. Cards and poetry can speak volumes about the truth of our love, so let me share the poet's words as mine, just as you did with your card. (I am putting the poem in paragraph form to save space). The title is "The Want of You."

"The want of you is like no other thing; / it smites my soul with sudden grasp; / it binds my being with a wreath of me— / This want of you. / It flashes on me with the waking sun; / it creeps upon me when the day is done; / it hammers at my heart the long night through— / This want of you. / It sighs within me with the misting skies; / oh, all the day within my heart it cries, / old as your absence, yet each moment new— / This want of you. / Mad with demand and aching with desire, / it leaps within my heart and you are—there. / God has not forgotten, for he always knew— / my love of you" (Ivan Wright, "The Want of You").

Don't need a crib sheet. My love for you is sure, pure, true, and forever.

Hymn: "Make me a captive, Lord, / And then I shall be free; / Force me to render up my sword, / And I shall conqueror be. / I sink in Life's alarms / When by myself I stand; / Imprison me within Thine arms, / And strong shall be my hand. / My heart is weak and poor / Until its master finds; / It has no spring of action sure, / It varies with the wind. / It cannot freely move / Till Thou hast wrought its chain; / Enslave it with Thy matchless love, / And deathless it shall reign" (George Matheson, "Make Me a Captive Lord").

Mediation: Dear God, Your perfection is not fully possible in this life because we are sinners at best. However, through the fathomless grace transferred to our lives through faith in Your Son, we can seek His ways and walk in His steps, not by human power but through the power of His presence in us. So thank You! Amen.

Devotional Sixty-One:

Greater than Our Hearts

In 1 John, we read, "God is greater than our hearts, and he knows everything" (1 John 3:20, NIV). I sometimes have trouble understanding people. When I get them figured out, they cross me up. And there are some people I can never figure out. So it's comforting to know myself. I ought to; I've been acquainted with me for more than eighty years. The trouble is, I know myself so well I sometimes push my faults and feelings onto somebody else. Jesus warns about calling other folk fools. I wonder what He thinks about me saying, "Fool!" to myself.

Well, it's not right to insult my neighbor's kids or other fellow believers. I am God's child. What right do I have to insult me, let alone someone else?

John says, "For God is greater than our hearts, and he knows everything (1 John 3:20b, NIV). That Father leads me to the stranger in my front room and says, "Jim, I want you to know Jim. He is one of My boys, and I think the world of him."

P.S.: I went to sleep in my chair again. I need you to keep me headed in the right direction. I did wake up wondering what I would write about tonight. As I have said to you, "I love our conversations." Some nights, we talk around the world and back. Sometimes, like tonight, I get lost in the malaise of the fundamentalist mentality. Dr. W. T. Conner, who taught theology at Southwestern Seminary, had to deal with that noisy crowd when J. Frank Norris and others at the start of the 20th century were trying to come in and take over the Southern Baptist Convention. They were on the outside then, now they are on the inside and in control.

When we are married, I want you to help me get over the anger and fret that developed in my "innards" when that crowd got rid of some of God's finest folk. I need to get over my distress about it. I have confessed my frustration to you several times. I always try to ask God to forgive my judgmental spirit, but you need to help me keep working on it. The changes in our denomination resulted in unnecessary disruption and pain. God cannot bless a broken people. Banking on God's love, I pledge, as we put our lives together, to live and love together through all the changing years. Above all, I want us to have "fun" and not be dependent on the past judgment of others. Or, let our lives be marred by the regrets of past disappointments within the Baptist family. Already, ours is a life given to us by God, and the focus should be on the celebration of our developing union and what is to come.

Hymn: "There's a wideness in God's mercy, / like the wideness of the sea; / there's a kindness in His justice, / which is more than liberty. / But we make His love too narrow by false limits of our own; / and we magnify His strictness with a zeal He will not own. / If our love were but more simple, / we could take Him at His word; / and our lives would be more loving in the likeness of our Lord" (Frederick W. Faber, "There's a Wideness in God's Mercy").

Meditation: Father, we thank You that in creation, You made unique creatures, and there are no two people exactly alike. Forgive us when we try to be somebody else. Let us blossom forth each day, allowing You to take us as we are and transform us into the goodness and likeness of Your perfect Son. Amen.

Devotional Sixty-Two:

The Lamb of God

In Matthew 12:12, Jesus observes that a man is of much more value than a sheep.

A sheep can produce a coat of wool a season, but men weave a thousand coats in a day. A sheep can learn to follow a trail, to lie down in the fold at night. Men blaze trails and fight off wolves.

Sheep are helpless. They have to be herded. Humans are shepherds of much more value than simple sheep.

But our Lord began His greatest drama in helplessness before the court of Pilate. The gentle Christ, described as "The Lamb of God which taketh away the sin of the world" (John 1:29b, KJV), gave His life to His enemies and brought the rebels of heaven, earth, and hell to their knees.

P.S.: I thought about several subjects for tonight but finally decided, in light of the Easter season, to just make a brief statement that gives a summary of the essence of the Easter celebration. It is a simple truth. God really loves mankind and developed a perfect plan for redeeming His very own creation. Jesus did pay it all, so all our fears and anxieties can be deposited in the empty tomb of Christ's triumphant resurrection. And, thank God, He is forever making all things brand new. The Old Testament begins with Isaac asking his father, Abraham, a simple question, "Where is the lamb?" The New Testament closes the book of Revelation with the simple statement, "Behold the Lamb of God, which taketh away the sin of the world" (John 1:29b, KJV). I am so happy and glad that this Easter, the two of us are believers and live our lives out of the arena of devotion to Him, who is above everything and knows us because of the trust we have in His sacrificial death on the cross for sin. How blessed we are to have that sure and true foundation now and forever. Happy Easter!

Hymn: "I heard the Savior say, / 'Thy strength indeed is small. / Child of weakness, watch and pray, / find in Me thine all in all.' / For nothing good have I / whereby Thy grace to claim; / I'll wash my garments white / in the blood of Calv'ry's Lamb. / And when, before the throne, / I stand in Him complete, / 'Jesus died my soul to save,' / My lips shall still repeat. / Jesus paid it all, / All to Him I owe; / Sin had left a crimson stain, / He washed it white as snow" (Elvina M. Hall, "Jesus Paid It All").

Meditation: Father, let all of our praise go to Calvary, the place of Your atonement for man's sins. You are the King of all creation and the Author and Finisher of our salvation. So, this Easter season, let us praise our eternal and living God and joyfully sing praises to our resurrected King and Savior. Amen.

Devotional Sixty-Three:

Reverse Hypocrisy

In Matthew 21:28–32, we read of two sons instructed by their father to go to work in a vineyard. One agreed but did not go; the other refused but at last did obey his father.

At the J and J Machine Shop near the Saline River in Harrisburg, Illinois, a certain guy named Harvey was one of the most profane, vulgar, and abusive shop owners you could find.

One hot day in the middle of the July harvest, a car smashed into the abutment of the narrow Saline River Bridge. I went to the crash as an ambulance driver for my father-in-law's funeral home. My wonderful father-in-law, Vernard Clayton, operated a fourth-generation family funeral home in Harrisburg. When we were in the ambulance and arrived at the scene, two children, badly bruised and bloody, wailed at the knees of their injured mother, who was cradled in the arms of Harvey. He had arrived at the scene before the ambulance. The family was from Mexico, and the father's name was Jesus! He stayed with the car, and Harvey soothed the victims as the mother quieted her children. He rode with them to the hospital to help with the details. This made my job twice as easy.

Harvey was a reverse hypocrite. Like the rebellious son in Jesus's story, he was better than he seemed. Harvey, at that time, may not have seen that the whole world lies wounded, and all of us sometimes have need of a tender word.

P.S. I don't know why this experience was on my mind, except we sometimes judge people in the wrong way. Harvey did not need to use profane words, but in the heart, he was a compassionate man. From that day onward, I had a different attitude toward Harvey. And, to make the story more complete, Harvey was later converted at a revival meeting in our church and became a lay preacher. I learned a lesson that day. God takes us right where we are to make us into what He wants us to be. Forgiveness and grace are always evident in the Father's love. There are a thousand reasons why I love you so. One of those is you model the act of forgiveness. One of your own friends has not necessarily conformed to God's design for marriage, but you have loved and cared for him all the while. Your sense of what is right could have caused you to question your friendship. Yet, you have understood his needs, even though his lifestyle is not God's ideal plan. There is good in every person. And, of course, there is the element of imperfection in each one of us. No human sin is greater than another. I am glad the Eternal Redeemer understands us better than we do.

Hymn: "I'm pressing on the upward way, / New heights I'm gaining ev'ry day; / Still praying as I onward bound, / 'Lord plant my feet on higher ground'" (Johnson Oatman, Jr., "Higher Ground").

Meditation: God of Perfection, help us to be pure in heart, and when we lose temper and allow anger to dwell, forgive us and move us toward a higher ground of fidelity and right living. In every circumstance, let us be free from an attitude of constant judgment of others, leaving the judgment to You. Amen.

Devotional Sixty-Four:

The Guests and the Presence

A meal is a pretty important event. If we don't eat, we don't live. People eating together do important business. When you break bread with someone, part goes into your lifestream, and part goes into the others; you carry a hidden unity between you. For a moment, if it is not already true, you are at least kin.

When people want to talk seriously, they share a meal. There's a feeling of trust, for we're at the gate of life together.

The Lord's Supper is the center of the life of the church. It was not intended to be a solitary exercise. People shared with each other because they were the mystical body of the present Christ. In 1 Corinthians 2:21, Paul warns Christians against disregarding each other during the Lord's Supper. Some churches are uptight about people talking during Communion. Maybe we missed the point. Jesus is our host at the table. But what host is satisfied when his guests speak only to him?

P.S.: Guess what? Notice the time. I went soundly to sleep in my chair again. What a "dumb bunny"! I dreamed about being with you for your Easter family meal. It was fun and delightful because we talked at length about our wedding and future. When I awoke, my thoughts drifted toward the importance of family and meals. At least three times a day during my growing up years, we had the opportunity to share with each other. Of course, when we started school and there were other parental demands, we were not together three times a day, but when we were, it was a happy time. Then, after the kids married, holidays became special because of meals together, like for us on Easter Sunday. Having gone to Maundy Thursday at church and participated with the church family in sharing the Lord's Supper, I could not help but think how important it is for families to share and communicate with each other. We should not honor only the host but each other as well. It all caused me to look forward to extending life with your family and you with mine. Creating a blended family from across the miles will have some challenges, but I am sure if we set the example and guide the process, an esprit de corps and friendship with our children will help them feel like kinfolk. Just like with my growing up years, as with yours, meals were important, especially meals on holidays. "Happy Easter to Yours, Mine, and Ours."

Hymn: "Christ the Lord is ris'n today! / Sons of men and angels say! / Raise your joys and triumphs high! / Sing, ye heav'ns and earth, reply! / Love's redeeming work is done, Alleluia! / Fought the fight, the battle won, Alleluia! / Death in vain forbids Him rise, / Christ hath opened Paradise, Alleluia!" (Charles Wesley, "Christ the Lord Is Risen Today").

Meditation: Father, You have declared the foundation of heaven and earth and, in the Trinity, have expressed Your intention for all mankind. That intention is for man's sinful ways to be redeemed by the redemptive power of Your Son's sacrificial death on the cross. May that witness be spread abroad to everyone. Amen.

Devotional Sixty-Five:

Imago Dei

It was a pleasant June day. Vacation Bible School was in full swing at Ash Creek Baptist Church in Azle, Texas. It was the church I served during seminary days. The air was filled with the cheerful voices of young matrons and the chatter of first graders in what was then called "the Beginner's Department."

Inez Kinchens watched the children trooping in from their curio hunt with stones, flowers, butterflies, and other of nature's royalties. They had learned that since God made everything, everything would tell something about God's creation. God was strong. God was beautiful. He made unusual things, and most of all, He was kind.

Jerry came in last, late for the morning activities, but had brought with him his two-year-old sister, holding her in his arms. "Well, Jerry, we have been outside looking for anything God made." The teacher asked, "Could you have found something God made?" Without hesitation, he said, "I found her," pointing to his sister. "He made her." Genesis 1 tells us God made man in His own image, male and female. Flowers, stones, and butterflies were hints of the Eternal. Jerry and Judy were His polaroids.

P.S.: Easter Sunday has been wonderful. The observance prompts a great reminder of the fact God is in the creation business, as well as the restoration business. He made man/woman the highest form of His creative powers, and though they turned their back on Him, He then developed a plan for redeeming mankind. His love for His own creation demanded fellowship with His own be reestablished. Being with family on this special day was a special blessing. Each one in "our family" is different, but as objects of God's creation, each is loved by Him and also by us because of some part we had in that creative act. Either by flesh or marriage, each one is ours. My prayer is God will give us the capacity to love each of them as He does and let our lives be an example of redeeming love that "will not let go."

Hymn: "'Tis finished! The Messiah dies, / Cut off for sins, but not His own. / Accomplished is the sacrifice, / The great redeeming work is done. / The veil is rent; in Christ alone / The living way to heav'n is seen; / the middle wall is broken down, / And all the world may enter in. / 'Tis finished! All my guilt and pain / I want no sacrifice beside; / For me, for me the Lamb is slain, / 'Tis finished! I am justified. / The reign of sin and death is o'er, / And all may live from sin set free; / Satan has lost his mortal pow'r; / 'Tis swallowed up in victory" (Charles Wesley, "'Tis Finished! The Messiah Dies").

Meditation: May the Lord Jesus's resurrection remind us all that life is to be lived as resurrected life. Help us to deposit all of it in the empty tomb of His resurrection. Living, He loved us, and dying, He saved us, and as the hymn text suggests, someday, He's coming again. Amen.

Devotional Sixty-Six:

Polishing a Melody

This event occurred several years ago while I was on the faculty at Southwestern. Because I was teaching courses on religion and aging, I was invited to speak to a meeting where a number of Texas Baptist church senior adult choirs were singing at a festival. I was sitting on a hard chair in a church recreation room prior to the festival, listening to an eighty-voice choir practicing for the concert. The director was putting them through the wringer. Everything had to be perfect: posture, dynamics, breathing. Do it over…again…again.

Then, the director led them through the whole song. I sensed the presence of music. So I cried. I don't know why, except it seemed the right thing to do. It was fantastic, and I was overwhelmed by the talents of these older persons. In Proverbs 22, we read that a man skillful in his work stands before kings. The Mission Belles won first place in the Houston Choir Festival. Here is a parable of Christian discipline. Polishing is hard work, but the shine is worth it.

P.S.: Two things "popped" into my head from our conversation while you waited for your grandson Tucker to finish his guitar lesson. We hummed a song that fits our love and relationship. I also thought about Tucker working to improve his ability to play the guitar. Obviously, one of the first songs that struck home with me when we first began to share a special friendship was a very popular song. In my mind, words from this song prompt me to say I think about you every night. Since then, we have sung or "hummed" many others, and as you know, at times, I can't help singing.

Hymn: There is a wonderful hymn by Carlton C. Buck entitled "O Lord May Church and Home Combine." This hymn clarifies church and home must work together to reveal the sovereign love, grace, and forgiveness of God.

Meditation: Dear Father, forgive us when, at times, we want to redo the past. The past life was precious indeed. Teach us to learn from the past, celebrate the good, and benefit from mistakes. Remind us life is short at best. Renew in us a fresh resolve to make every new day a loving day of self, others, and most of all, worship of You! Amen.

Devotional Sixty-Seven:

Who Has the Authority?

Saint Paul writes in 1 Corinthians, "The wife's body does not belong to her alone but also to her husband. In the same way, the husband's body does not belong to him alone but also to his wife" (1 Corinthians 7:4, NIV). In the marriage bond, each partner makes a gift of themselves. It should not be broken. Regretfully, soiled relationships end in divorce. God, in His perfect plan, intends marriage for life.

How is this best achieved or described? According to this Pauline statement, God developed the marriage relationship so partners could learn how to sacrificially serve others. Love in marriage is a triangle with God at the top, the husband on one of the two corners, and the wife on the other. The closer you get to God, the closer you get to each other.

That is a heavenly medley for a happy marriage!

P.S.: When I asked you what to do about tonight's sermon, you said to do something about marriage expectations. Apparently, we were at a point in our lives where we needed new love. I am not sure you could say we were famished. But, life's circumstances, losing Jo and LeRoy, caused us to be ready for new companionship. We both were and are overwhelmingly surprised by the magnetic draw of the growing love we share. It has grown so quickly, and so it seems, is here to stay. The proof is in the dynamic way it has multiplied. Who would ever imagine it could be like this? The inner and outer desires overwhelm me. Who would want to ration it or dole it out? That would be a prostitution of its reality. When so-called love takes on a tiresome sameness of routine, both partners feel a vague sense of dissatisfaction with unnamed longings. The thing that is missing, in that case, is the lack of a free and active expression of a "living love," one giving to the other. What keeps the relationship vital and moving is a joyous pattern of mutual response. Let it be true of us if, in God's will, marriage is consummated.

Meditation: Loving Father, just as You modeled for us by the giving of Your Son, grant to us a "living love" that knows no selfish bounds. To live this reality prepares us for earth's relationships, especially marriage. Amen.

Devotional Sixty-Eight:

Chores and Music

In Harrisburg, Illinois, where my father pastored First Baptist Church and later I served on the church staff before going to seminary, there was a man most people would call simple-minded. Strong as a yoke of oxen, harmless as a dove, Joe was grateful for anything you gave him or asked him to do.

There's a question about how simple he really was. Joe was a kind of dancer. When he pitched hay or worked on a neighbor's farm, he stepped in cadence, like he was at a Saturday night party. The arc of the hay swishing the air flourished in perfect time. Give him a new job, and he'd stumble around awhile. Then he'd find the cadence, and there he would go. Awkward as he was, Joe could make chores as graceful as ballet.

In Ephesians 2, Paul says we are saved by grace and not by works. If God's grace is like the grace of a skilled laborer, we need works. Ever see a graceful person who would not move or work?

P.S.: Grace, the above sermon I reworked some years ago came back to my mind after our conversation tonight. Obviously, from last Thursday till last night, we were enjoying a symphony of music. Together, we hit every note of the scale and created our own new melodies. And, abruptly, you had to return to your work and then face a long afternoon of chores related to the meeting tonight at your church. But I know how tired you must have been and how the good Lord gave you strength and spirit to fulfill your responsibilities. Knowing you, you did it with grace and charm like a ballet dancer. On and on, I could go remembering the confident ways you were always prepared, but more importantly, for the grand and gracious spirit you manifested in helping me and other organization leaders do their work. There are a "thousand reasons" why I love you as I do. But, certainly, one of those reasons resides in the spirit of your life. In so many ways, the same gift of disciplined duty was characteristic of Jo, my dearest first wife. So, I have been spoiled by very gifted women. You are not simple-minded like Joe, the hired man in the "sermon," but like him, you always seem grateful for anything you are asked to accomplish. Yes, *grace* and *works* go together like *love* and *marriage*. Am I ever grateful for the very thought of it!

Hymn: "There's within my heart a melody; / Jesus whispers sweet and low, / 'Fear not, I am with thee, peace, be still,' / In all of life's ebb and flow. / Jesus, Jesus, Jesus, / Sweetest name I know, / Fills my ev'ry longing, / Keeps me singing as I go" (Luther B. Bridgers, "He Keeps Me Singing").

Meditation: Orchestrator of the Universe, You intended for mankind to live pure and noble lives. It can't happen when we are left to our own sinful ways. Transform our behavior through complete faith in Your redemptive Savior and help us grow in maturity so that in Him, eternal music of praise rises from our voices, bringing disciplined purpose and fulfilling Your mission and calling. Amen.

Devotional Sixty-Nine:

The Oasis of Trust

In Jeremiah 44:5–8, we read those who trust in man are like shrubs in a salty desert, but those who trust in God are like trees by running streams.

Travelers flying over the desert can spot a year-round river by the winding strip of green trees upon its banks. Hidden springs keep the river flowing when everything dries up.

God writes in that green ink, "Stick with the deep springs and free yourself from the weather."

In every community, there are people sustained by year-round hope, flourishing on rainless days. They are orchards of fragrant fruit when their world seems a dustbowl! Trace on your map the trail of these strong and lovely people, and you'll camp every night in green pastures under the stars of a desert sky.

P.S.: Since we did not have our normal evening conversation, I wasn't sure about tonight's "sermon." Tomorrow, you will be on the "trail" with some of your dearest friends and members of your Sunday school class. I thought it might be good to be reminded how blessed we are to be surrounded by caring, loving friends. Your friend Toby, traveling with you, has also lost her beloved husband. It is another reminder life is precious. I know the trip to Ohio will be enjoyable, and it will be a blessing to have her as a roommate. Also, I could not help thinking about how good it would be to share this trip with you. Wish we had planned better, though it was fantastic to have you here last weekend. Already, I am looking forward to our trip to Hot Springs and then my trip to Memphis in May.

How good it is God has given us a close family, endearing church families, and a host of friends near and far. Most of all, the constant source of God's Spirit is guiding us through each of life's experiences. We certainly depend on human support, but what would we do without the abiding and empowering guidance of God's providential care? As we anticipate our coming together in marriage, it makes me glad that we are surrounded by people who love us, care for us, and want the best for us. Most of all, we are eternally blessed by absolute assurance we have God's protective hand leading the way. I am overwhelmed with excitement and joy in terms of what is happening in our lives. It indeed represents "new ground," posing a full set of "brand-new growth challenges." The lesson I would draw from the "sermon" is we have a vast interconnectedness to our lives. We do have an oasis of trust to lean on as we journey together. So, enjoy your friends, the trip, zip-lining, and thoughts of us blessed by the deep springs of God's love and care.

Hymn: "When we walk with the Lord / In the light of His Word / What a glory He sheds on our way! / Let us do His good will; / He abides with us still, / And with all who will trust and obey. / But we never can prove the delights of His love / until all on the altar we lay; / For the favor He shows / And the joy He bestows are for them / who will trust and obey. / Trust and obey, / for there's no other way to be happy in Jesus, / But to trust and obey" (John H. Sammis, "Trust and Obey").

Meditation: Creator and Father God, You have demonstrated through biblical heroes of faith and most supremely with Your Son's sacrificial death that a heart in fellowship with You creates thankfulness. How we do thank You for family, friends, and the faithful community of believers that challenge us to be friend and servant to all. Most of all, teach us to trust You and be obedient to Your leadership. Amen.

Devotional Seventy:

The Place

Freddy was a young person, probably still in his teens, who had offered to drive me across town to a Sunday afternoon preaching appointment at a mission's fair. On the way over, he said, "As we pass by this place, there's time to show you something special." Five miles out in the Texas flats, my young friend led me down a back trail through some small trees crowding a small riverbank. He stopped at a grassy bluff overlooking the stream below. Trees formed an arena of quiet, hollowed into the countryside.

"This is my place," he said. "It's where I go to be by myself." I was moved by his kindness. When I was young, I, too, had a place of my own in a wooded area behind the barn on my grandmother's farm. It is where I found peace and quiet and also a place where I did some first things like smoking a wild grapevine.

Wherever you are, all whose solitude claims a place uniquely their own are brothers and sisters, including Jacob, who, according to Genesis 28, slept at Bethel under a dream of angels. The next morning, he cried, "This is the house of God, and this is the gate of heaven" (Genesis 28:17, KJV).

P.S.: It may crowd the sermon a bit, but I could not help but think about your good day and "the place" where you tried something new. I did get to see the tape of your first zip-line experience.

It was a "first place" for you, and I was thrilled you were having a brand new "thrill." There are a lot of places you and I have been that stand out in grateful memory, yours with LeRoy and mine with Jo. So, your trip provided a new first-time experience. We now have some of our own, and across the years, there will be many more. I could tell by the excitement in your voice you had a very good day. You deserve many, many more of those days, and I can't wait until we can create our own special places, each of which reminds us of something special. I already have been counting "the places" that will be ours.

Hymn: "Master, Thou callest, I gladly obey; / Only direct me, and I'll find Thy way. / Teach me the mission appointed for me, / What is my labor, and where it shall be. / Willing, my Savior, to take up the cross; / Willing to suffer reproaches and loss. / Willing to follow, if Thou will but lead; / Only support me with grace in my need. / Living, or dying, I still would be Thine; / Yet I am mortal while Thou art divine. / Pardon, whenever I turn from the right; / Pity, and bring me again to the light. / Master, Thou callest, and this I reply, / "Ready and willing, Lord here am I" (Fanny J. Crosby, "Lord, Here Am I").

Meditation: Great Helper and Healer, our greatest hope here below is help from God above. We bow to acknowledge Your perfect ways and our own need to trust in You. Amen.

Devotional Seventy-One:

The Pot of Gold

In a recent sermon, I shared with you a reference about a man in my home church who was a very simple man. Never married, worked hard, always friendly, never missed church. But some people thought he had some quirky ideas about things. For one thing, he truly believed there was a pot of gold at the foot of the rainbow. So, whenever there was a storm, he threw a sack and his deposit book in his car and went rainbow hunting. He was a top rainbow spotter but never did find any gold.

Since he was on the simple side, he never got discouraged. He was a cheerful, hardworking handyman who worked on various farms in the county. He whistled a lot, slept well, and avoided ulcers, strokes, and community politics. He was just dead sure that somewhere, that pot of yellow gold was waiting for him. Not too unlike those who are convinced they will win the Publishers Clearing House sweepstakes.

Genesis 9:13 tells how, after the flood, God gave the rainbow as hope the world wouldn't be washed out again. What a pot of gold that rainbow brought! How about your own? Watch the next storm and check out your heart, for that's where your treasure is.

P.S.: Sermon ideas come from all sorts of conversations we share. Obviously, we talked about your experiences in the Creation Museum and the intention for them to finish the building of Noah's Ark. We also talked about the wealth some of our friends may have accumulated and agreed life is more than gold. It's nice to have it, but it doesn't buy peace or happiness. We also discussed how much fun it would be for us to share neat experiences together, like another zip-line event, a Grand Canyon trail, or a Wilderness Dude Ranch in the Rockies. Or, better still, a trip to the Rhine River, a vacation in Hawaii, or perhaps a cruise to Alaska. We could dream all night. Those are indeed "legitimate searches" for happy times together. But my "pot of gold" is together with you. Regardless of where we go or where we are, I will have more than enough if I have you. Each passing day has added a "shine and glow" to my and our treasure. And, what's more, we don't need a "deposit book" to add up the value. It is priceless.

Hymn: "O Christ, our hope, our heart's desire, / Redemption's only spring, Creator of the world art Thou, / Its Savior and its King. / How vast the mercy and the love / Which laid our sins on Thee, / And led Thee to a cruel death / To set Thy people free. / O Christ, be Thou our lasting joy, / Our ever great reward; / Our only glory may it be To glory I the Lord!" (Latin Hymn, Translator John Chandler, "O Christ, Our Hope, Our Heart's Desire").

Meditation: God of the heavens and the earth, make our lives as lovely as Yours, our actions flowing from Your commands and opportunities in new ventures to share Your message of redemption. We thank You for a beautiful world. Help us to be good stewards of its treasures, like the rocks of towering grandeur make us strong and pure. Amen.

Devotion Seventy-Two:

Members of the Flock

The psalmist praises God because "we are his people and the sheep of his pasture" (Psalm 100:3, KJV).

You'd think the psalmist could find a better animal than sheep to compare humans to. Take your ordinary garden variety sheep. Look him in the eye. Not a lot of luster there. A voice that couldn't make a volunteer choir! Talents: eating and sleeping.

A sheep's keenest instinct is to do the wrong thing in an emergency. To circle and save the wolf unnecessary steps, to drown in drinking water.

How strange that intelligent, self-sufficient humans claim with one voice the psalm that begins, "The Lord is my shepherd, I shall not want!" (Psalm 23:1, KJV).

P.S.: What a thrill it was to hear about the Bob Hills and learn they are still doing well. One of the best devotions I have ever heard on Psalm 100 was given by Bob in Japan when we went with Rusty Griffin to do a check visit on Project Tokyo. You may remember we worked with the Glory Construction Company in Tokyo to build missionary houses and apartments away from the inner city. The Japan Baptist Convention sold its downtown headquarters for 60 million US dollars and used the money to buy new office space in the suburbs. The extra money was used to build new apartments for their convention staff, new church buildings, and missionary houses. It was a great project and the only time in the Brotherhood Commission history we paid volunteers to go, provided they stayed a minimum of six weeks. It was a great reminder God's flock covers the earth, and anywhere and everywhere you find fellow believers, you feel at home. Surely and truly, we are the "sheep of His pasture." Though we share that sense of kinship with each fellow follower of Christ, there is something uniquely special between the two of us. That would and should be true of all soul mates. But for us, there is a dynamism and sense of oneness that cannot be contained in mere words. I just know that we are the "sheep of His pasture." Now that we have found each other, it is thrilling for me to know I can be most totally my true self with you. Thanks for the touch of your life on mine. I love "Ewe."

Hymn: "O God to Those Who Here Profess." This is a wonderful hymn by Charles P. Price that lifts up the importance of the home embodying lasting love for husband and wife and their offspring and then extending that love to others, both the loved and the unloved. The profession of our faith in God is empty if we do not convey His kind of love to others.

Meditation: Lord, teach Your servants that mutual submission to one another is the pathway to growth and learning. Forgive us when our own desire for self-expression takes precedence over our need to listen and learn from others as well. Also, remind us that the closer we draw near to You, the closer we get to each other. Amen.

Devotional Seventy-Three:

Scum of the World

Paul writes in 1 Corinthians, "When we are slandered, we answer kindly. Up to this moment we have become the scum of the earth, the refuse of the world" (1 Corinthians 4:13, NIV). Paul and his followers shared the gospel in a first-century world fraught with evil. He makes it plain the Christian experience is never free from conflict. Paul compares their situation to scraps left on the plate after a banquet. He shares a lengthy list, like becoming a spectacle, being fools without honor, oft times hungry, thirsty, poorly clothed, roughly treated, reviled, persecuted, slandered, and being scum. When you consider the list, you see the possibilities of why there can be hesitation to sign up for the journey.

C. S. Lewis said, "The real problem is not why some pious, humble people suffer, but why some do not." John Bunyan said, "In times of affliction, we commonly meet the sweetest experiences of the love of God."

The overarching question for us remains: "How much of a 'scum' are we willing to be?"

P.S.: Sermon ideas come from all sorts of conversations we share. We talked about many of the African-American pastors you work with. Many of them are bi-vocational. Yet, in spite of struggles, they are happy in their walk with the Lord. You have identified with them, and many hold you in high regard as a friend and helper. In a real sense, we have had it easy. We have more than we need. I have never gone hungry. There are many believers who are considered "so-called scums" because of the sacrifices they endure to take the gospel to difficult places. So, as we anticipate our lives being joined in marriage, may we resolve to keep the "first things first"! People first, whatever their race, creed, or personal needs. Next time we eat, think of our plenty. Next time we crave something, remember we already have all we need. The next time we seek power and status, remember Jesus did not have a place to lay His head. A thousand years from now, it will not matter what titles we have held or what status the world may have given us. May a part of our marriage covenant be "God make us 'scums'" like the apostle Paul.

Hymn: There is a great hymn by E. Margaret Clarkson entitled "Burn in Me the Fire of God." The essence of the hymn is to admonish believers to allow Christ's image to be formed in them to provide the kind of example that will lead others to follow Him.

Meditation: Father, You have ordered that ultimate destiny is based on choice, not chance. May we flee from the cloak of evil and seek after righteousness, godliness, faithfulness, loving-kindness, perseverance, and gentleness with self and others. May the witness of the apostle Paul prompt us to empty ourselves and, like Jesus, put first the needs of other persons. Amen.

Devotional Seventy-Four:

Against the Grain

When I was a young person, the visiting evangelist for a church youth revival was giving an object lesson to young children on Sunday morning. He put a block of wood on the floor, placed a log on the plank, took an axe, and tried to split it. He wasn't getting anywhere. But before he swung three times, the children were shouting, "Turn it on its end! Turn it on its end!"

He was trying to split the block against the grain.

Genesis 1:28 tells us when God created man in His image, He commanded him to subdue and replenish the earth. Today, this isn't working out too well. Things sometimes get out of control because man thinks He knows more than God and goes against the grain of the Creator.

P.S.: We talked about a friend of ours and his frustrations regarding a work associate who thinks he knows more than everyone else. Egotism is an acceptable trait if you also know your weaknesses. But some people think they can do no wrong and, by attitude and actions, try to prove their infallibility. A truly wise person is one who is intellectually humble and knows his or her limitations. Karl Barth, the great German theologian and the author of many books, was asked on one occasion, "What is the most significant theological insight you have had?" He must have knocked his questioner off his or her proverbial feet when he responded, "Jesus loves me this I know, for the Bible tells me so."

In our conversation tonight, you asked me if I would like to attend Merry Makers or Sunday school with you. The answer is *yes, yes*! To be with you will be part of the motivation, but more importantly, I need to keep learning. I am very much looking forward to both "living" and "learning" with you. An important byproduct will be the friendship and fellowship with others of our age and interests. Grace, God has given us each good bodies but also good minds. I have been fortunate to be in an "academic world" for a long time, but there is much that I do not know. You have knowledge and skills I do not have. Just think how good it will be for us to help each other explore answers to both the profound and simple questions that will be a part of sharing life together. Most of all, our "bonding love" will strive to search for the best answers to life's questions and not "go against the grain."

Hymn: "Master, Thou callest, I gladly obey; / Only direct me, and I'll find Thy way. / Teach me the mission appointed for me, / What is my labor, and where it shall be. / Living or dying, I still would be Thine; / Yet I am mortal while Thou art divine. / Pardon, whenever I turn from the right; / Pity, and bring me again to the light, / Master, Thou callest, and this I reply, / 'Ready and willing, Lord, here am I'" (Fanny J. Crosby, "Lord, Here Am I").

Meditation: Dear God, we recognize that the nation and our world cannot change for the better until we change for the better. Revive us again and renew the right spirit within us. We remem-

ber the words King David used in Psalm 51. Even though he had broken Your commandments, he exclaimed, "The sacrifices of God are a broken spirit and contrite heart" (Psalm 51:17, NIV). As David renewed fellowship with You, so let it be with us. Amen.

Devotional Seventy-Five:

Is Your Eye in the Right Place

The dancing girl swirled before the hot eyes of Herod the Tetrarch. Like a startled fawn, light as the air that clasped her, she spelled with her body the ancient symbols of joy, of pain, of desire.

Flashing limbs now still as chiseled marble, Salome bowed before the king. "Name your treasure," the stunned king whispered to his stepdaughter. She rose. Coached by Herodias, her mother, the girl challenged the eyes of the monarch.

"The head of John the Baptist on a platter," she chanted to the frowning king. Herod juggled his pride and his fear. Matthew 14 reports he beheaded John so Salome could dance to her mother with the tongue of the desert prophet stilled in blood and silence.

This is a terrible story. But how many living prophets have sealed their lips at the whim of a beautiful but deceitfully selfish woman?

P.S.: I was a bit pressed to think about a theme for tonight's "sermon." The one I chose is another from the Roger Carstensen collection I have redone. The book you are reading about the temptress Cleopatra, as well as the maneuvering episodes of Herod, made me think how desperate some people can be to have their own way. Ambition and the need to control can be a deadly arsenal. I am so glad that our love is not based on conniving, manipulative motivations but rather a bonding mutuality that attracts each to the other. For instance, there cannot be a "boss" in the mutuality of coming together. Each partner can be most truly himself or herself, with neither locked into a role that has to be played or manipulated for self-aggrandizement.

Power-seeking people put the desire for power above the need to give to or serve another. And, of course, the union of two who totally love each other is uniquely and amazingly personal—not public. They share their own experience, which no others can match or enter into. No one else can tell us just how to share life with each other. The dynamics are for us to explore, experience, and develop into a harmony as near to perfection as possible, knowing that each must keep working to improve it. Unlike the selfish power of a Salome, godly love will include spontaneity of life, respect for each other's feelings, freedom of expression, the expectancy of mutual pleasure, sensitivity in caring, and leading onward to completion.

Hymn: "We are climbing Jacob's ladder, / We are climbing Jacob's ladder, / We are climbing Jacob's ladder, / Soldiers of the cross. / Ev'ry round goes higher, higher, / Ev'ry round goes higher, higher, / Ev'ry round goes higher, higher, / Soldiers of the cross. / Sinner, do you love my Jesus? / Sinner, do you love my Jesus? / Sinner do you love my Jesus? / Soldiers of the cross. / If you love Him, why not serve Him? / If you love Him, why not serve Him? / If you love Him, why not serve Him? / Soldiers of the cross" (Spiritual, "We Are Climbing Jacob's Ladder").

Meditation: Father, we are aware, painfully at times, that determination and discipline control our destiny. We are what we choose or decide. Sometimes, selfish pursuits interfere with growth and success. Forgive us when ours is a commitment with lip rather than life. To serve another and to serve You is not done apart from sacrifice. So, empower us to serve. Amen.

Devotional Seventy-Six:

Burning Hearts and Cold Days

What a winter! The memory of it ought to air-condition us into July. "Energy" is on everybody's tongue. We know if we had enough oil and natural gas or could make the sun and wind cooperate with us a little, our economic troubles would pretty much be over.

What about the church's energy? The church can have a cold service on a hot day in August. What about personal energy? The unknowns of life can sometimes limit motivation and drive. It may happen, especially when fears are based on the imaginary rather than the real. It is important to be aware and not in denial, but anxiety over the unknown turns a positive spirit into a ghostly one. What is the formula for happy living?

In Luke's Gospel, we learn that the disciples who walked with a resurrected Jesus they had not recognized said, "Were not our hearts burning within us while he talked with us on the road and opened the Scriptures to us" (Luke 24:32, NIV). Let the Bible be opened by our Lord's Spirit, and the energy of resurrection will warm and lift us when other fires burn low.

P.S.: Receiving information about some of your health concerns made me more aware of the depth of my love for you. It appears what you thought might be a major problem is something easy to deal with. At least, it seems so. We both count on it. But, as I said, even hearing you had some serious thoughts about what it could have been caused me to shudder. Our love has grown so deep I would be devastated if there was a major illness or life-threatening challenge facing us. So much of me is now wrapped up in you.

I know you remember Elizabeth Barrett Browning's "Sonnet 43," *How Do I Love Thee?* from *Sonnet of the Portuguese*, perhaps one of the world's most famous love poems. She wrote my words for you and our love when she said, "I love thee to the level of every day's / most quiet need, by sun and candlelight." That phrase encapsulates any need you have anywhere our minds and bodies are loved because they are our own possessions, not mechanisms that can be used for satisfaction and discarded at will but treasures of eternal value. Even though you have a beautiful face, beauty is not in the face but is a light in the heart. Just as the disciples were stirred by the Lord's presence and His interpretation of Scripture, let us always feel the energy of resurrection because not only are we His eternally, but we now belong to each other, and that love is eternal, regardless of what may come our way.

Hymn: "Purer in heart, O God, / Help me to be; / May I devote my life / Wholly to Thee: / Watch Thou my wayward feet. / Guide me with counsel sweet: / Purer in heart, / Help me to be. / Purer in heart, / O God, Help me to be; / Teach me to do / Thy will Most lovingly; / Be Thou my friend and guide, / Let me with Thee abide; / Purer in heart, / Help me to be. / Purer in heart, / O God, Help me to be; / Until Thy holy face / One day I see: / Keep me from secret sin, / Reign Thou my soul with: / Purer in heart, /

Help me to be" (Fannie Estelle Davison, "Purer in Heart, O God").

Meditation: May the impact of great poetry, learning from life's experiences, and, most of all, the inspiration of the Holy Scripture provide the source of our decisions. Let our actions be constant with Your great wisdom. Amen.

Devotional Seventy-Seven:

The River of God

After my paternal grandfather passed away, Dad and Mom moved into my grandmother's beautiful farmhouse in Ledford, Illinois, just a few miles from Harrisburg. We lived there until my dad moved to a church that had a parsonage. Even though the farm had ponds, it was seven miles to the nearest river. And in those boyhood years, Southern Illinois went through a drought. It was not as bad as Oklahoma's Dust Bowl, but water was scarce. There were ditches and ravines, of course. After a heavy rain, a brown river would form in the pasture, backing up to the barn. But summers were dry, and crops suffered.

Texas has been in a similar drought for the past few years. But this winter, there were heavy snows and ice storms, and this spring, we have had heavy rains, including six inches just today. There was a heavy stream running down the ditches on either side of my house. I have to admit it. Streams are magic. I love the mountain streams that flow endlessly to the sea. It is magical to watch the water flow. Streams speak of refreshing vegetation to follow but also to the spirit of the depths of God.

So you can understand why I love Jesus's teaching in John 7, "If anyone is thirsty let him come to me and drink. Whoever believes in me, as the scripture has said, streams of living water will flow from within him" (John 7:37b–38, NIV). And in the book of Genesis, we learn that rivers were the boundaries of paradise.

P.S.: It is obvious that today's rains and the recent wet Texas spring have brought a lot of joy. Not only are my lawn and garden refreshed, but the Texas countryside looks more like the Dells of Michigan in early summer. I have never seen the wildflowers as colorful. It is refreshing to breathe the air washed in the bath of a heavy thunderstorm. Wish it could stay this way the rest of the year. But August comes. All through the day, as I watched the streams of water flow to the neighbors' lake and onto the West Fork of the Trinity River just beyond the "across-the-street properties," my mind and heart were drawn to the refreshing life and love that came to me because of you. And, unlike the seasonal nature of Texas weather, our love is like the mountain stream continually flowing and flowing, and yet it is always there. It is always the same, and yet every moment is new! The stream of our love is an emblem of eternity. It will never run dry. Like the Genesis passage, the river of our love is like the boundaries of paradise. I am forever refreshed by the rushing waters of our love!

Hymn: "Eternal Father, strong to save, / Whose arm does bind the restless wave, / Who bids the mighty ocean deep its own appointed limits keep; / O hear us when we cry to Thee for those in peril on the sea. / O Savior whose almighty word the winds and waves submissive heard, / Who walked upon the foaming deep, / And calm amid the rage did sleep; / O hear us when we cry to Thee / For those in peril on the sea. / O Holy Spirit, who did brood upon the waters dark and rude, / And bid their angry tumult cease, / And die for wild confusion peace; / O hear us when we cry to Thee / For those in peril on the sea. / O Trinity of love and pow'r, / Your children shield in danger's hour; / From rock and tempest, fire, and foe, / Protect them whereso e'er they go; / Thus, evermore shall rise to Thee glad hymns of praise from land and sea" (William Whiting, "Eternal Father, Strong to Save").

Meditation: We thank You that all creation, both sunshine and rain, represent an outstretched finger pointing us to You, the Giver of nature. Grant us the discipline to be good stewards of all of it. In Your name, we pray, amen.

Devotional Seventy-Eight:

A Profanity Rehabilitated

There is an amazing instruction that comes from the lips of King David. "Let Him alone, and let him curse, for the Lord has hidden him" (2 Samuel 16:11, KJV).

An old enemy cursed, swore, and stoned David as he fled before the troops of Absalom, his own beloved yet rebel son. One of David's bodyguards asked permission for David to get even by beheading his enemy and to muffle his cursing forever.

David knew that Absalom's false rebellion came not just from his son's ambition but from his own failure as king. The cursing and stoning really served the purposes of divine justice. But David also knew that in God's own time, He could turn the penalties His children drew upon themselves to higher purposes of His own.

David, a man after God's own heart, and yet one who also knew his human weaknesses, knew that God made his enemy curse him, buying that curse as something good for him, and then David translated it into a *benediction*.

P.S.: I told you about a conversation with our election judge, a pianist for a Weatherford, Texas church, who was bragging about her new pastor. She was excitedly illustrating how he was going to "preach the Bible." (Certainly, he should do that and preach all of it.) Then, she illustrated his intent by telling about a young couple in their church who were living together. The woman partner had joined the church, and both were attending regularly, but her male companion did not want to marry just yet because he had two children and was dealing with pains related to dealing with his first wife, who had asked for a divorce. So, immediately, as she explained, the new pastor met with them and told them to either marry or leave the church, and if they did not, he would ask the wife's membership be withdrawn. My response was based on the need for God's people to be biblically firm in holding up God's ideal but also biblically forgiving and redemptive, not cutting people off from the nurturing influence of Christ's body, the church. My question was, "How long is redemption?" With Jesus, it was always "people first." With His opponents, the religionists of His day, it was always about legalism and cultic claims. Rescue and redemption is the brightness of the love and forgiveness of God, a caring that, across a sea of human "lostness," illuminates the world with mercy and grace.

One of the joys of our love is the openness and trust we have in each other and our own ability to acknowledge our weaknesses. Even though there are things that could be redone, there is within us a lasting desire to translate all the strengths and weaknesses of the past into a benediction. In my statements to others about you, I have always commended you as being a godly woman and aptly named Grace because you indeed demonstrate the love, grace, and forgiveness of the One who perfectly modeled those divine attributes. I love you for those traits. I always want our marriage to bless each other, bless others, beginning with family and beyond, and most of all, bless the God who made us, saved us, and called us into His service. I thank Him for all of this and more. That, indeed, is a *benediction*.

Hymn: "He's got the whole world in His hands. / He's got the whole world in His hands. / He's got the whole world in His hands. / He's got the whole world in His hands. / He's got the wind and the rain in His hands. / He's got the wind and the rain in His hands. / He's got the wind and the rain in His hands. / He's got the whole world in His hands. / He's got the little tiny baby in His hands. / He's got the little tiny baby in His hands. / He's got the little tiny baby in His hands. / He's got the whole world in His hands. / He's got ev'rybody here in His hands. / He's got ev'rybody here in His hands. / He's got ev'rybody here in His hands. / He's got the whole world in His hands" (Spiritual, "He's Got the Whole World in His Hands").

Meditation: Our prayer of thanksgiving is that the Creator of the Universe knows no power failure. Indeed, we rejoice that You've got the whole wide world in Your hands. That means us, too! Amen.

Devotional Seventy-Nine:

Like the Dream of a Tree

In Isaiah, the prophet promises, "For as the days of a tree so will be the days of my people; my chosen ones will enjoy the works of their hands" (Isaiah 65:22b, NIV).

When our son Jeff was finishing high school, we took him on a trip to California, including a great deal of the west and northwest. It was his first extensive coverage of a beautiful part of the United States. One of the things we did, which I, too, had always wanted to do, was a trip into the redwoods of Northern California. The weather was fantastic, the air was fresh, and the skies were blue as we toured the forest. We were completely overwhelmed by the size and majesty of those magnificent trees. The trunk of one tree was big enough for a car to drive through.

I walked to the biggest tree near us and touched its towering trunk. I watched the massive, easy rhythm of the tall spar swaying against the clouds. The wind-song above us was like the sigh of the organ in a European cathedral.

Later, I learned from a park ranger that in its many centuries, that tree inscribed in expanding rings a calendar of every season it had grown. In the memory of the first gigantic redwood I had ever seen, I prayed, "O Lord, let my days make me as tall, as strong, as timeless as my dream of a redwood tree. And may my life cause my children and their children to respect the expanding rings marking the seasons of my life."

P.S.: Grace, the motivation that prompted the memory of this experience with Jeff was hearing you respond to the disappointment you felt when you learned Nicole could not take enough time off to do the cruise you had planned. I could tell how difficult it was for you to give up another memory trip with your grandchildren. At the same time, I was impressed with your understanding of her summer schedule challenges, especially the added pull of her "young love." You have been a towering strength to both Nicole and Tucker; like the giant redwoods, the "expanding rings of each season of your life" have endeared their love for you and yours for them. That will not stop, regardless of how this summer trip works out. I also promise as we blend our lives together, we will work hard to be like the redwoods for yours and mine soon to become "ours." Both Tucker and Nicole are growing adolescents. In many ways, Nicole is taking on adult roles. Both of them are learning to pick up what is being laid down and learning to walk forward as more self-directing persons without walking away from their heritage. Stretching and expanding a relationship so everything becomes bigger, without snapping or exploding the bond, is the challenge adolescence poses. May God give us the strength and steadfastness of a redwood tree.

Hymn: There is a penetrating and poignant hymn by F. Pratt Green called "For the Fruit of all Creation." Its message is that in every aspect of life, our thanks to God are expressed in the help we give to neighbors, the food we give to the hungry, and the harvest we share with our world. Such acts of generosity represent our thanks to God, the provider of all things.

Meditation: Dear Lord, help us remain rooted in our heritage and faith. We thank You that while sleeping or awake, You are watching over us and calling us to be grateful for the wonders that surround us and for the truths that challenge our best behavior with self or others. Let us look at the giant trees You made and also the giant men and women that stand before us, all bearing evidence of your unique and powerful creative order. Amen.

Devotional Eighty:

Verna's Dream

In John's Gospel, the author says of the Christ, who was Word made flesh, "From the fullness of his grace we have all received one blessing after another" (John 1:16, NIV).

Let me briefly tell you about Verna. She was alive, and she wanted everyone to sense the aliveness of God's nature. Her name was Verna Cook Garvan. The wife of a well-known Arkansas businessman, she developed a dream of creating a botanical garden on Lake Catherine near Hot Springs. The two of us experienced a walk through this "dream" over the weekend. We were blown away by nature's beauty. Trees of all types, vegetation from around the world, flowers of nearly every color and season, flowing streams and cascading waterfalls, vistas of beautiful Lake Catherine, birds, animals, comic presentations, an outdoor café, and a magnificent Gothic-appearing chapel made from towering wood beams and glass in a canopy of towering native trees. Her dream is now continued, thanks to the University of Arkansas, other state agencies, and a number of foundations, including the one by the "dreamer."

It is obvious Verna loved nature, and when she died not long ago, in a way, it was hard to grieve, for she is too alive in her dream to be gone.

I thought about this fantastic natural display and immediately thought about Jesus. He had this in common with Verna. He lived life to its fullness, and from its overflow, He made gardens out of the hearts of men.

P.S.: A little longer than 50 seconds, but it is a summary of one of our most thrilling times. We had a fantastic day traversing Verna's "dream" garden. It was an absolutely beautiful day. We were *together*! The happiness, hope, and love beams brightly in our lives, anticipating our own wedding. Such feeling was made stronger when we walked through the garden and especially experienced the "eternal presence" of God's creative powers, especially when entering the chapel. It was a spellbinding day! From the start of the day till the day's end, we were overjoyed by the reminders we are blessed to be together, connected in heart, mind, and soul. Add the joy of our deep, profound, and confessed love for each other to the beauty of God's creation; you can understand why we both felt like we had a symphony of divine love poured out on us.

What a renewing time it was for reflecting on what is really important in life. Three things came to my mind. First of all, we rejoice God has gifted us with each other. Second, we are anxious for our marriage to be as eternally beautiful as Verna's garden so those who live on after us will have reason to be thankful for the fruit of "our dream." Since my first love's, Jo's, first name is Verna, I was deeply connected to Verna Garvan's dream and the enduring quality of our first love. And third, however long God gives us to be together, every season of our lives, year by year, will manifest the remarkable diverse color and creativity of "Verna's dream." But beyond Verna, there is a divine dream God arranged for His children. So, we eagerly await the coming of our own marriage given to us by the One who made us and, in His redemptive plan, brought us together to dream our own new and fruitful "garden."

Hymn: "Sing to the Lord of harvest, / Sing songs of love and praise; / with joyful hearts and voices / Your alleluias raise. / By Him the rolling seasons / in fruitful order move; / O sing to the Lord of harvest, / a song of happy love. / Your hearts lay down before Him / When at His feet you fall; / and with your lives adore Him / Who gave His life for all" (John S. B. Monsell, "Sing to the Lord of Harvest").

Meditation: The beauty of a botanical garden is a reminder, O Lord, that in all things, You are the Creator. It reminds us that Your nature is filled with unique seasons, dramatizing varied colors of plants and flowers. In it all and through it all, there is a "harvest" from the seasons that brings blessing and pleasure to the beholder. Grant that we may never tire of the wonders of Your creation. So, help us adore creation and You, the Giver of it all. Amen.

Devotional Eighty-One:

Loving God and Each Other

There is a most interesting message in 1 Corinthians 8. We read, "If anyone supposes that he knows anything, he has not yet known as he ought to know; but if anyone loves God, he is known by him" (1 Corinthians 8:2–3, NASB). What a probing statement. I take it to mean that if I had more real knowledge, I would have been less confident in thinking I knew it all.

The Phillips translation says, "[T]hat while knowledge may make a man look big, it is only love that can make him grow to his full stature" (1 Corinthians 8:3, Phillips). The Living Bible paraphrases verse 2: "If anyone thinks he knows all the answers, he is just showing his ignorance" (1 Corinthians 8:2, TLB). The apostle Paul wrote this passage to combat the idolatry of his day. Someone has expressed it this way: "Isn't it odd that a being like God who sees the façade still loves the clod He made out of sod? Now, isn't that odd?"

Loving God provides the substance for loving each other. Lord, let me love You more and more!

P.S.: Grace, it is true from this passage of Scripture I learn I cannot love you as I ought without first loving God. That means He must be first. That does not make you or anyone else second. It just means real love grows for anyone, in any human relationship, when he or she is best-loved, when the lover loves God. That makes it possible for the one loved to be affirmed in godly love. That means love esteems and affirms the unconditional and unique value of the one loved because it is the way God loves. Love forgives and forgets the failings of the one loved because that is how God loves. Going forward, I will work hard to read your heart, not your lips. I will try to understand rather than judge you. I would never demand you meet my expectations as the price of admission to my own heart. That is the way God loves. The hymn evokes eternal praise to Him who first loved us.

Hymn: "Sing to the Lord of harvest, / Sing songs of love and praise; / With joyful hearts and voices / Your alleluias raise. / By Him the rolling seasons / In fruitful order move; / O sing to the Lord of harvest, / A song of happy love. / Bring to His sacred altar / The gifts His goodness gave, / The golden sheaves of harvest, / The souls He died to save. / Your hearts lay down before Him / When at His feet you fall; / And with your lies adore Him / Who gave His life for all" (John S. B. Monsell, "Sing to the Lord of Harvest").

Meditation: It is with great adoration we join in celebrating God's great creation. Amen, and amen.

Devotional Eighty-Two:

The Hidden Paragraph

Having just experienced the creative power of God in nature, I was reminded that Genesis 1:26 tells us man is made in the image of God. Ever wonder what God looks like? In John, we read, "No one has ever seen God, but God the One and Only, who is at the Father's side, has made him known" (John 1:18, NIV). But we have no real photograph of the face of Jesus. Artists across the years have attempted to portray Him. We just don't know. Maybe He looked a little like the best of all of us.

Once in a while, I try to find a hint of what God is like from the faces of people I know. Strange? Sometimes, I find more clues of God in just plain people than the handsome or beautiful. Maybe God has a sense of humor and hides His likeness in strange places to add excitement to the discovery. Or, maybe He shows the color of His magnitude in the indescribable beauty of a place like Garvan Gardens in Hot Springs, Arkansas, which you and I just visited. No one or nothing can fully describe the Creator of the Universe.

But why not join the hunt? However, beware—if you find God, things won't ever be the same!

P.S.: Even though we discovered who God is as children, we really came to know Him when we placed our faith in His Son.

However, through the years of our lives, we have had rivers of reminders about His creative powers. We have seen Him in nature, certainly through the lives of spouses, children, grandchildren, and many other sources. We have been swept over by the beauties of His handiwork in people and places around the world. The majestic powers of His creativity are all around us. And, without question, our recent walk through one of His gardens in Hot Springs brought the two of us closer together. For a moment or a "day-in-time," we were caught up in a lofty inspiration of His power and blessing. It was as if we heard Him saying, "I have brought you together, and as you walk through the pathway of life, remember, I have prepared the way."

I hope I am not allegorizing too much about the experience, but it just seems at this point in our journey, we were given a 'hidden paragraph' of God's blessing and power. It was as if He was saying, "This day, this experience is for you. Look at Me, look at each other, look at life, look all around you, remember it was Me as Creator who made you and in My redemptive powers have saved you to eternal life. Walk with Me and forever be blessed by the beauty of My world."

I do know life here on earth is not all colorful flowers or cascading streams. There will be hills and valleys of pain and disappointment, like those riveting grief moments that occurred at the death of our first spouses. However, the larger-than-life feelings we shared with each other are symbolic of the creative power of God. They move us from the temporal to the eternal aspects of love. I will forever be captivated by His powerful and beautiful character and for making it possible for two of His children to be drawn to each other. Thank God, and thank you for being such a blessing to me.

Hymn: "Now thank we all our God / with heart and hands and voices, / Who wondrous things hath done, / In whom His world rejoices; / Who, from our mother's arms, / hath blessed us on our way / with countless gifts of love, / and still is ours today. / O may this bounteous God/ Thro' all our life be near us, / with ever joyful hearts / and blessed peace to cheer us; / and keep us in His grace, / and guide us when perplexed, / and free us from all ills / in this world and the next. / All praise and thanks to God / the Father now be given, / the Son and Him who reigns / with them in highest heaven, / The one eternal God, / whom earth and heav'n adore; / for thus it was, is now, / and shall be evermore" (Martin Rinkart, Catherine Winkworth, "Now Thank We All Our God").

Meditation: "Many, oh Lord my God, are the wonders you have done. Things you have planned for us no one can recount to you; were I to speak and tell of them, they would be too many to declare" (Psalm 40:5, NIV). That does capture our praises of gratitude for every living thing. For that and much more, we give thanks. Amen.

Devotional Eighty-Three:

Listen to the Music

On one occasion, I went with Jo to a music store for her to purchase some sheet music, and while there, I looked over the merchandise. I wandered over to a beautiful grand piano with a most familiar trade name. "Hey, what luck?" I sat down to sample a chord or two. (People who know me well know I play the piano strictly for my own "amazement.") It was Jo who had all the musical gifts. She was not with me. So, who could refuse to touch the keys of such a well-known instrument? Not me!

What a disappointment! The instrument had been designed by the manufacturers to play "honky tonk" at the push of a button or pedal. There was no way good sound could come from that box, especially by me.

Somebody had bought an honored name and looted it.

You can't always identify a Christian by a name tag. On the other hand, it's possible to buy into the brand and cash in on the goodwill it brings. Want to find out whether someone is genuine? Check the music they make with each other for the signature of the Master.

P.S.: I know we are caught up in the melodic strains of love and devotion for each other. It is one of the evidences of its reality.

And unlike a "honky tonk" noise, our love is a symphony of beautiful tempo and sound. Anywhere you touch, the sound beams out in harmony, providing pleasure and joy not only to the ear but to the heart and mind as well. I am still thinking about last weekend and all the melodies we made. As you said in conversation tonight, from start to finish, it was a "perfect" composition. It wasn't just the beautiful surroundings and all the people that added to our enjoyment of Hot Springs. Ultimately, it was the sounds we made with each other in response to the beautiful world God has made for us. It was beautiful music!

I could not help but think of words from Johann Wolfgang von Goethe, who wrote, "This is the true measure of love: when we believe that we alone can love, that no one could ever have loved so before us, and that no one will ever love in the same way after us." That unique and very personal composition is made by us. It cannot be created by anyone else or claimed by them. It is ours, and I want to spend the rest of my life adding "verses" and "movements" to our symphony. Thanks for plucking the harp strings of my heart and bringing the signature of the Master into our lives.

I look forward to the moment when, with vows, our longing is finally complete.

Hymn: "Day by day and with each passing moment, / Strength I find to meet my trials here; / Trusting in my Father's wise bestowment, / I've no cause for worry or for fear. / He whose heart is kind beyond all measure / Gives unto each day what He deems best— / Lovingly its part of pain and pleasure, / Mingling toil with peace and rest. / Ev-'ry day the Lord Himself is near me / With a special mercy for each hour; / All my cares He fain would bear, and cheer me, / He whose name is Counselor and Pow'r, / The protection of His child and treasure / Is a charge that on Himself He laid; / 'As thy days, thy strength shall be in measure,' / This the pledge to me He made. / Help me then in ev-'ry tribulation / So to trust Thy promises, O Lord, / That I lose not faith's sweet consolation / Offered me within Thy holy Word. / Help me Lord, when toil and trouble meeting, / E'er to take as from a father's hand, / One by one the days, the moments fleeting, / Till I reach the promised land" (Caroline V. Sandell-Berg, "Day by Day").

Meditation: Dear God of Redemption, may we ask Your Spirit to confirm the reality of our trust and belief in You. Forgive us when we seek to play savior and "go it on our own." Let us remember and forget never that genuine faith expresses itself in true works of righteousness, led by the Spirit's direction. Amen.

Devotional Eighty-Four:

How about Another Poem

Inspiration for another short sermon did not rise to the top of my thoughts, but all day long, I have relived the countless ways your life has touched mine. Especially noteworthy is how I have been so strangely blessed by the presence and influence of your friendship. Tonight, we had fun thinking about the events of our "journey." We wondered if it could even be possible to anticipate them. The answer, of course, was no, but the answer also includes a postlude that reflects how in God's providential "surprising grace," we can now say "for all that has been *yes*." So, rather than a sermon tonight, let me share some lines from a poem by Roy Croft. There isn't enough energy in my bones to include it all, but here are some verses that capture the gratitude I have for you. Starting at the time you worked for me in an executive role and now reconnected in these later years, you have made a significant difference in my life. The poem is entitled "Love," and it certainly captures my feelings of gratitude for each step of the journey.

> I love you,
>
> Not only for what you are,
>
> But for what I am when
>
> I am with you.

I love you,

Not only for what

You have made of yourself,

But what

You are making of me.

I love you

For the part of me

That you bring out;

I love you

For putting your hand

Into my heaped-up heart

And passing over

All the foolish, weak things

That you can't help

Dimly seeing there,

And for drawing out

Into the light

All the beautiful belongings

That no one else had looked

Quite far enough to find.

I love you because you

Are now helping me to make

Of the lumber of my life

Not a lectern,

But a temple;

Out of the works

Of my every day

Not a command

But a song

I love you

Because you have done

More than any creed

Could have done

To make me thrilled.

And more than any fate

Could have done

To make me fulfilled.

You have been and now are a special "pearl of great price" gift to me.

Hymn: "Of the Father's love begotten, / Ere the worlds began to be, / He is Alpha and Omega, / He the source, the ending He, / Of the things that are, that have been, / And that future years shall see, / Evermore and evermore? / O ye heights of heav'n adore

Him; / Angel hosts, His praises sing' / Pow'rs, dominion, bow before Him, / And extol our God and King; / Let no tongue on earth be silent, / Ev'ry voice in concert sing, / Evermore and evermore! / Christ, to Thee with God the Father, / And, O Holy Ghost, to Thee, / Hymn and chant and high thanksgiving, / and unwearied praises be: / Honor, glory, and dominion, and eternal victory, / Evermore and evermore!" (Aurelius Clemens Prudentius, "Of the Father's Love Begotten").

Meditation: God of all beauty and wisdom. We thank You for the inspiration of poetic verse that prompts reflection and meditation on life's most intimate relationships. It reminds us You are the Alpha and Omega, the source of unending life. May we bow before You in the grandeur of creation and be blessed by those whose gifts express Your eternalness through the sung and spoken word. Amen.

Devotional Eighty-Five:

The Odor of Moab

When my friend Roger Roark was a boy, he had a dog whose name was Socks. As dogs go, Socks was a sorry hound. But he had a keen nostril. Roger never got tired of trying to lose Socks. He'd double back and jump off the railroad track. He'd mix his trail with a dozen others. It didn't matter to Socks. He'd sniff and slobber his way to Roger every time. Roger had his own odor. Everybody does.

In Chapter 48, Jeremiah says of Moab, "[H]is taste remained in him, and his scent is not changed" (Jeremiah 48:11b, KJV).

What do you think? Could a good hound, given a sniff of the Constitution, sort out today's Americans through the mixed trail of their passage? Is there still in this country a distinct flavor of justice, of absolute belief in the separation of church and state, a special aroma of freedom? Is there a strong urge to be independently responsible for one's own behavior? Is it surely a time for the country to be united rather than politicized? Is there someone left who is "dead sure" our country is not the servant of all? Empower individual responsibility. May the odor of Moab fill our nostrils with self-reliance and patriotism.

P.S.: I am worried that creeping socialism is once again raising its ugly head. It invaded the former Soviet Union. It is rampant in some Latin American countries, like Venezuela, and certainly in Castro's Cuba. How well I remember Mark Twain's definition of a socialist as "someone who likes to spend someone else's money." Massive government control destroys individual liberty.

Obviously, it is time, once again, for freedom-loving citizens to stand up and speak out, or we will lose our basic tenets of democracy. What has this to do with us? We will love each other regardless of how social and governmental issues develop. But our precious kids and grandkids will face a different nation than the one that produced us. Unless we exercise citizen power and vote for a president more committed to social justice and economic prosperity for all, the nation will find the government in charge, not the people. We need leadership that is proud of the nation, not apologizes for it. Let the USA bring jobs and factories back to our own people. It is good to outsource some labor efforts but not at the expense of those wanting to work and earn but have no opportunity. When Aristotle asked the Sabine farmers why they continued to plant new trees in their old age, the response was "for the generations to come." It is time for America to think again about its primary economic purpose. It is, and should be, American citizens first for this generation and the ones that follow. Forgive me for moving away from the personal to the corporate, but I just had to "get it off my chest."

Hymn: "God of our fathers, whose almighty hand / leads forth in beauty all the starry band. / Of shining worlds in splendor thro' the skies, / our grateful songs before Thy throne arise. / Thy love divine hath led us in the past, / in this free land by Thee our lot is cast; / Be thou our ruler, guardian, guide, and stay, / Thy Word our law, Thy paths our chosen way. / Refresh Thy people on their toilsome way, / lead us from night to never ending day; / fill all our lives with love and grace divine, / and glory, laud, and praise be ever Thine" (Daniel C. Roberts, "God of Our Fathers").

Meditation: Father of the nations, we give thanks that in America, religious liberty has been a sacred and defended value. May Your strong arm of defense continue to empower free religious expression. May Your bounteous goodness nourish this nation with peace and harmony with one another and with You. Amen.

Devotional Eighty-Six:

Geography of Faith

My sister Phyllis moved with her physician husband from Illinois to Florida, and after six months, she developed a Southern accent. I could not believe how quickly she learned the dialect. Surrender a Southern Illinois accent in six months? I hate to think the environment is that powerful.

What are we, a mixture of everything that happens to us? I have to admit I can't escape my surroundings. I'm affected even when I fight or challenge them. I do business every day with many things, including geography and weather.

In Isaiah, we learn, "How beautiful upon the mountains are the feet of Him that bringeth good tidings, that publisheth peace; that bringeth good tidings of good, that publisheth salvation; that saith unto Zion, my God reighneth" (Isaiah 52:7, KJV). The Creator looms in all He has made. To faith, God is the horizon under distant skies. He is the air we breathe. His intelligence is our geography, His smile our weather.

P.S.: It was obvious tonight you were still anxious and a bit frustrated by all the challenges facing you over the weekend. As you opined, it includes a trip to Jackson, a passport dilemma, and an air conditioning issue. I can't say I blame your frustrations because I, too, would be anxious. But the thought occurred to me:

God is very aware of all those things, so rather than be pulled by them, let God push you through it all. It is so easy, like my sister Phyllis, to be pulled by a different accent. That was not her speech, even though some of the motive was to identify with a new Southern language. Just as you got good news from the dentist, relax and let these other challenges be given over to God, who is the air we breathe and the intelligence of our geography. Our love isn't based on geography, and though we are apart for now, I am with you in spirit. Most of all, I am looking forward to the time when our faith in God's care for us won't be affected by geography at all. In the meantime, please know my thoughts and prayers reach across the miles from Fort Worth to Memphis.

Hymn: "Let all things now living / a song of thanksgiving / to God the Creator triumphantly raise, / who fashioned and made us, / protected and stayed us, / who guideth us on / to the end of our days. / His banners are o're us, / His light goes before us, / a pillar of fire shining forth in the night, / 'Til shadows have vanished / and darkness is banished, / as forward we travel from light into light. / His law He enforces, / the stars in their courses, / the sun in His orbit, / obediently shine. / The hills and the mountains, / the rivers and fountains, / the deeps of the ocean / proclaim Him Divine. / We too, should be voicing / our love and rejoicing, / with glad adoration / a song let us raise, / Till all things now living / unite in thanksgiving / to God in the highest, hosanna and praise!" (Katherine K. Davis, "Let All Things Now Living").

Meditation: In moments of frustration and anxiety, help us lift our drooping hands and strengthen weak knees. Our innermost desire is to walk in peace and harmony. Heal what is lame within us. As the scriptures say, "May we worship the Lord in the spirit of His Holiness" (Psalm 29:2b, NIV). In His name, we pray. Amen.

Devotional Eighty-Seven:

Rain for All of Us

Texas has been in a drought for several years, but this spring, the drought has ended, and we are now having extremely wet weather with flash flooding. In reflecting on flooding, my mind went back to a time when I was a small lad. We were still living on my grandmother's farm, and before my dad went to seminary, he taught school and pastored a small church. In the summer months, when school was out, he worked for the REA, installing electric lines in the rural areas of Southern Illinois.

My memory is about a Model A Ford clattering to a stop in front of the house. A stranger in overalls stepped out. "Son, what's your name?"

"Jim."

"Jim, is your daddy home?"

"No, but Mother is."

My mother told the stranger Dad would be in soon. He sat beside me. "How are your crops doing this year?" he asked quietly. I remember Mother saying, "My husband says if we don't get rain in a few days, the garden is gone, and there won't be another hay cutting." I remember as if it was yesterday, he said, "Let us pray about it," and right there in our living room, this stranger prayed rain would fall on our place.

It wasn't long until Dad came home, and almost at the same time he opened the door, thunder struck, and heavy rain began to fall. Dad greeted the stranger, and I heard him say, "I met Jim, and he invited me in, and I just had prayed God would send rain your way. Looks like He did." After a brief conversation, the stranger excused himself, and when he left, he turned to me and said, "Jim, it was nice to meet you and your dad, and I hope we all get lots of rain." In Exodus 33, we read, "The Lord said to Moses, 'I'll do the very thing you have asked, because I am pleased with you and I know you by name'" (Exodus 33:17, NIV). When a farmer in overalls called a five-year-old by name and sat beside him to talk and pray for rain, God seemed so real and personal for this lad.

P.S.: I knew you had to drive to Jackson, Mississippi, on a rainy afternoon, and I'm so glad you made your Vaiden stop before it started. It is pouring here tonight, and because it is extremely wet, we might need another "stranger" to pray for the rains to stop before there is major flooding. Not really, because we still need the lakes and underground streams to fill. However, as we talked today and again with your conversation with Val Roth, I was reminded how God's power and sustaining presence have guided us through life's journey. You know we have often thanked God for bringing us together. These past months have "drenched" us with His refreshing "showers of blessings." It has been overwhelming; I could not help but be reminded how friends and maybe even a "stranger" we don't know about are praying God's "full and running-over" reservoir of blessing be ours. From the parched days of trauma and difficulty of caring for our mates and then you with your mother, the desert days are now being filled with abundance and indescribable joy! Speaking for myself, caring for Jo until the end of her precious life has made me more sensitive to human needs. What's more, as we walk through to the *light* of our union, we have not only the prayers of family and friends but even the surprises of strangers.

Hymn: "Lead on , O King Eternal, / The day of march has come; / Henceforth in fields of conquest / Thy tents shall be our home; / Thro' days of preparation / Thy grace has made us strong, / And now, O King Eternal / We lift our battle song. / Lead on, O King Eternal, / Till sin's fierce was shall cease, / And holiness shall whisper / The sweet amen of peace; / For not with sword's loud clashing, / Or roll of stirring drums / With deeds of love and mercy / The heav'nly kingdom comes. / Lead on, O King Eternal, / We follow not with fears; / For gladness breaks like morning / Where'er Thy face appears; / Thy cross is lifted o'er us; / We journey in its light: / The crown awaits the conquest; / Lead on, O God of might" (Ernest W. Shurtleff, "Lead On, O King Eternal").

Meditation: May every reminder of the showers of God's blessings cause us to grow in grace and mercy for the rich gifts of family, friends, and even strangers. Dear God, the world of Your creation is a beautiful world, and we thank You, Father, for giving us these rich resources of grace and blessing, "even strangers within the gates." Amen.

# *Devotional Eighty-Eight:*

The Sweetest Poison

Medicine is extremely expensive these days. The most expensive kind costs nothing in money. Act like you want it, and you can get it from anyone. That medicine is sympathy.

Why is sympathy expensive? It tells me my problem is not my fault and robs me of helping myself. It soothes my aches and puts off a real diagnosis. Sympathy not deserved helps me enjoy a whipping and ask for another. It turns a man or woman into a helpless child.

God is not all that sympathetic. When poor Job, the sickest man of all, complained of his mistreatment, God spoke through the roar of a tornado, "Gird up now thy loins like a man; for I will demand of thee, and answer thou me" (Job 38:3, KJV). Sounds unsympathetic? Maybe! But God told Job to stand up. And, these days, that's just what the doctor ordered.

P.S.: Tonight's conversation about submissiveness was good, and it gave us the opportunity to affirm again how much we want our marriage to be characterized by growth. It will require a willingness to change. That can't happen if a defensive attitude develops and we nurture the need for "false sympathy." It will not happen if one of us feels one is being treated more unfairly than the other. There are traumatic times in life when sympathy is helpful, and the empathetic love of someone helps heal a wound. But, you can nurse self-imposed sympathy into a disease.

In a dynamic marriage, there is trust and understanding based on shared needs and wants. Hopefully, they are rationally evaluated, and the give-and-take provides stability. Our marriage will not be a patriarchy, where the husband rules as a dictator, or a matriarchy, where the wife rules as the awesome power behind the throne. It will not be an anarchy where no one has answered the question, "Who's in charge?" Where there are no accepted rules, others, usually children, end up in control. Instead, you and I have already committed to a mutual submissiveness. Our desire is for it to be a theocracy with God directing traffic and giving wisdom for decision-making. That commitment will also produce not just stability but security and serenity. In that case, both of us find pleasure in each other as two among equals. Obviously, as the woman on TLC said, empathy, not sympathy, is the best medicine. I will work hard to not violate your need for autonomy. I already know, through our courtship, you have the same desire.

Hymn: In the remarkable hymn by Wilhelmina D'A. Stephens "Jesus Was a Loving Teacher," we are reminded that Jesus, the Master Teacher, was a loving teacher and showed it by teaching His followers how to love and pray; in patience, He waited for us to learn God's love will and telling stories that prompted our praise and service.

Meditation: Dear God of the nations and people, it is awesome to know that in Your creative power, You ordered only one DNA for each of us. No two people are exactly alike. Help us to respect differences and learn how to mediate mutuality in word and deed. Mutual submissiveness cannot be achieved apart from Your guiding wisdom. Let that be our resolve. Amen.

Devotional Eighty-Nine:

The Tent-Cord Within

I remember the first time we went camping; I was probably about five years old. Uncle Elmo, my father's only brother, my favorite uncle, and my dad put up the tent in the steady breeze of an Illinois evening. The pegs were driven into the ground with quick, sure strokes. Then the cords were tightened, and the tent, trim and taut, sprang into form before our eyes,

The next morning, the pegs came up, and the proud tent collapsed at my feet. I remember I cried at the loss of my new house. Years later, when Uncle Elmo had a coronary collapse, I again remembered the tent. He sort of collapsed, like an inner cord to his tent was broken.

Eliphaz, Job's friend, says in Chapter 4 that frail humans have their tent cords plucked up within them. In the crash of the winds where we walk these days, Lord, anchor our tent cords within us!

P.S.: Grace, your compassionate concern for your gravely ill friend prompted a sermon response. We are at the stage in life when life itself is fragile. That is true for all people, but the law of averages rates us higher. We have been bountifully blessed with good health. I must admit I live life as if it will last forever. And, of course, right now, we are basking in the glow of new and fresh love. I may be acting like an adolescent, especially when it comes to thinking about all the good things God has brought into our lives. I want to keep those thoughts active. But I also know critical illnesses of family and friends can come at any moment. The same is true for us. The last days of life are not so different than what we have already faced. (It hurt deeply to lose Jo.) Beginning in early childhood, we do have to die to smaller worlds if we are to reach bigger ones. But in every case, there is life on the other side of those crises of risk. No exit ever leads us out to nowhere. As I said to you before, every exit is also an entrance, and learning this fact gives a person hope and the ability to trust God with the whole of life.

Life for us is destiny, and in all things, the bitter and the sweet, God is at work for good. Trusting in His goodness and grace is the anchor point for everyday living. That is one of the purposes of this book, *Surprised by Grace*. Hopefully, it will be helpful to each reader, but especially those like us considering a second marriage. Moving forward, I know there are things we are used to that will need to change or have to be given up. But, beyond the change comes new experiences. God, give us grace to receive them.

Hymn: "Is your life a channel of blessing? / Is the love of God flowing thro' you? / Are you telling the lost of the Savior? / Are you ready His service to do? / Make me a channel of blessing today, / Make me a channel of blessing, I pray; / My life possessing, my service blessing, / Make me a channel of blessing today" (Harper G. Smyth, "Make Me a Channel of Blessing").

Meditation: Whether a candle in a corner or a lighthouse on a hill, may we walk as "children of the light," blessing the world with love and friendship. People around us are watching us. May they not be disappointed in our care for them regardless of life's circumstances. Amen.

Devotional Ninety:

A Favor from My Enemy

One of the things I have struggled with in recent years is how to love the unlovely. In Matthew 5:44, Jesus tells us to love our enemies. I want to ask Him, "Jesus, do You realize how things really are?" If folk in His day were like folk now, they had trouble loving friends and even getting along with themselves.

When I try to love my enemy, I don't get any help from him. He has no smile to warm me, no gift to enrich me, no encouragement to strengthen me. He trips me up, he knifes me and others in the back, and then he laughs at my disgrace.

My enemy wants to engineer my catastrophe.

The only reason I have for loving him is that Christ told me to. The only kind of love Jesus was trained in was the truth, which sends rain to the just and unjust. If I can love my enemy, the Lord would have to be real.

P.S.: I have struggled in dealing with the influences that brought change and division in our Baptist world. Neither I nor we can change the events of the past, including the motives of key leaders in that effort. They used controlling actions to achieve their objective. The effort was to root out Liberalism in Baptist life. It was a scare tactic. There were a small number of Liberal theologians who could have been terminated by existing trustee structures. You only had to be the victim of their aggressive agenda to appreciate the damage that a so-called enemy can "heap on you." Not only me but my dearest and godliest friends were damaged by their agenda. There are times when I think I have gotten past the righteous indignation that wells up in me.

We cannot erase the memories from the past but must move forward with hope. One of the things I need your help with is getting me past the disgust for some of that crowd. I want us to go forward in our marriage focused more on the future than on our past, especially those elements from the past that trigger disappointment. It was Zechariah who stressed, "[W]hen evening comes there will be light" (Zechariah 14:7, NIV).

My prayer for us is we can take the best of the past with us and leave the unpleasant behind. Going down the mountain of life is altogether different from climbing up it. People are prone to think of the last part of life as "night." In my abounding excitement and gratitude for our love, I can only think of the rest of our years not as the darkness of night but rather filled with the "light of abiding love." That could be called "authentic intimacy." Yes, I am *surprised by grace*, God's grace and yours.

Hymn: "Blessed be the tie that binds / our hearts in Christian love; / the fellowship of kindred minds / is like to that above. / We share our mutual woes, / our mutual burdens bear; / and often for each other flows / the sympathizing tear" (John Fawcett, "Blessed Be the Tie").

Meditation: Lord, some people in my life are difficult to love.

May we ever remember You showed Your love to us even when we were Your enemy. Please direct us into ways to love with Your power and grace. In the name of the one who wants us to make friends of enemies. In Jesus's name, amen.

Devotional Ninety-One:

The Day Frosty Preached

In Mark 13:11, Jesus teaches that when His followers are on trial, they should not be anxious about what they say. For the Holy Spirit will speak through them in that hour. This sermon is another one by Roger Carstensen but based on a similar experience that occurred at Southwestern Seminary. Call his name "Frosty." He stood before twenty fellow students. Nineteen had already preached a required sermon in preaching class. He had put off the ordeal as long as possible.

He violated every rule of speaking—eyes down, hands twisted behind him, body stiff as a fencepost in winter. Frosty tried to preach. All he had prepared to say, he could not recall. He opened his mouth, but nothing came out. Finally, he rallied and spoke to the audience of fellow students. "It's too big," he said. "I read the Bible, I read the books, I talked to the professor. It's too big. I am not enough of a man to preach."

In the silence, fellow students looked at each other and saw the first tears of the semester. Something had been given to Frosty, something of the heart, something of the spirit, something from the divine hand of God.

P.S.: What a great day we shared. In every way, it was outstanding. The fellowship was endearing. There was good food, good friends, good worship, good entertainment, but most of all, the absolute fresh delight from new and amazing love. So deep have our moments together become.

As you know, I could not hold back the tears of joy and happiness for you. It was overwhelming, and the only way I knew to express my gratitude for our love was in tears. I thought about how this young seminarian felt when he stood to preach a "simple sermon." The power of our love is overwhelming. It is much bigger than the mere words of men. It defies explanation. It is bigger than I am, and its power is greater than the simple words I might render. But the significance of love needs no verbal explanation. Our love is from the heart, from our spirits. I am convinced it is something given by God's redemptive plan for undeserving persons like us. As the subtitle of this book suggests, we have experienced "grace and reconnection in an unexpected journey." It has happened; it is real, and I say again, it is "near heaven."

Hymn: "Spirit of God, descend upon my heart; / Wean it from earth; thro' all its pulses move; / Stoop to my weakness, mighty as Thou art, / and make me love Thee as I ought to love. / I ask no dream, no prophet ecstasies, / No sudden rending of the veil of clay, / No angel visitant, no op'ning skies; / but take the dimness of my soul away. / Teach me to love Thee as Thine angels love, / one holy passion filling all my frame; / the kindling of the heaven descended Dove, / My heart an altar, and Thy love the flame" (George Croly, "Spirit of God, Descend upon My Heart").

Meditation: Dear Lord, teach us the patience of unending praise for planting seeds of love within the human heart. Because of that source of love, help us to love You more. Amen.

Devotional Ninety-Two:

The Night I Felt Sorry for the Lord

Last night's sermon was about Frosty, a great sermon from a tear of unworthiness. It made me think about how a lot of preachers have their own hang-ups. One is many dearly love to be listened to. I feel the same. We like to have warm bodies and eager ears out there in the pews. So, when people don't come, it feels like a conspiracy.

I remember, as a young minister in Southern Illinois, being asked to be a supply preacher for six Sunday nights while the minister was on sick leave. An older retired pastor was asked to do Sunday mornings, and I was recruited for Sunday nights. I never will forget the nervousness and anxiety it prompted within me to think more people came to hear the older minister than me. I remember one Sunday evening, the pianist was not there. The faithful deacon was on vacation. The youth—who knows where they are? Why were they not there to hear one of their own age? Hardly anyone was there.

I looked at the lights of that rural Southern Illinois town and felt sorry for the Lord. Jeremiah 15 came to mind. "I sat alone because of Your hand for you have filled me with indignation (Jeremiah 15:17b, NKJV). Thank God I have a sense of humor. That night, I realized I was not God Almighty after all. My sermon wasn't all that much to miss. This young minister had to admit if the hand of God had been on him, the people would have been there, and like when Frosty preached, there would have been tears. It was a gut check for me!

P.S.: I don't know why this experience popped into my mind. Unless it was thinking about Frosty and reliving unforgettable moments with you, as cited in last night's sermon, one of the subtle temptations of preachers is getting wrapped up in their own expertise, not relying on God's Spirit to manifest Himself through their promptings. You have to empty yourself in order to fully discover the power of God's empowerment. I know it is not necessarily the same comparison, but in a sense, the dynamic is the same. That is, yesterday morning, in the midst of expressions of fervor and devotion to one another, I became so utterly empty of myself. But, I was also filled with gratitude, recognizing that the love of our lives was not based on anything either of us could boast. Rather, it was the gift of complete commitment to one another. Thank God for the gift of each other. We are two, but we shall soon be "one."

Hymn: "I'll praise my Maker while I've breath; / and when my voice is lost in death, / Praise shall employ my nobler pow'rs. / My days of praise shall ne'er be past, / while life, and tho't, and being last, or immortality endures. / Happy the man whose hopes rely on Israel's God! / He made the sky, and earth, and seas, with all their train: / His truth forever stands secure; / He saves th' oppressed, He feeds the poor, / and none shall find His promise vain. / I'll praise Him while He lends my breath; / and when my voice is lost in death, / Praise shall employ my nobler pow'rs. / My days of praise shall ne'er be past, / while life, and tho't, and being last, or immortality endures" (Isaac Watts, "I'll Praise My Maker").

Meditation: Dear Father, when we think of Your great compassion for the "children of men," it overwhelms us with praise and gratitude. As the hymn writer expresses in another verse, "he sends the laboring conscience peace." That surprising awareness makes us rejoice. Keep revealing Your eternal wisdom to Your needy children. In God's good name, we pray. Amen.

Devotional Ninety-Three:

Emancipation

In 1 Corinthians 3:21–23, Paul teaches that all things are ours, and at the same time, we belong to Christ.

Did you ever feel you belong to your possessions? Take your house. Every month, it tells you to make the payment. If it is paid up, you still get orders to pay taxes. It orders you to replace plumbing, worn water heaters, dishwashers, and air conditioning units.

Your car is also your boss. No matter what gas costs, you have to pay up. Change the oil, change filters, and buy license tags. On cold mornings, I ask my car permission to ride.

When I belong to Christ, I don't have to have a car or even a house. Belonging to the Eternal, I don't even have to limit my living to the earthly. Only when I am free to do without it can I own anything. In the freedom of the love of God, the whole world is mine.

P.S.: Grace, you know, in recent nights, the sermons have been triggered by reminders of "union." Or change of word references: "I" and "Me" to "We" and "Us." There is also another important pronoun. It is "Him." A part of the message I tried to convey in the last "sermon" is this sense of "oneness" we share. I have thought about it a lot, especially following the fantastic time last weekend. Also, in recent days, we each had reason to "belong to our possessions," like a new air conditioning unit for your house and blown down trees at my Texas home.

Also, in our conversation tonight, we talked about paint for your house. That kind of need never stops as long as we have possessions. But for me, all those things seem insignificant because I can truthfully say I am not bound by my possessions. A house that once was important and furnishings and collections that cost money and time, once valued, are no longer important to me. The point is, I said to myself. "There is nothing in this grand old house of mine I could not live without." We will have things, houses, and cars, but all of those possessions cannot begin to compare to the value of *us*, and most of all, *Him* who is at work forever creating and recreating the "new" in life. I have long advocated the command, "Seek ye first the Kingdom of God…and all these other things will be added unto you" (Matthew 6:33a, KJV). I have believed and practiced that reality, but it is time to reaffirm the commitment. I really believe the promise stated above. "When I am free to do without it, can I own anything." Our love has done many things, but for sure, it has anchored me more deeply in kingdom reality. For you and "all those other things," I am being *surprised by grace*.

Hymn: "Jesus, I my cross have taken, / All to leave, and follow Thee; / Destitute, despised, forsaken, / Thou, from hence, my all shall be; / Perish ev'ry fond ambition, / All I've sought or hoped or known; / Yet how rich is my condition: / God and heav'n are still my own! / Haste thee on from grace to glory, / Armed by faith, and winged by prayer; / Heav'n's eternal days before thee, / God's own hand shall guide thee there; / Soon shall close thy earthy mission, / Swift shall pass thy pilgrim days; / Hope shall change to glad fruition, / Faith to sight, and prayer to praise" (Henry F. Lyte, "Jesus, I My Cross Have Taken").

Meditation: May we never forget that Your great commandment is to love You with all might, power, and spirit and to love our neighbor as we love ourselves. How the obedience of that command would make this world what You want it to be. Help us to live and love. It is in Your matchless name we pray. Amen.

Devotional Ninety-Four:

A Samaritan in Naples

Several years ago, I led a Spiritual Emphasis Week for a church in Naples, Florida. Jo and I were guests in a motel provided by the church. At 4 a.m. and sound asleep, I heard a knock at the door and a loud noise coming from the portico between the door and the parking lot. I went to the door and found a dirty, swaying man, eyes bloodshot, standing stooped at the door. "You a preacher?" he said.

"Yes."

"Help me!"

The motel clerk told him I might be of help. Obviously, this man was an alcoholic out of booze. Half the time, he was doubled over with the dry heaves. He gasped out a number for me to call. He gave me his name and the name of the person I was to call. I called and sketched the situation to the voice on the other end, "Get him a mug of hot coffee to hold him till we get there." I went to the motel lobby and got two cups of hot, black coffee.

In 15 minutes, a distinguished man and his lovely wife, members of Alcoholics Anonymous, were in the room. They embraced the drunk, cleaned the motel porch where he had heaved, paid the bill for the room he was in just down from us, thanked the motel clerk for putting him in touch with me, and took him home with them. In Luke 10, I had long ago read of the "Good Samaritan." In Naples, Florida, in 1980, by the grace of God and Alcoholics Anonymous, I met him.

P.S.: Tonight, we talked about Sabbath laws and the strict environment in which we grew up. We talked about the strict observance of Jewish law and the condescending attitude of religious leaders of Jesus's day. In archaic Jewish law, there were hundreds of laws and sub-laws that restricted Sabbath behavior. Of course, Jesus's response to His critics for dipping grain on the Sabbath was, "The Sabbath was made for man, not man for the Sabbath" (Mark 2:27a, NIV). We now appreciate the Jewish mindset to keep Sabbath laws, but we are not torn by the legalism that prompted a lack of compassion. We certainly can laud our parents and their legacy, which held up high standards, but sometimes, in the midst of strict legalism, the needs of persons go unmet.

With Jesus, it was "people first." With His followers, it was always "work" and "Sabbath observances first." To win the "Jesus way" battle is to win it all. In His realm, He always comes down on the importance of every single person without regard for religious affiliations or cultic claims. While religious leaders passed right on by, the man was robbed and left in a ditch. It took a Good Samaritan to illustrate the way believers should behave. Of course, this truth is practiced first with each other, then at home, and then with others. I do so much look forward to walking with you "in His way."

Hymn: "Rescue the perishing, / care for the dying, / snatch them in pity from sin and the grave; / weep o'er the erring one, / lift up the fallen, / tell them of Jesus the mighty to save. / Down in the human heart, / crushed by the tempter, / feelings lie buried that grace can restore; / touched by a loving heart, / wakened by kindness, / chords that are broken will vibrate once more. / Rescue the perishing, / care for the dying; / Jesus is merciful, Jesus will save" (Fanny J. Crosby, "Rescue the Perishing").

Meditation: Father, grant us the spirit of the Good Samaritan who had compassion for someone in need. Forgive us when, in our haste, we "pass by on the other side" in order to avoid involvement in service to others. Amen.

Devotional Ninety-Five:

Sweet Wine for the Soul

During the summer of my junior year in high school, I worked on my uncle Earl's farm. It was fun because, by that time, I was old enough to drive his great big John Deere tractor. Halfway to the hay field on a July Illinois morning, I saw the water jug had tipped over. The corn-cob stopper had jiggled out, and over half our water was gone. Through the hot day, we rationed water—Uncle Earl, my cousin Glen, and a neighboring farmer helping us. I policed the water jug, but by the end of the day, the jug was empty.

Usually, heading home after a hard day, I had a lot of things on my mind, like jumping in my uncle's lake and having a refreshing swim. This time, there was only one thing on my mind: water. Good old tasteless water. Not soda pop. Not lemonade, just water.

I pulled up the tractor, headed to the outside well, and hammered up the crystal stream of the best drink one could taste.

In Matthew 5, Jesus said, "Blessed are those who hunger and thirst for righteousness, for they will be filled" (Matthew 5:6, NIV). At various times in life, when the jug of my life has tipped over, the tasteless good water not available on that hot July day becomes the sweet, sweet wine of the soul. There is a thirst that only Christ can fill.

P.S.: As mentioned in our telephone visit, I was searching for a subject for tonight's sermon. So, I chose another one I adapted a long time ago from Roger Carstensen. A lot of memories of last weekend could have been rehearsed. Actually, we did! And what great fun and fantasy to recall them. But this sermon tonight picks up on my last confession to you. Namely, I wanted to reemphasize what a blessing it was to reconnect with you. The "jug of life" had turned over, and I was lonely, restless, and searching. And there you were. Other options could have been available, like remaining single. But given our history and the remembrance of the sweet water of the thirteen years together in a structured work relationship, my entire being was convinced we were meant for each other. It was a C. S. Lewis "stab of joy." And, after these months we have shared, I want to spend the rest of my life drinking from the well of love. The outside well at Uncle Earl's had to be pumped. But with us, there is no wait. The sweet, sweet wine of the soul is always on and running over.

Hymn: "There is a balm in Gilead / to make the wounded whole; / There is a balm in Gilead to heal the sin sick soul. / Sometimes I feel discouraged, / and think my works in vain, / but then the Holy Spirit / revives my soul again. / If you can't preach like Peter, / if you can't pray like Paul, / just tell the love of Jesus, / and say He died for all" (African American Spiritual, "There Is a Balm in Gilead").

Meditation: The deep well of meaningful human relationships is the source of happy human behavior and endeavor. May we live in praise of You, our Creator and Redeemer. Amen.

Devotional Ninety-Six:

A Window Named Andromeda

Once, on a clear night, an astronomer showed me the galaxy Andromeda. He told me Andromeda is the only object outside the Milky Way, our own galaxy, visible to the naked eye.

To see Andromeda, most folks have to glance at each side. Suddenly, like a moonbeam on water, hangs the faint glow of a distant universe, a window into infinity. Andromeda, of a million suns, is our neighbor, more than 1,000,000 light years away. Beyond that universe are myriad others.

It does us good to feel small once in a while. Join the singer in Psalm 8. "When I consider your heavens, the work of your fingers, the moon and the stars, which you have set in place, what is man that you are mindful of him, the son of man that you cared for him" (Psalm 8:3–4, NIV).

Guess what? I went to sleep in my chair again, and it is now late, late. I took Stevie outdoors for his necessary relief. I was dazzled by the stars. It was the first night in nearly a month that was not cloudy, and the stars seemed to be right on top of me. The air was crisp and bright, and it appeared as though the glowing of the stars was magnified a hundred times. Beautiful! The first thing I thought of was us. I thought how nice it would be if we were both looking at that heavenly gaze. Then, my thoughts quickly turned to you, and like a flash, it occurred to me that you have become a star in my life.

I could hardly get past that thought until I was almost teary-eyed in thanking God. He is mindful of us, and by His mercy, grace, and loving-kindness brought us together. We have other stars in our lives, especially dear family, but yours has brought a new sense of significance to my life.

Of course, Psalm 8 came flooding across my mind. It is a reminder of God's creative power. So, in the form of a "sermon idea," I want the whole world to know we have been connected by the one who made the moon and the stars and "is mindful of us."

Hymn: "When upon life's billows you are tempest tossed, / When you are discouraged, thinking all is lost, / Count your many blessings, name, them one by one, / And it will surprise you what the Lord hath done. / When you look at others with their lands and gold, / Think that Christ has promised you His wealth untold; / Count your many blessings, money cannot buy / Your reward in heaven, nor your home on high. / So, amid the conflict, whether great or small, / Do not be discouraged, God is over all; / Count your many blessings angels will attend, / Help and comfort give you to your journey's end. / Count your blessings, name them one by one, / Count your blessings, see what God hath done; / Count your blessings, name them one by one; / Count your many blessings, see what God hath done" (Johnson Oatman, "Count Your Blessings").

Meditation: Dear Loving Father, gazing at the star-filled

heavens, we are reminded of the vastness of Your love. It makes Your Spirit burn within us. May we always look to the light of Your creative power for strength and courage for the living of each day. Amen.

Devotional Ninety-Seven:

How Much Are You Worth

I heard an interview tonight with a British actress, the star of the film based on Thomas Hardy's *Far from the Madding Crowd*. In the movie, her first proposal for marriage was from a neighboring farmer who brought her a lamb from his flock and asked for her hand in marriage. In the movie we saw together, she discounts the man and the lamb till the end when she recognizes the symbolism of the lamb, which also represents the willing sacrifice of a man who truly loved her—one who was willing to sacrifice his own life for her sake.

In Matthew 12:12, Jesus observes a man is of much more value than a sheep. There is no way to place a value on human life nor on the willing sacrifice of one who sacrifices for another. In John 15:13, we are told, "Greater love has no one than this, that he lay down his life for his friends" (John 15:13, NIV).

Jesus showed us how to do this, not by settling disputes or negotiating conflicts. Rather, we see Him cultivating inward harmony through acts of a shepherd's love, like washing the feet of men He knew would betray Him, lunching with a corrupt tax collector, and honoring a sinful woman society had scorned. Finally, He gave His life so lost sheep could find salvation. The gentle Christ is indeed the "Lamb of God" who takes away the sins of the world.

That is the kind of love a marriage proposal should represent.

P.S.: Need I say more? The strength of the movie we saw was that it was filled with life lessons. In the Hardy novel, the heroine had the choice of three different types of marriage. Each had different appeals for her. But redeeming, persistent, sacrificial shepherd's love for someone he loved more than himself won out. In the end, the man with a "shepherd's heart" was chosen.

I want to be that kind of husband for you. I did not bring a lamb, or an estate, or the dashing sword of a soldier to our marriage proposal. But it happened in God's house, in the presence of two believing disciples, both of whom have sought to follow the "Lamb of God." We have each committed to loving each other to the end. And I am confident because He has known us for a long time, we will strive to be "servants to one another." Each day, I am having fresh reminders of how very good we are for each other. Six months from tomorrow, we will formalize a love that has become bigger than both of us. We have developed a coherent view of life that lifts up individuality but expresses it outwardly in sacrificial love, like the one who "laid down His life for His sheep." I have so much to learn about the Shepherd's love, but I want to grow to be like one for you and us and for our families we love so dearly.

Hymn: "In heavenly love abiding, / no change my heart shall fear; / and safe is such confiding, / for nothing changes here: / the storm may roar about me; / my heart may low be laid / but God is all around me, and can I be dismayed? / Wherever He may guide me, / no want shall turn me back; / my Shepherd is beside me, / and nothing can I lack; / His wisdom is forever, / His sight is never dim; / His will forms each endeavor, / and I will walk with Him. / Green pastures are before me, / which yet I have not seen; / bright skies will soon be o'er me, / where the dark clouds have been: / my life I cannot measure, / the path of life is free; / my Savior has my treasure, / and He will walk with me" (Anna L. Waring, "In Heavenly Love Abiding").

Meditation: Great Shepherd of the Sheep! Your sacrificial atonement for man's sins cannot be measured in human terms. Truly, You have shown us how to sacrifice and serve one another and those who are significant others, like spouses, children, and friends. May we gladly bear such witness to these and to a world needing to be loved by Your eternal desire for redemption and renewal. Amen.

Devotional Ninety-Eight:

Watch Out Who You Call Fool

In 1 John 3:20 (NIV), we read, "God is greater than our hearts and he knows everything."

Tonight, we talked about "Bruce Jenner." It is hard to understand human motives, and I have trouble understanding some people. When I get them figured out, they cross me up. So it's comforting to know myself. I ought to since I've been acquainted with me for over eighty years. The trouble is, I know myself so well. I am now more aware of shortcomings and foolish things. I know myself, and I still try to forget known weaknesses. Jesus warns about calling other folk careless fools. I wonder what He thinks about saying "Fool" to me!

Well, it's not right to insult my neighbor's kids. I, too, am God's child. What right do I have to insult me?

John says, "My Father is greater than my heart and knows everything." That Father leads me to the stranger in my front room and says, "Jim, I want you to know Jim. He is one of My boys, and I think the world of Him."

P.S.: There are some things we will never figure out, including transgender operations. But then there are things about me that are not perfect. As much as I try to improve the quality of my life, there are weaknesses that keep cropping up. The freer society becomes, the more difficult it will be to understand new norms of behavior. Of course, human nature has not changed since the first Adam sinned in the Garden, and "Cains will keep on killing Abels" until the "second Adam" comes again.

Loving the unlovely is perhaps one of the greatest challenges of Christian living. I need to start with me. Then, will I have the compassion to understand others. It is so easy to start judging others. To be sure, our heroes in society and sports should be better examples. No one has ever lived up to the full intention of the Creator God, but "He is patient with you without wanting anyone to perish, but everyone to come to repentance" (2 Peter 2:9b, NIV). As we build our lives together, may the compassion and love we have for each other and the love of Christ give us the capacity to understand the things we don't understand. Most of all, may He give us the courage to hold the imperfect to the "light of the gospel." We are not judge and jury. That power belongs to God.

Hymn: "I sing the mighty power of God, / that made the mountains rise, / that spread the flowing seas abroad, / and built the lofty skies. / I sing the wisdom that ordained the sun to rule the day; / the moon shines full at His command, / and all the stars obey. / I sing the goodness of the Lord / that filled the earth with food; / He formed the creatures with His Word, / and then pronounced them good. / Lord, how Thy wonders are displayed, / where'er I turn my eye, / if I survey the ground I tread, / or gaze upon the sky" (Isaac Watts, "I Sing the Mighty Power of God").

Meditation: Thank You, dear Father; in Your wisdom, You pro-

vided life for plants, flowers, trees, animals, and all creation. We gratefully acknowledge all who borrow life from You are forever in Your care. Wherever we are, You are present there. Help us live this eternal reality. Amen.

Devotional Ninety-Nine:

There Is a Spiritual Famine in the Land

When I was a boy, I read everything I could get my hands on. I remember a picture in a *Farm Journal* magazine.

There was a sad-looking horse standing at a manger it had been chewing on. A big piece of the manger was gone. The horse had a case of hidden hunger. Its feed lacked something vital, so the horse chewed on the food manger, and its insides, a latticework of splinters, would shortly depart this life.

The hunger that drives folk to fill their lives with junk is starvation of spirit. The breath of life is in us, and man, with or without Christ, has a deep hunger for deity and is incurably religious. But, without the Word of life, we starve. America is in days described in Amos 8, where we read there will be "not a famine of food, or a thirst for water, but a famine of hearing the words of the Lord" (Amos 8:11b, NIV)."

P.S.: You have heard me say, "It is time for another trustworthy Billy Graham type to call America back to God." The effective force of believers praying for such a thing is very encouraging.

We must pray God will use the desires of His people to turn the spiritual famine in the land into spiritual revival.

In the meantime, I miss you already. Our visit was too short. But the thought of not being able to hear your voice almost any time of the day or night makes me feel lonely and sad. Yet, I know you will be having a good time with Tucker and Nicole, so enjoy every minute of your trip with them and hurry home. I am already hungry to hear your voice, but more importantly, to see you once again two weeks from now. Can't wait!

Hymn: "We praise Thee, O God! For the Son of Thy love, / for Jesus who died, and is now gone above. / We praise Thee, O God! For Thy Spirit of light, / Who hath shown us our Saviour, and scattered our night. / All glory and praise to the Lamb that was slain, / Who hath borne all our sins, and hath cleans'd every stain. / Revive us again; fill each heart with Thy love; / May each soul be rekindled with the fire from above. / Hallelujah! Thine the glory. Hallelujah! Amen. / Hallelujah! Thine the glory. Revive us again" (William P. Mackay, "Revive Us Again").

Meditation: Dear God, in every age and generation, those of Your highest creation have repented and believed but also have sinned and strayed from Your salvation. But You have promised that when our hearts are humbled and turn from evil, You will not withhold Your grace. May it happen in a spiritual revival of our land. Amen.

Devotional One Hundred:

Happy Birthday

Even though you and your grandkids are sailing on the Caribbean Sea and we are far apart, you are so very close to my *heart*. Yes, you are close to my heart when I think about the good times we've shared and, in recent months, the love that keeps on growing.

Close to my *heart* are the plans we have made for our marriage and the hopes that we've both called our own.

Close to my *heart* is each moment with you, the dreams in which you have a part, and throughout the future, God has opened to us; *you* will always be close to my heart.

Close to my *heart* forever is *you*; the sea you sail has its pearls, the heaven its stars, but my *heart*, my *heart*, my *heart* has its love, *you*.

Happy birthday!

P.S.: I know you do not want your age made public, but we both know. As I said before you left on your trip, I have a special card and birthday remembrance. I will give it to you next week when we see each other again. However, instead of a typical "50-Second Sermon," I just needed to say you are "my sermon." Indeed, I have been *surprised by grace*. Nothing I have ever thought or written brings me more inspiration or satisfaction than having you in my life. We have shared birthdays through office parties and many years with Jo and LeRoy. But this is your first birthday since last

August and the surprising reconnection of our lives. So much has happened in these months. It is absolutely incredible how bonded and glued we are. I hope and pray we will enjoy the very best of God's blessings, knowing two souls with but a single thought and two *hearts* that beat as one. Heaps and gobs!

Hymn: "The God of Abraham praise, / all praise be to His name, / who was, and is, and is to be, fore'er the same! / The one eternal God, before what now appears; / the First, the Last: beyond all thought His timeless years! / His Spirit flowing free, high surges where it will: / in prophet's word He spoke of old, / His voice speaks still. Established is His law, / and changeless it shall stand, / it lives upon the human heart, on sea or land" (Daniel ben Judah Dayyan, Newton Mann, William Channing Gannett, "The God of Abraham Praise").

Meditation: Thank You, Father, for the gift of life. And, on this day, I give thanks for the life of Grace Atchley. You have brought us together in a surprising way following the passing into the eternal hands of our first marriage partners. We pray You will supply each of us with Your strength. So, our family heritage will grow increasingly strong. We want to build on the best of our past but will need Your grace and blessing to guide us now and in the future. We also pray for our children, who are handling abrupt changes related to the remarriage of their parents. Bless them and us as we face these challenges. We pray in the "name of the one whose name is above all others." Amen.

Devotional One Hundred One:

Let the Shining Loose

It is June 5, and it is your birthday. I know you must have had a good time watching the kids swim with the dolphins and doing other fun things. All day, I have thought about how you must certainly be enjoying the thrill of sharing with your beloved grandkids. Hope the cruise goes well. Also, my mind thought about the shining sea and, most of all, the shining of our love. It radiated all the way to me.

I guess everybody knows the speed of light is 180,000 miles per second. That is a fast time. A spaceship at 30,000 miles an hour is fast by today's air speeds. But the speed of light makes a spaceship a horse and buggy.

The speed of light is so effortless. Turn on a flashlight, and there it goes. Light a match, and a tiny probe lances the sky. Shining a light isn't anything we do. It does itself.

Maybe that's why Jesus said, in Matthew 5:16 (KJV), "Let your light so shine …that they may see your good works, and glorify your father which is in heaven." We can do the works all right. But when something shines, that's more than us. We just let it go.

P.S.: Even though we are thousands of miles away, the speed of love and the "light" of its radiation surround me with the knowledge of love for each other. I have missed you, especially not getting to talk at any moment of the day. But the extended time away from the phone has given me the opportunity to reflect on the breadth and depth of our love. One thing I did tonight was go back and read "sermons" and your response back to me. Also, I looked at all the photos on file. They are numerous, like your reclining pose on your sofa, the picture for the Mid-South Baptist Association directory (magenta sweater), and pictures we made at the French restaurant and in Hot Springs. You can imagine all the wonderful thoughts each photo brought to mind. As fast as the speed of light, the touch of your love was there, lighting the synapsis of mind and memory. God willing, I won't have to be away from you on your next birthday. As I said in last night's greeting, your birthday is the first since our reconnection last August. Once again, let me say *happy birthday*! Cruising with your grandkids adds to the excitement.

Hymn: "Our Father God, who art in heaven, / all hallowed by Thy name; Thy kingdom com; / Thy will be done in heaven and earth the same. / Give us this day our daily bread; / and as we those forgive who sin against us, / so may be forgiving grace receive. / Into temptation lead us not; / from evil set us free; / and Thine the kingdom, / Thine the power, and glory ever be" (Adoniram Judson, "Our Father God, Who Art in Heaven").

Meditation: God, the Author of all life, thank You for the life of Grace Atchley. On this, her birthday, help each of us give thanks for Your majestic creation of her life and all of life. Grant her many more. We acknowledge all truth and creative being and all authority is in Your hands. We want to tell of Your greatness, for there is no other like You. May endless praise be our song. May the life of Grace Atchley be blessed by Your guiding hand. Amen.

Devotional One Hundred Two:

Doing What Comes Naturally

In Psalm 51:6, the writer asks God, "and in the hidden part thou shalt make me to know wisdom" (Psalm 51:6b, KJV).

This afternoon, to escape the loneliness of the house, I went to my back lawn and enjoyed the beautiful sunny afternoon. While there, I watched a squirrel playing in the grass. Squirrels always amaze me! They can't simply plod along, saving energy for when Stevie, my dog, shows up. When that happens, they put their bodies through curves and arcs that would shame an Olympic gymnast.

I asked one of the squirrels of my acquaintance about his locomotion. "We have to undulate," he explained. "It's the way we are."

I asked, "But when do you have time to practice?"

He paused for a split second of immobility. "Practice; what's that?"

He smiled a toothy grin, flicked his tail, and flowed up a tree, especially after Stevie barked.

If I am granted wisdom in my secret heart, I can be right. There is absolutely no doubt, from inside, by instinct, like a flourish of the saving finger of God.

P.S.: The absence of your voice these past four days has been difficult. It caused me to spend a lot of time reflecting and praying for your safety. Obviously, I am counting the minutes till we are back in telephone range. I can't wait to hear your voice and know you are alright and all is well. We have been absent from each other before, but the phone has kept us in constant touch. I have certainly missed you. This is the longest we have been beyond voice range. Even though you were having fun with Nicole and Tucker and though I was finding plenty to do in the house and the yard, I was absolutely in the doldrums. The good from it is in my innermost being (the psalmist called it the "secret heart); there resides an eternal "wisdom" given by God. We are His in Christ. In His will, we are blessed in love and confidence of anticipated union. I don't like absence from you, but it reinforces the strong bond of our love.

Hymn: "Here, O my Lord, I see You face to face; / here would I touch and handle things unseen; / here grasp with firmer hand eternal grace, / and all my weariness upon You lean. / Too soon we rise; / the symbols disappear; / the feast, though not the love, is past and gone. / The bread and wine remove; / but You are here, nearer than ever, still my shield and sun. / Feast after feast thus comes and passes by; / yet, passing, points to that glad feast above, / giving sweet foretaste of the festal joy, / the Lamb's great bridal feast of bliss and love" (Horatius Bonar, "Here, O My Lord, I See You Face to Face").

Meditation: Thank You, Abba Father, that in Your eternal activity, You created in man a desire to know You. We know from experience that all mankind is born with powers of rational affection, which intuitively seeks the divine. The truth is, You seek us, and we rejoice, knowing spiritual birth represents the leap of faith to Your divine redemption. Amen.

Devotional One Hundred Three:

No Sermon but a Psalm

I did not think to mention this tonight, but one of the things I did to pass the time while you were gone was to read through some of the psalms. There are five collections, or five volumes, in what we call the Psalter. There are ceremonial psalms like Psalm 24. Then there are those called communal laments, like 44, 79, and 80. Next are the private laments, like Psalm 22:1a (KJV), which begins with, "My God, my God, why hast Thou forsaken me?" (Where have you heard that before?) The fourth group is private praise songs, meant to be a kind of prayer book like 18, 30, and 66. The people, learning them by heart, would be able to use them as they recovered from illness or praised God for acts of deliverance. The fifth group is the royal cultic psalms. It is necessary to understand the place of the king in ancient Israel. His title was "Messiah." So, literally, He was the anointed of Jehovah to be the representative man embodying God to the people and the people to God in Psalm 89.

And, has anyone ever found a better picture of God than the simple picture that brings comfort to people on their wedding day, their dying day, and all stations in between? Psalm 23. It was the rereading of this psalm that prompted the sermon about servanthood. The true Messiah was a servant, and certainly, husbands should be. It is the best of the royal cultic ones.

But, the one I want to share with you tonight is the great royal wedding song—Psalm 45, which even tells what they were wearing when they were at the ceremony. So, rather than a "50-Second Sermon," read through Psalm 45. In reading it, think about our wedding, the intent of our hearts, and the sense of majesty to be framed as one. I do love you, and to use a word from a praise psalm, "hallelujah," the Hebrew word for "Praise Jehovah" or "Praise the Lord."

Hymn: "Holy God, we praise Your name; / Lord of all, we bow before You; / all on earth Your scepter claim, all in heaven above adore You. / Infinite Your vast domain; / everlasting is Your reign / Hark, the glad celestial hymn angel choirs above are raising; / cherubim and seraphim, in unceasing chorus praising, / fill the heavens with sweet accord: / holy, holy, holy Lord" (Ignaz Franz, Clarence Walworth, "Holy God, We Praise Your Name").

Meditation: Dear God and Author of Scripture, we thank You, with all praise, that You gave us the Psalms. These hymns are filled with all praise to You. Even in the midst of sorrow or gloom, or in praise to Your holy name, You speak so that we may understand Your grace and forgiveness to the children of men. Let us learn to live the eternal message of these great hymns inspired by Your hands. In the Creator and Redeemer's name, we pray. Amen.

Devotional One Hundred Four:

Things Old and New

I have a friend who is something of a "would-be" philosopher. Recently, he observed that it takes money to make money. Another buddy with us put him in his place. "So what's new? I've heard that a thousand times."

This would-be philosopher would be the first to admit he's not the world's most original mind. But our friend's critical response speaks for all who think unless a thing is new, it is not true.

The book of Acts tells us in 17:21 that the people Paul talked to at Mars Hill in Athens "spent their time in nothing else, but either to tell, or hear some new thing" (Acts 17:21, KJV).

Paul pointed out that their new altar to an unknown God was, in fact, a shrine to an old idea. After all, there is "Something" out there, bigger than we are, forever mysterious, forever new. Christians call it "God." He is older than creation but as new as the morning dew or the saving act of His Son, who is forever making all things new for those who believe.

P.S.: We both agreed to read selected psalms. I could not get away from a fresh reading of them. The one big idea staying with me is whatever your condition, whatever your need, you'll find the deepest level of experience already expressed in the Psalms. The old becomes the new, and something doesn't have to be "new" to be better than the "old." But the absolute truth is that the "old" can, and is most often, the source of something "new." I am not trying to be a philosopher, but the truth of it all speaks directly to us. We are old friends; we have been blessed to live a number of years and have been formed and influenced by the "old, old story of Jesus and His love." We have formed values that are rooted in old traditions and feel more at home with the familiar.

But all of that has become building blocks for something new and beyond our wildest dreams. As we walk forward together into a new world, we do not walk away from a continuing relationship with our sources. And the thing that stands out from the rereading of the Psalms is that our lives are shaped by those sources. Not everything from our past is perfect, and there will be mistakes in the future, but we have the steadfast assurance that His rod and His staff will guide us. Especially is that true if we are open to each other in response to God's ever-abiding presence. To sum it all up, we have already experienced "newness of life and vitality." Each time we are together stretches into "new" excitement and joy beyond the last. Each "new" day brings a deeper sense of covenant and commitment to each other.

I look forward to expanding the "newness" of each passing day and growing together till we dwell in the house of the Lord forever. In the meantime, may God help us not waste a single day creating something "new" from the "old." All of life has both in it.

Hymn: L. W. Terley has written a hymn entitled "Servant of the Least." In the hymn, he highlights the magnificent truth that

Calvary tore the view that hid God's face from male and female, Jew or Greek, and made it plain that eternal salvation is for all. Let us sing that praise forever. That is the heart of the gospel.

Meditation: Dear God, we acknowledge You as the Author and Sustainer of life. Grant us the desire to walk by faith and less by sight. Lead us with heavenly light and teach us Your way. Make something new within us until earth's race is won. In Christ's name, we pray. Amen.

Devotional One Hundred Five:

The Secret of a Good Climate

My grandmother Williams loved her father, and as a small child, I loved her stories about my great-grandfather Barnes. He was a white-bearded, gentle patriarch of ninety-five years. A picture of him and his wife graced the walls of her bedroom. Later, it hung in an antique bedroom in our house. (Our grandson Michael, as a little boy, would sleep in the antique bedroom when he came for a visit with his parents. He was afraid of the bearded old man, so he covered the picture with a towel.) My grandmother used to tell me how her father gathered his children and grandchildren around him and described what heaven would be like. She showed his photograph so her children could understand how he looked. She was vague on details, but there was no doubt the heaven she and now we heard about was the place to go.

Somehow, I got the idea my great-grandfather would be at home there. This made heaven special to my grandmother. After all, climate does mean a lot, but the people who live in a place are what make living there worthwhile. My great-grandfather Barnes went to heaven before I could understand eternal existence, but because he was there, I wanted to be there, too.

In 1 John 3:2, we read, "[I]t doth not yet appear what we shall be: but we know that, when he shall appear, we shall be like him;

for we shall see him as he is" (1 John 3:2b, KJV).

When I, or anyone, really discover the "who" of heaven, the "where" will take care of itself.

P.S. I am still sorry I woke you tonight, though I loved our conversation, as I always do. It is so easy and so very natural for us to talk with each other and share whatever comes to mind. Usually, something one of us says is the inspiration for the "50-Second Sermon." Since we talked about Chicago, I thought about sharing my first trip there, but after spending some time telling you about my grandmother Williams's farm, it seemed appropriate to dwell on the subject of heaven and home.

My first few years were spent on her farm. Her husband, my grandfather Elijah Williams, died at age fifty-one. My father did not want his mother to live alone, so Dad and Mom moved from their honeymoon house, which was built on one acre of land from my grandparents' farm. They moved into the "big house" where my grandmother lived. At least, it seemed big to me. There were large rooms, five fireplaces, and a huge warm-air stove in the central room (it would be called a den today). The kitchen was at the back of the house, and before electricity, there was a wood-burning stove. There was a kerosene-fueled refrigerator as well as a wooden ice chest. The formal parlor was most impressive with leather furniture and the beautiful hand-knit wool rug I told you about tonight. The farm had several very nice buildings: a huge barn, a smokehouse, a chicken house, an external garage, and, of course, an outhouse. I was born on that farm, and my earliest childhood memories center around the activities of that special place. It was there I became aware of family, including my great-grandfather Barnes. I learned he was kind and gracious. He was a godly man, and it became obvious he had a strong influence on his children, grandchildren, and his "greats," like me. So, my first awareness of heaven came from hearing about his death and my grandfather Williams'. I can barely remember the details, but when I learned they were in heaven, I sure did want to go there, too.

Since then, of course, you and I have experienced the death of many of our family members, including the deaths of our own first spouses. So heaven has far greater meaning now than it did when we were children. God has led our dear ones on, and now those experiences of death and loss will greatly enhance our need to make our earthly home a bit of heaven. I wish we had several "lifetimes" with each other. You have brought a lot of heaven into my life. Let's make every day count. And, if God should so choose to let me live as long as my great grandfather Barnes, I would like to be like him, helping others want to go where he now lives.

There is a verse from "The Eternal Goodness," a poem by John Greenleaf Whittier, that says, "I [We] know not what the future hath, / Of marvel or surprise, / Assured alone that life and death, / God's mercy underlies." Let's promise to live each gifted day, making our new home a place that points to God's place and will also be ours someday. Jo and LeRoy, our first spouses, will be there, and all of God's faith-filled children. If we do that, heaven is always close by.

Hymn: "Come, we that love the Lord, / and let our joys be known; join in a song with sweet accord, / and thus surround the throne. / Let those refuse to sing who never knew our God; / but children of the heavenly King may speak their joys abroad. / The hill of Zion yields a thousand sacred sweets, / before we reach the heavenly fields, / or walk the golden streets. / Then let our songs abound, and every tear be dry; / we're marching through Immaneul's ground, / to fairer worlds on high" (Isaac Watts, "Come, We That Love the Lord").

Meditation: Dear Father, You have promised You have made a place for us. It is through faith in Your own Son, Jesus Christ, that we can claim that eternal reward. We are kingdom-bound, now on earth, and then in the place of Your abode. We have the assurance that You will go to glory with us. Hallelujah and praise to You. Amen.

Devotional One Hundred Six:

In Constant Repair

Not long ago, I supplied the pulpit and delivered a message from the book of Ephesians. I entitled the sermon "The World at One (In Christ the Hope of Glory)." In his letter, Paul sees the misery of our divided planet, the whole world at odds and divided against itself, alienated, disintegrating; he sees erected walls and frontiers and the creation of every new alliance causing even greater division than before.

As Paul notes, God has declared His hidden purpose for redemption in the coming of Christ, whose mission is to unify, to gather together, to mend, to reconcile, and to unite the world. He uses a wedding analogy in describing how Christ established the church. It is the agent for helping God repair a broken and divided world. In describing the mission of the church, Paul looks toward the church not as some religious institution but as a "community of unity," which is learning to love like people who get married. He calls it "the bride of Christ," learning the rule of adequate resources. Likewise, a well-drilled and equipped army keeps its power lines in constant repair as God's colony on earth.

P.S.: In tonight's telephone call, you kept saying you didn't want our marriage to end up dull and like a routine. It needs to be forever new, exciting, and creative. Of course, I certainly agree with you and affirm how important it is to initiate "surprises." Like in all good partnerships, there needs to be a plan for growth and change. Dullness and routineness should be replaced by carefully planned intentions that add purpose, fire, mystery, excitement, and "surprise."

It is at that point that the marriage of Christ to the church is the best example for understanding the dynamic role of husband and wife. First of all, we both agreed we want our marriage to be like the church, a "community of unity." Also, a good partnership is open to learning the rule of adequate resources and being disciplined to use them. In the spirit of the "sermon," it is very important the power lines be in constant repair. That means many things, but most importantly, it means being open to each other and willing to work together to make amends. It means affirming each other's leadership and creating a union that could be like God's colony on earth, the church. Constant repair certainly does not mean constant carping and complaining, putting the other person down. On the contrary, deep abiding love in marriage means it is a ruling passion. In the mind, it is a close sympathy. In the body, it is a wholly secret and delicate longing to possess and claim each other's love. In that spirit, there is wholeness and completeness. That is a beautiful picture of what the church is and what I am confident our marriage will be. I am in need of constant repair and need God's help and yours!

Hymn: "I sing the mighty pow'r of God, / That made the mountains rise, / That spread the flowing seas abroad, / And built the lofty skies. / I sing the wisdom that ordained the sun to rule the day; / The moon shines full at His command, / And all the stars obey. / I sing the goodness of the Lord, / that filled the earth with food; / He formed the creatures with His Word, / and then pronounced them good. / Lord, how Thy wonders are displayed, / Where'er I turn my eye, / If I survey the ground I tread, / or gaze upon the sky! / There's not a plant or flow'r below, / but makes Thy glories known; / and clouds arise, and tempests blow, / By order from Thy throne; / While all that borrows life from Thee Is ever in Thy care, / And ev'rywhere that we can be, / Thou, God art present there" (Isaac Watts, "I Sing the Mighty Power of God").

Meditation: Gracious Father, we joyfully recognize Jesus Christ, Your Son, as head of the church and pray that His gospel is proclaimed with boldness. Empower each of us, Your followers, to become partners in Your passion for every person of every clime, creed, or race. Give to all our days commitment, courage, hope, and endless praise. In Your name, amen.

Devotional One Hundred Seven:

Not Ego-Driven

One of the highest compliments I could pay my chosen fiancé and soon-to-be wife is she is not ego-driven. She has a God-given capacity to build me up, whether I deserve such praise or not. Tonight's telephone visit is an example of lofty praise of me, whether or not deserved. But she always makes it a point to pass along words of encouragement. I want to be worthy of that praise.

Before getting ready for sleep, I needed to thank God for the gift of Grace. Not only is she a surprise, but also a gift. There are so many people in our world who think they can build themselves up by tearing someone else down. They are experts at spotting the weaknesses of others and prophesying doom. They expect the worst in people and are a little grieved if they don't come through. Many of them think they are not egotistical. Somehow, they believe they are about all anyone can depend on. It's sort of like the U.S. Cavalry in a Western movie, ready to rescue a bumbling world.

In Romans 11:2–4, Paul recalls how Elijah got discouraged and asked to die, saying as God's only faithful man, he was on the way out. God responded He had 7,000 faithful left, indicating He could actually get along without Elijah. A host of God's special people are "doing His news." Thank God, Grace is one of them.

P.S.: You can tell by the time that I finally got to my bedroom

I had already slept awhile in my chair. So the sermon and P.S. was sent late in the night. That won't be a habit once we are together. After our very "personal" sharing tonight, covering a host of happy moments as our love for each other was reviewed, it made me aware of how you encourage me and make me feel like I am the greatest guy in the world. I truly want to be like you think I am. Unlike many other selfish-driven folks we both know, you have an unusual gift of encouragement. At a time in my life emptied because I had lost my companion, you have given me new strength. I am indeed a "Grace-blessed" person!

Hymn: "Gracious Spirit, dwell with me, / I would gracious be; / help me now Thy grace to see, / I would be like Thee; / and, with words that help and heal, / Thy life would mine reveal; / and, with actions bold and meek, / for Christ my Savior speak. / Holy Spirit, dwell with me, / I would holy be; / show Thy mercy tenderly, / make me more like Thee; / separate from sin I would / and cherish all things good, / and whatever I can be / give Him who gave me Thee. / Mighty Spirit, dwell with me, / I would mighty be; / help me now Thy power to see, / I would be like Thee; / 'gainst all weapons hell can wield, / be Thou my strength and shield; / let Thy word my weapon be, / Lord, Thine the victory" (Thomas Toke Lynch, "Gracious Spirit, Dwell with Me").

Meditation: God of all creatures, we acknowledge our need for help and support, not only from You but significant others who prop us up. Lead us all to be a bridge of care connecting people everywhere. We need Your enabling power to act. In Your matchless name, we pray. Amen.

Devotional One Hundred Eight:

The Arsenal of the Presence

We just had a terrible auto accident in our neighborhood. Don Daniels, longtime Aledo School Superintendent, and his fifteen-year-old grandson were killed on I-20 in a head-on collision after one car crossed the median and hit his car head-on. Daniels and his grandson were killed instantly.

The havoc brought back a memory. It was a hot July day in Texas. I was a fairly young driver. My air conditioner and car radio were on. Windows were up. I was dulled by the straight road and fast rocky terrain.

Suddenly, I saw a diesel engine bearing down on the crossing ahead. I heard the banshee whoop of the whistle. My car slid on smoking rubber just three feet from the thundering train. Maybe my guardian angel was on duty that day, or maybe not.

Satan asked Jesus to let angels keep him out of trouble, and Jesus turned him down. Later, He dismissed twelve legions of angels when He went to the cross alone.

In Matthew 18, Jesus said, "That in heaven their angels do always behold the face of my Father which is in heaven" (Matthew 18:10b, KJV). If my angel can lead this child into the Presence, I will handle bruising rocks and railroad crossings. But God expects me to be on angel alert. I truly am, and I am certain you are one of my "angels."

P.S.: The only thing I can think about right now is coming to see you. I have several things to do tomorrow and then a drive to Memphis. Between now and then are "thousands of cars" and a lot of distractions. Right now, I have only one main agenda. It is the anxious and growing desire to see you. I hope I arrive safely. Yes, I do believe in God's angels who hover over us in perilous times, like railroad crossings. But you are now my "shining angel." Every step of the way, I will imagine you in our "hello again hug." My prayer is I may know God's watchful care and protection until I am in your presence.

Hymn: "Sometimes a light surprises / the child of God who sings; / it is the Lord who rises with healing in His wings. / When comforts are declining, / He grants the soul again a season / of clear shining to cheer it after rain. / It can bring with it nothing / but He will bear us through; / who gives the lilies clothing / will clothe His people, too; / beneath the spreading heavens / no creature but is fed; / and He who feeds the ravens / will give His children bread" (William Cowper, "Sometimes a Light Surprises").

Meditation: Dear Guard and Protector, thank You that You are the Source of all being, the Creator of color, shape, song, and silence. You are the Revealer, the Author of all wisdom. You are the Redeemer, the fountain of forgiveness and grace. You are the Sustainer, like manna in the wilderness. You are the Protector, guarding us through anxiety and fear. For these blessings and many more, we find security in knowing You watch over us. Amen.

Devotional One Hundred Nine:

Counting Eternity

In Psalm 90, the author asks God, "So teach us to number our days, that we may apply our hearts unto wisdom" (Psalm 90:12a, KJV).

Long ago, I heard a preacher tell of a granite mountain off in a corner of a trackless sea where nothing lived. Once every thousand years, a swallow flew around that mountain and brushed it with a wing.

"When by the brushing of a bird's wing every thousand years that mountain should be worn into the sea," the preacher intoned, "eternity would have just begun."

Impressive illustration, I thought, but untrue. Eternity does not begin, nor does it ever end.

But when under God we number our days, we find in each moment a touch of the everlasting. Faith is the timetable of the Eternal. Did not Jesus promise that if we had a mustard-seed faith, we could speak to a mountain, and it would tumble into the sea?

P.S.: Obviously, our longest telephone conversation to date had many flourishes! I don't need to remind you our years are precious, at best. Certainly, twenty good years would be a wonderful gift. Each day should give us a chance to say at the end of the day, "We gave it our best." You can't cram the real meaning of life into needless activity, but as we talked, it would also be a sin and disgrace to lose life because we settle into a "comfortable routine." That leads to boredom and dullness. I do want us to have "the best we can afford." Most importantly, I want to experience the security of Christian love.

I have been asked how my relationship with you has become significant. My first answer was, "At a personal level, she is now number one." With Jo, she was number one. The memory of my first marriage unity inspires my intention for you and me. Then, I went on to say, "I am safe and secure in our love because, in a very real sense, it is the same kind of love God has for me." I know I can talk to you about anything, and I also feel you can trust me to be the spiritual leader of the family God will create. As we have become used to pouring out our hearts together, we now are free to communicate about anything.

We are not afraid to expose ourselves, both strengths and weaknesses. We know we accept each other just as we are. How wonderful it is to know I am not on a performance basis, and I hope you feel the same. Regardless of the subject or concern, I am still going to be loved for eternity. That makes me want to perform better, not for an act or action, but to love you eternally for the person you are. I have said to husbands-to-be who came for marital counseling, "Many a man does not realize the wife he has been given is a reflection of his own behavior toward her." That lesson given to others is for me, too, because beyond the years God may give us, our love is eternal, just as it was for our first spouses. I want each day to reflect a bit of such a never-ending reality. So, as we live each day, let us live it counting eternity!

Hymn: "Great God, we sing Your guiding hand / by which supported still we stand; / the opening year Your mercy shows / that mercy crowns it till its close. / With grateful hearts the past we own; / the future, all to us unknown, / we to Your guardian care commit, / and peaceful leave before Your feet. / In scenes exalted or depressed, / You are our joy, You are our rest; / Your goodness all our hopes shall raise, / adored through all our changing days" (Philip Doddridge, "Great God, We Sing Your Guiding Hand").

Meditation: Dear God, we confess even at our best, our faith is weak. That is true because we do not fully trust in Your eternal plan to be Redeemer, Guide, and Defender. Forgive us for not accepting Your eternal promises. Those abiding truths inspire us to place our confidence in the eternal gift of salvation offered by faith to those who believe in You. Therefore, help us live each day knowing it is stamped with eternity. So, give us "mustard-seed faith." We pray this in Your name. Amen.

Devotional One Hundred Ten:

Bertie Slickpates's Invention

This story is for real. The names have been changed to protect the innocent. It is an "old" sermon but "new" tonight. It is the story of the magnet in "Sleepy Meanwell's" easy chair. Bertie Slickpate was responsible for it. Bertie was a good friend to "Sleepy" and aggressive as a "Watkins salesman."

Bertie had sold Sleepy's wife, "Moodie," the magnet. She aimed the magnet to hit Sleepy's chair about the time he got home from work. He'd get a funny look on his face, skid over, and get stuck in his easy chair. That magnet wouldn't let up on him till maybe 1 a.m. when he'd stagger off to bed. Sleepy's wife, Moodie, wanted him to be out of her hair, so she would bring his food to the chair. It also helped when she aimed the TV at him. The local beer also eased him a lot, maybe with salted peanuts or pretzels.

The rumor around town was that Bertie was so successful with selling his magnets that he was able to buy a new gold Cadillac every year, and for all I know, that is true because I've seen men all over the country stuck in easy chairs in front of TVs.

Proverbs 26 tells how the sluggard turns in his bed like a "rusty hinge." Maybe Bertie Slickpate got his patent from whoever dreamed that up.

P.S.: The "story"—or maybe a fable—may not be true, but it was told in one of Roger Carstensen's sermons. Since I spent far too much time in my easy chair last night, the thought hit me: I certainly would not want to become a "Sleepy Meanwell." I am sure part of my temptation had to do with a tender back and lack of sleep. But for some reason, over the last 24 hours, the recliner felt like it had a magnet in it, drawing me to "ease." The point I want to make is just as you don't want to get bored with nothing to do, I, too, want our days (time) to be used fruitfully. Given our temperament and inventiveness, I don't ever see it happening. So a theme song for us, when we are together 24/7, is "No Ruts on Us!"

I have said to you before sometimes the most spiritual thing one can do is "take a nap." But, on the other hand, it would be so easy for some people to "skid" into a dull routine. I used to say to my students one anecdote for retarding aging "is to do fewer things for the last time and more things for the first time." I promise not to be a Sleepy if you likewise will not be a "Moodie." I have not seen any of those tendencies in either one of us. Based on how we have shared life when we are together, I can't wait for the fun to begin.

Hymn: "There shall the Child lie in a stall, / This Child who shall redeem us all. / How great our joy! / Great our joy! / Joy, Joy, Joy! Joy, Joy, Joy! / Praise we the Lord in heav'n on high! / Praise we the Lord in heav'n on high! (Traditional German Carol, "How Great Our Joy").

Meditation: Great God of strength and power, challenge us daily, move us toward discipline and fortitude. Keep us mis-

sion-minded, carrying out noble life goals in keeping with Your plan and guidance. We want to walk as worthy citizens of our great land and as stewards in Your kingdom. In our later years, wipe away foolish fears so we may continue exploring the new before us. In Your name, we pray. Amen.

Devotional One Hundred Eleven:

The Wrong Time to Smile

This morning's news told that one of the escaped prisoners had been shot and killed, and the other man was surrounded. When I heard the news, I smiled and said to myself, "Thank heavens, they got them."

In Ezekiel 18:32, the writer says God has no pleasure in the death of anyone. No pleasure in anybody's death? That seems a little strange. Surely, a God of true holiness would view with satisfaction the execution of a murderer.

We may not be all that nice, but there are some people who really have it coming. What would decent people do if they couldn't say from time to time, "She is asking for it," or "It finally caught up with him"?

Apparently, God respects the spark of life flaming in vicious men. He does not smile when that light flares out. All day, my thoughts went back to the morning news. I have a horrible feeling that at the news of the prisoner's death and the capture of his partner, I smiled. If I did, I, too, am in need of mercy, for I smiled in the presence of the grief of God.

P.S.: Grace, the news today was filled with questions for me. We talked about some of them. It has caused me to reflect and think a good bit. How shall we respond to ISIS executioners, murderers, and people whose sexual preferences run contrary to biblical ideals? How will we react to thieves, exploiters of children, and on and on? All of it is a reminder man cannot legislate human behavior. I have been driven back to the question, "What is my personal response to those who profane God's plan for human life?" The answer that has stayed with me all day included a powerful directive on forgiveness. The answer is found in the Great Commandment, "Love the Lord your God with all your heart and with all your soul and with all your mind and with all your strength. The second is this: love your neighbor as yourself. There is no commandment greater than these" (Mark 12:30–31, NIV).

Some people are hard to love. However, some may never get to God's love for them unless I love them. God loves us for more than ourselves. His name reaches others through us. He keeps us on our feet and holds us together not just for our welfare but for those who read our lives. The only way some people can sense the light of God is through our human lamps, flickering and smoky though they be. The central theme of tonight's phone visit was how God brought blessing to the two of us, imperfect though we are. That blessing is the gift of power, the gift of oneself to the other. Blessing is our permission with each other and forecasts our destiny. (An engagement and a wedding could not work without it.) Blessing is both material and spiritual, the gift of what we are, along with our openness to possibility. God's blessing sets us free. Blessing is given with our hands held open, a symbol for emptying self to fill the other. And the source of that blessing is "we have sought to apply the Great Commandment." It is never applied perfectly, but in our heart of hearts, we do want to love God supremely and love others just as we love ourselves. It is God's pathway for all human behavior.

Hymn: "Where cross the crowded ways of life, / where sound the cries of race and clan, / above the noise of selfish strife, / we hear Your voice, O Son of Man! / From tender childhood's helplessness, / from woman's grief, man's burdened toil, / from famished souls, from sorrow's stress, / Your heart has never known recoil. / Till all the earth shall learn / Your love and follow where Your feet have trod; / till glorious from Your heaven above / shall come the city of our God" (Frank Mason North, "Where Cross the Crowded Ways of Live").

Meditation: Our Father, may our love for You be made vivid in our love for neighbor, as for self. Forgive us when selfish desires trump our need to care for others with the same or greater need. Teach us Your ways and Your commandments. We pray this in the name of who perfectly demonstrated how this is done, in the name of Your Son, the sacrificed one. Amen.

Devotional One Hundred Twelve:

God Gave Me "Grace"

A new, bold, powerful, engaging force has broken into my life. Her name is Grace, and, wonder of wonders, she said yes when recently, I asked her to become my bride. The mystery and miracle for me is that she said "yes." We now are in the process of putting our lives together.

Though we are separated geographically until marriage, we have committed to seeing each other at least once per month, if not more often. Each visit builds on the last, and after several months of spending quality time with each other, we find ourselves opening up. The more we have learned about each other, the deeper our love has grown. In emptying ourselves, we have discovered that an event of openness is not something that happens only once. It is a process that happens day by day and over time. It has made me aware of my own needs. And only as we are in touch with our own needs will we be able to give love. We have discovered a breathtaking romance, but the maturity of the years has helped us define love as something larger than romance. We are building it on the best experiences with LeRoy and Jo, our first mates.

We are also aware we cannot worship the past but gain strength and insight from its reality. Going forward, we have purposed to become channels of blessing to each other because our lives will require new priorities. We can and will bless the past but honor the future with mutual commitment.

Text and P.S.: So, to get to the text (after a bit more time than 50 seconds), the reality of God's gift of "Grace" to me has driven me back to Proverbs 20:6. The writer says, "Many a man claims to have unfailing love, but a faithful man who can find?" (Proverbs 20:6, NIV). In the P.S., let me summarize some answers to this question that have cascaded on me in fabulous days just spent with Grace but also reinforced in the most recent weeks and months of getting to know her. So, the P.S. is a list of praises.

Because God gave me Grace:

- I know faithfulness is a man, not a word.
- I've experienced the luxury of being cherished and nourished.
- I know how it feels to share laughter, tears, unspoken thoughts, changes, surprising dreams, struggles, family support, and inside jokes that go way back and others of more recent vintage.
- I've learned to respect each other's needs and even delight in our differences.
- I now know how many miles a full bladder can still go.
- I have come to more fully understand God loves a woman very well through a godly man.
- I am a better, stronger person, even separated from her for a while than I ever would have been without her.

- I am becoming rich with shared memories not only about our first spouses but with each other.
- I will be eternally grateful.

And, without question, the writer of the above Proverb could have written, "My heart has found a home outside its own skin."

I must say once again, I have been *surprised by grace*. You have helped me grow and become a better person. Going forward, I will delight in the growth of this "surprising new partnership."

Hymn: "O for a closer walk with God / a calm and heavenly frame, / a light to shine upon the road that leads me to the Lamb! / The dearest idol I have known, / what e'er that idol be, / help me to tear it from Thy throne, / and worship only Thee. / So shall my walk be close with God, / serene and calm my frame; / so purer light shall mark the road / that leads me to the Lamb" (William Cowper, "O for a Closer Walk with God").

Meditation: Dear Father, teach me how to bless others by practicing the elements of trust and forgiveness. To be loved by another means, I must risk loving too. Let that be a firm pledge in my growing relationship with Grace. Certainly, relationships demand mutual commitment. So, challenge, strengthen, and guide us to such a mutual resolve. Amen.

Devotional One Hundred Thirteen:

Something Better than Soup

I started to fix soup for my noon lunch but decided instead to do hamburger steak. But the thought of soup brought back an important memory. During my student days at Southwestern Seminary, preaching at a downtown Fort Worth mission was a requirement. Each of us took a turn. Soup and sandwiches for the men were provided after preaching.

I rang the bell of the gospel as clearly as I could for my weary, experienced audience. I waited for responses. The men rose and headed for the soup.

One listener tottered over to me, smelling of rotgut whiskey. He dug a sharp elbow in my ribs. "You can lead a horse to water but can't make him drink!" Overwhelmed by his own wit, he cackled in evil joy as he pushed into the soup line.

It really came home to me that my task was bigger than talent. Paul says in 1 Thessalonians 1 that his readers were chosen by God "Because our gospel came to you not simply with words, but also with power, with the Holy Spirit and with deep conviction" (1 Thessalonians 1:5, NIV). People can preach, but only God can save.

P.S.: In my earlier years, I had the tendency to think God's calling and anointment meant it was for me to think the goal of faithfulness was "I do work for God." The truth is, "He will do His work through me." God calls all believers to His service and places on each tremendous responsibility. He expects no complaining when people do not respond to His message.

Oftentimes, the way we count results is man's terms, not God's. That truth came back to me in forceful ways last Sunday morning. Our pastor preached a powerful sermon, one of the best a believer could hear. My first thought was there would be a large number of people making public decisions. But the only one I saw was just one person who came to the altar. That response was a worthy one, but hundreds of hearers who applauded the sermon content were also encouraged in their faith. That, too, represents a significant response.

How do you measure spiritual response? Obviously, it is God's business, not ours. He measures how each person responds to His message, delivered by imperfect messengers. I have also learned through the year that just like a tree grows down before it can grow up, I have spent too much time concerned about fruit but not as much about the root. And who knows, maybe in time, the overly "whiskey-drunk listener" to my sermon may have responded to the call of the gospel. As the two of us blend our lives together, I am very much looking forward to sharing ministry with you. It is going to be "something better than soup."

Hymn: "Savior, Thy dying love / Thou gavest me, / Nor should I aught withhold, / Dear Lord, from Thee: / In love my soul would bow, / My heart fulfill its vow, / Some off'ring bring Thee now, /

Something for Thee. / All that I am and have, / They gifts so free, / In joy, in grief, thro' life, / Dear Lord, for Thee! / And When Thy face I see, / My ransom'd soul shall be. / Thro' all eternity, / Something for Thee" (Sylvanus D. Phelps, "Something for Thee").

Meditation: Dear God, only without Your mercy and grace I, too, could be homeless and in great need. Help us remember Your Son came to redeem all mankind but gave special attention to the poor and needy. Let us show God's love to everyone in need by word and deed, just as You ask us to do. Amen.

Devotional One Hundred Fourteen:

Ain't Gonne Study War

Today, on one of the TV news reports, the question was asked of the U.S. Military Chief of Staff, "How much longer will the war between ISIS [fundamental Islamists] and the Western world last?" He indicated this terrorist mentality will never be completely destroyed, and there is no way to know how long the current warfare will last.

In Isaiah 7:16, the prophet Isaiah tells King Ahaz of Judah not to fear armies about to stamp out his kingdom. By the time a child soon to be born would learn to "refuse the evil and choose the good," the threat of invasion would be over. In other words, in two years, time enough for a child to choose between good and bad, the danger would disappear.

Sometimes, when you look at a verse of scripture a second time, another meaning comes out. When a child learns to decide, a war in one time and one place is called off. Do wars come because people won't grow up?

If God's grownup children could tell the difference between good and evil, maybe enemies everywhere would forsake the skills of war. Isaiah says in another place, "Nation will not take up sword against nation, nor will they train for war anymore" (Isaiah 2:4b, NIV).

P.S.: If I could be a mediator to stop all the anger between individuals or groups or nations, war would cease. I wish I had that kind of magical influence and strength. Compassion for other persons requires extraordinary selflessness. Those around us who are angry and upset about various controversial issues may not always appreciate our help.

One Boy Scout told his mother he had done his good deed for the day.

"What did you do?" she asked.

"Joe, Phil, Tom, Richard, Judd, and I helped the little old lady across the street."

"Why did it take so many of you?"

"Because," her son replied, "she did not want to go."

Some wars are fought because of ignorance and lack of understanding. When people are forced against their will, they respond to efforts to fix their problem, like the response of the scouts. Being a Christian in a warring environment means dealing with the battle where it occurs. T. D. Studd, a brilliant British Christian minister in the last century, said, "Some wish to fight their battles within the sound of church or chapel bells, but I want to run a rescue shop within a yard of hell." After World War II, following the atomic bombing of Hiroshima and Nagasaki, the U.S. poured billions of dollars into the reconstruction of those cities. Who really wants to be on top?

A young schoolboy came running to his teacher one day shouting, "Teacher, two boys are fighting, and I think the one on the bottom would like to see you now." Tonight, we talked about how compassion for each other removes barriers and difficulties that always produce tension and dispute. Wars between individuals and nations could be solved overnight if each side would show compassion. It is always the basis for compromise. As we move forward in life together, we alone will not solve the war between radical fundamentalism found in radical Islam and the Western Christian world. But closer to home, we can be agents of peace between ourselves, our family, and our neighbors—and who knows how far the influence of that kind of spirit will reach?

Hymn: "O God of love, O King of peace, / make wars thro'-out the world to cease; / Thy wrath of nations now restrain. / Give peace, O God, give peace again! / Remember, Lord, Your works of old, / The wonders that our parents told; / Remember not our sins' dark stain. / Give peace, O God, give peace again! / Whom shall we trust but You, O Lord? / Where rest but on Your faithful word? / None ever called on You in vain. / Give peace, O God, give peace again!" (Henry W. Baker, "O God of Love, O King of Peace").

Meditation: Great Creator God, You have written Your great name on humankind for our potential growth into Your likeness. May our vision for life's destiny be found and exhibited in the life of Your Son, the Lord Christ. Amen.

Devotional One Hundred Fifteen:

Any Stretch in Me?

Jesus said in Matthew's Gospel, "Neither do men pour new wine into old wineskins. If they do, skins will burst, the wine will run out and the wineskins will be ruined" (Matthew 9:17, NIV).

I regularly attend my home church. I am at home there. Everything is familiar. We have a familiar order of worship and sing familiar new and old hymns from the hymnal. The choir always sings a familiar, beautiful, harmonious anthem or hymn arrangement. My pastor always preaches a powerful sermon from a familiar text. I always look forward to seeing familiar smiles on the faces of fellow church members.

Last Sunday, I worshiped in a church where previously I was a member. I heard an outstanding sermon from my former pastor, who preached for the present pastor, who was on vacation. I heard special music from the former minister of music who served the church during my time there. It was an outstanding medley of familiar hymns popularized by George Beverly Shea. Both were powerfully blessed by God's Spirit and presence.

However, there were some unfamiliar things, like very loud contemporary praise music, which had a rock sound. There were worshipers demonstrating praise by standing, waving hands heavenward. There was audience applause for Jesus. I am not comfortable with some of this kind of celebrative atmosphere. However, I was at home because I felt God's presence in worship.

Since last Lord's Day, I have asked myself, "Jim, suppose the new wine of Pentecost bubbled up among us? Is there any stretch left in the old skin?"

P.S.: I know we talked about this before, but I needed to get it out of my skin. You have already accommodated yourself to contemporary worship at our Germantown church. It is a stretch for me and will continue to be. However, I do realize the way people respond to worship styles is enormously varied. And I must be non-judgmental about other styles of worship in the same spirit. We must not cut other people off from the gospel witness because of their sexual preferences or any other reasons outside of biblical ideals. A church, at its best, is not a sacred society of sad saints but a body that rejoices in the fact that Jesus is Lord. Neither is the church a sacred society of isolated saints but a body of believers who sustain each other. A church should be a seeking church, open to serve everybody. Most of all, as we have discussed, a church should be a compassionate church reclaiming rather than condemning. As long as Germantown Baptist Church demonstrates those qualities, I will be at home there. Your history there, and mine, for a time, add to the attachment we have. Your history is much richer than mine, but we have reasons to love our church. I promise to do the same for you. Above all, I pledge never to make those matters a test of fellowship, even though I may be uncomfortable at times.

Hymn: "Grant, Lord, that with Thy direction, / 'Love each other: we comply, / aiming with unfeigned affection / Thy love to exemplify; / let our mutual love be glowing / so that all will plainly see / that we, as on one stem growing, / living branches are in Thee" (Translator Frederick W. Foster; Author Nicholaus L. Graf von Zinzendorf, "Christian Hearts, in Love United").

Meditation: Dear Father, may our fellowship with You and with others not be limited by personal preference, but the light and brightness of Your eternal love becomes the object of our worship. Amen.

Devotional One Hundred Sixteen:

Lions and Prophecy

Tonight's sermon could be about a wedding dress, but that can come later when I see it. Actually, the inspiration comes from a TV documentary I saw late this afternoon on the city of Chicago. Obviously, the city is searching for ways to improve its PR in light of the murders and crime that plague America's second-largest city. Seeing the documentary brought back my first boyhood visit to Chicago in 1943. I hadn't even been to Springfield or Peoria when our family rattled our way to what was then a more "dirty city" because of coal soot and steel manufacturing.

I remember the stockyards were frightening, the Field Museum fascinating, the skyscrapers of that era unbelievable to this country boy. I especially remember Wrigley Field, the Lincoln Park Zoo, and the lions.

I was "scared" of lions, and they had a whole convention of lions there, switching their tails, showing their teeth, and eyeing people to figure out who had the best flavor. Just after I turned to see the monkeys, all those lions roared at once. Did that ever make an impression! They spoke to something in me that went back past my parents and grandparents, to caveman days. In boyhood response, I rose effortlessly in the air and yelled back at those "ferocious" lions.

In Amos, we read, "The lion has roared—who will not fear? The Sovereign Lord has spoken—who can but prophesy" (Amos 3:8, NIV). Who has never trembled in the fear of God has done no business with the Eternal.

P.S.: Today, in worship at my church, reflecting on its message and meaning, I was reminded of my childhood visit to Chicago. The essence of the sermon emphasized the fact before all things and in all things, life is held together by the Eternal God. I am very confident it is in Him we were first brought together and are now being held together. The apostle Paul stated to the church in Colossians, "He is before all things, and in Him all things hold together" (Colossians 1:17, NIV). That means God is the principle of cohesion in the universe. He impresses upon creation, even for a lad visiting Chicago, the unity and solidarity that make His world a "cosmos instead of a chaos."

Even though the two of us are imperfect saints, there is a cohesive love for each other that moves far beyond the physical. It reaches in praise and gratitude for the God who made us and, through His providential guidance, brought us together. It remains a marvel and a mystery. It is real. It is His majesty symbolized by "roaring lions" that makes one aware He is in charge of all things. The empty cup, the empty cross, and the empty tomb of His Son bear witness. He has done all His justice requires for persons to be reconciled to Him. The worship of this Lord's Day, our happy telephone visits about a "wedding dress," and the anticipation of life together make me so happy and glad. I literally want to roar like the lion.

Hymn: "Lift up your heads, you mighty gates; / behold, the King of glory waits; / the King of kings is drawing near; / the Savior of the world is here! / Fling wide the portals of your heart; / make it a temple, set apart from earthly use / for heaven's employ, / adorned with prayer, and love, and joy. / Redeemer, come, we open with our hearts to You; / here, Lord, abide; / Your inner presence let us feel; / Your grace and love in us reveal" (George Weissel, "Lift Up Your Heads").

Meditation: Dear Father, may every follower of Your divine way serve others in Your love and wisdom, reaching out to all we know and see. Even if we are strangers in a new place, grant us the courage to serve in power from the one who gives us life. Amen.

Devotional One Hundred Seventeen:

Look What God Gave Me

The people who influence us most are not those who buttonhole us and seek to manipulate us but those who live their lives like stars in heaven and the lilies in the field. Those are the lives that mold us. A great mistake is to think that a Spirit-filled man or woman must always be casting sermons at people. (I do hope my sermons have a salutary effect.)

Being "filled with the Spirit" is merely a refusing of self and a taking by faith of the life of Christ as wrought in us by His Spirit. God has given me that kind of friend and life partner to be. She is now *priority number one*.

She is a godly woman and reflects the picture found in Proverbs 31:15–19. The message translates the verses like this, "She's up before dawn, preparing breakfast for her family and organizing her day. She looks over a field and buys it, then with money she's put aside, plants a garden. First thing in the morning, she dresses for work (does her hair), rolls up her sleeves, eager to get started. She senses the worth of her work and is in no hurry to call it quits for the day. She's skilled in the crafts of home and hearth, diligent in homemaking." My partner, Grace, is kind and exhibits a quality of love that is godlike, and it can be seen in her actions and attitudes. How grateful to be given a gift like that. She is a surprise indeed!

P.S.: After such a sweet time in phone communication, I just needed to give special thanks for bringing such happiness to my life. Please let me put it as simply as possible. We talked about obedience, and I tried to say our obedience would be mutually determined, one with the other and in the spirit of what seems best. That does not mean we won't have differing opinions, but in spirit and attitude, we will always seek the best compromise. My desire for our decision-making is to honor our love for each other and honor God. A true wife is her husband's better half, his lump of delight, his flower of beauty, his guardian angel. To quote from the Genesis account of God's creation of Eve, I truly feel that my "rib for you is the best bone in my body." Women are too frequently found fault with for often looking into the glass, but it is not nearly as bad as a glass in which men drown their senses. In past years of working together and now in months of careful interaction with each other, there has never been any attempt to find fault with each other or each other's weaknesses. Rather, there is already a spiritual and emotional union that "*fits*," that is *real*, and leaves us *comfortable* and wanting to grow in a shared love. Just as we have already committed our vows in friendship, I am very much looking forward to writing my part of our wedding vows, expressing how two lives are so united.

Hymn: "How lovely and how pleasant, / when people dwell in peace, / and love is ever present to bind them each to each. / As dew upon the mountain refreshes every flower, / so love springs like a fountain / for those who know its power" (Slovak versification of Psalm 133; Translator Jaroslav J. Vajda, "How Lovely and

How Present").

Meditation: Dear Father, words are inadequate to fully convey my gratitude for reconnecting my life with Grace. Like sweet oil pervading the temple and flowers joyfully unfading, we have resolved to marry. May the vows we write and state at our wedding be more than ceremonial words but life commitment, "till death do us part." Amen.

Devotional One Hundred Eighteen:

The Wrong Question

In Matthew 19:17 (NIV), Jesus said to one inquirer, "'Why do you ask me about what is good?' Jesus replied, 'There is only One that is good.'" Two struggling parents are beset by pain and anxiety.

"Brother Jim, Jonathan has been arrested! They say he's selling drugs!" The mother was on the edge of tears.

"Something's been wrong for the last five or six years," the Father added.

"Tell us. Where did we go wrong?" Jonathan's mother inquired as she wept. "He had a Christian home in every way, every advantage we could afford. We set a Christian example every day. What makes children act this way?"

This happened many years ago now. I remember how difficult it was for the parents and the awkward way I may have handled their burdened frustrations about their son's behavior. I did the best I could to encourage them, but I have thought about that for a long time. Jesus Himself would not claim the title "good" for Himself. Perhaps the son of these noble parents found them too "good" to be real. I do not know it to be true, but perhaps so.

P.S.: I watched a Trinity Broadcasting church service one afternoon, and one of the pastor's illustrations was along similar lines to those experiences described above. Sometimes, in our own spiritual smugness, we do not see the whole world lying wounded, and each of us has need of a tender word of encouragement. The names are not given, but the family that was known so wonderfully well as faithful members of our church was extremely strict with their children. Too often, they saw themselves on a spiritual pedestal before others, including their children.

It brought to mind a statement from Dr. W. T. Conner I shared with you the other night. He said, "Sometimes we can be so heavenly-minded that we are of no earthly good." I am not saying "Jonathan's" behavior was caused by his parent's overzealous attitude. It is highly possible that Jonathan felt he could never be as "good" as his parents, so "why bother." If Jesus would not even allow the word "good" to be used to refer to Him but only to the Father, how much more should we likewise be careful to "live mercy and walk humbly with your God" (Micah 6:8b, NIV). As we join our lives, let us certainly lift up high standards, but not higher than our compassion for those we love.

Hymn: "Lord, I want to be a Christian / in my heart, in my heart, / Lord, I want to be a Christian in my heart. / Lord, I want to be more loving in my heart, in my heart, / Lord, I want to be more loving in my heart. / Lord I want to be more holy in my heart, in my heart, / Lord I want to be more holy in my heart. / Lord I want to be like Jesus in my heart, in my heart, / Lord, I want to be like Jesus in my heart. / In my heart, in my heart, Lord I want to be a Christian in my heart. / Lord, I want to be more loving in my heart. / Lord I want to be more holy in my heart. / Lord I want to be like Jesus in my heart" (African American Spiritual Adapter John W. Work, Jr., and Frederick J. Work, "Lord, I Want to Be a Christian").

Meditation: Dear God, give us wisdom to parent children in a way that reflects Your kind of love. It is the way of sacrifice and service. It is the way of intellectual humility where one recognizes that in earthly relationships, no one is perfect. It always models grace and forgiveness. That is Your way, and let it be ours. Amen.

Devotional One Hundred Nineteen:

Saline River Sanctity

For your advance information, this is an older sermon from a series I did. The ideas came directly from Roger Carstensen. The names are fictitious, but they represented some folks each of us may have known.

Ray Holyheart was by consensus the nearest to a saint in his town of Harrisburg, Illinois. The Saline River ran through my home county. The county is named after the river. Roy was the terror of sinners and the scourge of the lukewarm. He'd had a vision. They say an angel with a golden crown and silver feathers showed up as clear as the movies over Ray's head during a camp meeting and brushed a cherub's smile across his face.

Ray went to work on the less fortunate. "Where is your smile? Where is your angel?" If you couldn't ante up a molted silver feather or flash a cherub's smile, Ray would tell you where you should go…smiling!

In 1 Corinthians 12, we read the apostle Paul had vision trouble. His trip to the third heaven was too bright to live with. So God gave him a "thorn in the flesh" to keep him real. I guess it takes a thorn to keep somebody close to God enrolled in the human race. Why did Ray not have one? Maybe his community needed a pain, and Ray was it.

P.S.: Ever know somebody who seemed called by God to be a pain? Typically, they have a "kickative" mentality and enjoy being fault-finders rather than fact-finders. If I wanted to know something about a land of beauty and poetry with verdant valleys and cascading streams, I would not send a vulture out to provide a portrait of the terrain. In all probability, he or she would come back to report, "I found a dead carcass beneath a tree."

We see what we want to see, and people who have a low self-image have no appreciation for their own gifts and talents. They are typically ready to find fault with someone else. They try to build themselves up by tearing down someone else. For, after all, we do have the power of choice and self-determination. So, choose to love rather than hate. Choose to smile rather than frown. Choose to build rather than destroy. Choose to praise rather than gossip. Choose to heal rather than wound. Choose to give rather than grasp and, most of all, as Jesus did, choose to forgive rather than curse.

As we enter our lives together, I want to move beyond the hurt personalized by the persecution of dear friends and the distress brought into my own life by strife and division. I never want to be a faultfinder and always let God be the judge of other people's behavior. Most of all, I want to be a peacemaker inside our own home, family, church, society, and a world that anxiously looks for a better way to live life. Though this sermon was originally shared with students, it is even now a reminder and lesson for me, like the ticking of today's clock. I want always to practice what I preach, so help me.

Meditation: Dear Father, help us always to live the words we say. Blot out the temptation to see ourselves as better than others. May we have the grace to seek the power Your peace imparts to us and to each one of us, Your children. Amen.

Devotional One Hundred Twenty:

The Saline River Invalid

Another Saline River sermon: Uncle Flanagan was the worst patient the Harrisburg Hospital ever had. He swore at the nurses, threw his breakfast tray across the room, and bit his thermometer in half. Why? He had never been sick a day of his life. He got up at 5 a.m. singing and jumping. Worked fourteen hours and danced in the evenings. Never had an ache in his bones, a cavity in his teeth, or glasses on his nose.

Uncle Flanagan understood God Almighty had made him special. He sympathized with poor fools who got sick. So he made a fool of himself at the hospital.

Jesus said in Matthew 9:12 that we who are righteous have no need for a physician. He reserved His ministry for the sick. Uncle Flanagan didn't know he'd been sick when he was well. He had an overdose of good luck. May God grant us that Beloved Physician who, companion of our happy days and moments, sustains and redeems us when we write the bitter pages of our own diary.

P.S.: An insightful sermon from the inspiration of Roger Carstensen. We have talked about how blessed we are to be in good health. It is evident our abilities and activities belie the chronological years. I thank the Lord each day for energy and internal drive. You, likewise, have been wonderfully blessed. You are still working. I can't imagine you without a "plan" for the day. Much of your drive we both share has kept us "young at heart." I have come to care for you for many reasons. One of those reasons is your caring spirit. I realize, at some point, one or the other may need special care. You have had ten years of caring for LeRoy and your mother. In a similar timeframe, I had the privilege of caring for Jo. If and when either of us is hampered by physical or mental challenges, my pledge is to handle it by trusting the Great Physician and our resources no matter what may happen. I want to make sure the love we share shines through each day, regardless of limitations. I look forward to caring till the end. (Oh yes, holding hands going together.) We are at a time in life when the loss of family and friends is occurring too rapidly. In the meantime, let us resolve to make every day His day but also ours.

Hymn: "Children of the heavenly Father / safely in His bosom gather; / nestling bird nor star in heaven / such a refuge e'er was given. / Neither life nor death shall ever / from the Lord His children sever; / unto them His grace He showeth, / and their sorrows all He knoweth" (Translator Ernest W. Olson; Author Caroline V. Sandell-Berg, "Children of the Heavenly Father").

Meditation: Eternal Father, in life, You give and take away. Yet, You do not forsake us, and Your loving purpose is to preserve us for eternity through the accepted gift of Your Son, our Savior. So endow us with Your security of salvation and reward us with Your promise of eternal life. Thanks be to God. Amen.

Devotional One Hundred Twenty-One:

It's the Thought That Counts

The Grange was in session. Singlehead Dewberry addressed the chair, "Washington don't know this village exists. I move we send a gift to the president and get this place on the map." The motion carried. The chair appointed Morton Squinchmerit, the miser, to do the honors.

Morton believed that in giving, it was the thought that counted. So he found a pale-wattled, listless chicken that had been gasping around a day or two and looked ready for chicken heaven. He wrapped it in gold foil and red ribbon and sent it to the president. The message, "Dear Mr. President, let this gift represent what our folks think of you." There's economy, if ever you needed to know about it. Of course, Morton got a free audit from the IRS that year.

In Malachi 1, the prophet asks whether the governor would be pleased with the blind animals the people were offering to God. Since God is the Lord of Excellence, He demands the best. On earth as it is in heaven, our best is the only thing we can really afford.

P.S.: Grace, it may be a bit of a stretch from this doggerel to a wedding dress, but in looking over old files, this "50-Second Sermon" idea from Roger Carstensen was already done, and I am kind of sleepy and ready for bed. I know you are struggling with the wedding dress, whether it is too expensive. Cindy thinks it may be too much for a private wedding. If the dress was four thousand or even seven hundred, you might quarrel a bit about the price. We both want our wedding to be characterized by dignity and beauty, providing a lasting memory. My advice? Don't be a Morton Squinchmerit! If you or "we" could only afford a near-dead chicken, that would be one thing. You are more important than the president, and you won't get an IRS audit. So go for it and remember the only thing we can afford is our best. Given the picture of the back of the dress, it certainly defines the dress and *you* as the *best* (without commenting about how great you look from the back). So, in the grand scheme of things, I would say, compared to other wedding dress price tags, it is a 65 percent deal. I love what I see, but the groom is not supposed to see the dress till the wedding.

Hymn: "If you will only let God guide you, and hope in Him through all your ways, whatever comes, He'll stand beside you, to bear you through the evil days; who trusts in God's unchanging love builds on the Rock that cannot move. / Only be still, and wait His leisure in cheerful hope, with heart content to take what-e'er the Father's pleasure and all discerning love have sent; nor doubt our inmost wants are known to Him who chose us for His own" (Translator Catherine Winkworth; Author Greg Neumark, "If You Will Only Let God Guide You").

Meditation: Dear Father, this moment of reflection reminds me You are the Author of marriage, beginning with Adam and Eve. Since that signaled moment of Your creation, You have sought to bless the marriage ceremony, and Jesus Himself began His earthly ministry demonstrating His divine power by changing water into wine to enhance the celebration. May we each enter into that sacred moment with gratitude for Your blessing and with offered praise for our own written vows. Amen.

Devotional One Hundred Twenty-Two:

The Growl of a Preacher

When the patriarch Jacob was on his deathbed, he called his twelve sons to his side and blessed them. Each had a destiny to suit his nature.

Rueben had lost his self-control and thus lost his birthright. Judah led his brothers and thus would be king. Joseph was a fruitful bough and would prosper. Benjamin was a ravenous wolf and would divide the spoil of the prey.

The fierceness of Benjamin burst out in Saul, warrior king of Israel. Acts 9 tells how another Benjamite, Saul of Tarsus, breathed threats and murder against the disciples of the Lord. It is strange that such a brutal person could become a preacher, really an evangelist. But in its own way, the gospel is brutal, for it attacks weakness, sin, and hopelessness. It attacks death and produces eternal life.

P.S.: I meant to mention to you a conversation I had with my internist today. She knew I was a minister and made a point to share with me a "spiritual miracle" that occurred in her brother-in-law's life. My physician is from India, as is her husband. His brother has been a drug addict and is apparently involved with a drug gang. Her father-in-law is an active Christian and was converted in India from his Hindu faith. The family settled first in the

Eastern part of the U.S., where the parents still live, but after she and her husband both finished medical school, they opened their current practice in Texas.

She told me her father-in-law had been praying for his delinquent son for years with no positive response. The father is gravely ill with cancer, and she said he has just a few days to live. Sometime over the last conversations while at his father's bedside, the son made a profession of faith and asked the Lord to remove the drug addiction. They know it will be hard, but she said you would have to be very familiar with Indian culture to know how a promise to a dying father becomes a trust. It reminded me of the "sermon" from Roger Carstensen I shared with students many years ago, but this testimony brought it alive in my memory. The gospel is indeed a divine miracle, and though man cannot control someone else's behavior, the power of the gospel working through God's Spirit can change a brute into a preacher.

Hymn: "We cannot measure how You heal / or answer every sufferer's prayer, / yet we believe Your grace responds / where faith and doubt unite to care. / Your hands, though bloodied on the cross, / survive to hold and heal and warn, / to carry all through death to life / and cradle children yet unborn. / So some have come who need Your help / and some have come to make amends, / as hands which shaped and saved / the world are present in the touch of friends. / Lord, let Your Spirit meet us here / to mend the body, mind and soul, / to disentangle peace from pain, / and make Your broken people whole? (John L. Bell and Graham A. Maule, "We Cannot Measure How You Heal").

Meditation: Dear Miracle-Working God, You do create a cosmos out of chaos, and You redeem sinful man through belief in the miraculous virgin birth of Your Son, His sinless life, sacrificial death on the cross, and His triumphant resurrection. That can only be known for sure by repentance, faith, and trust in Him as the only way to redemption. Thank You for Your saving power. Amen.

Devotional One Hundred Twenty-Three:

The Eager Listener

Have you ever met an eager listener? You'd think the eager listener would be the conversation's richest blessing. So many people do not listen at all.

The eager listener has a bright and beaming eye, a broad smile, and a nodding head. He starts agreeing before you end your first sentence. He slaps you on the back in the middle of an infinitive. If you recite the alphabet backward, he'd swear that was the best poetry he'd heard since Eddie Guest. A really good, eager listener is so positive he starts nodding affirmatively before you even speak.

Jesus told His disciples in Mark 6:11 that if the citizens of a town refused to hear them, they were to shake the dust of that place off their feet and leave for good. If you're on serious business with the words you speak, watch out for the eager listener. He has the deafest ears of all.

P.S.: I have a "friend" who is a former student. He seems to thrive on being "top of the class" and make sure those around him know it. And to make matters worse, his "easy listening" is usually followed by the words "That's nothing!" and then attempts a "bet you can't top this" story. I was with him tonight, seated at the same table. I am always glad to be recognized. The worst blow was when other people passed by our table; he would say, "By the way, Dr. Williams was my favorite seminary teacher." Sometimes, he would quote something I said in class. After a while, it was embarrassing, and I was ready to crawl under the table. Then, it dawned on me that I goofed with this student by not helping him handle his ego-driven need for recognition. But it was a reminder for me to listen carefully so I may respond honestly.

The eager listener, it seems, has put forth little effort in cultivating his own inwardness and uniqueness as a person. Their thoughts are someone else's opinions. Their lives are a mimicry, and their passions are a quotation from somebody else. However, is that a fair judgment for this student? Were there some things I should have learned from him? I have previously stated I learn more from my students than any other source. In what ways did I miss such an opportunity with him?

It is to say, going forward, I want to hear what you are saying, handle your thoughts openly, and learn from each other. Though I have been in a teaching role for a long time, I want you to be my wife but also my teacher, a formal plea and pledge from an inquiring mind!

Hymn: "I gave My life for thee, / My precious blood I shed, / That thou might'st ransomed be, / And quickened from the dead; / I gave, I gave My life for thee, / What has thou giv'n for Me? / I gave, I gave My life for thee, / What hast thou giv'n for Me? / And I have brought to thee, / Down from My home above, / Salvation full and free, / My pardon and My love; / I bring, I bring rich gifts to thee, / What hast thou brought to Me? / I bring, I bring rich gifts to thee, / What hast thou brought to Me?" (Frances R. Havergal, "I Gave My Life for Thee").

Meditation: Father of all knowledge and wisdom, grant us a humble mind that places utmost value on gaining an understanding of the realities of Your creation. To know is to want to know more. That means I need an open mind to join You in creating a cosmos out of chaos. It means we need to be open to learning from others as well as teaching others Your way. So grant it for this day and every day. Amen.

Devotional One Hundred Twenty-Four:

A Detour to The Altar

In Matthew 5:23–24, Jesus teaches that if I remember my brother has something against me, I get reconciled to him before I offer a gift or partake of the Lord's Supper.

Sometimes, the long way around is the shortest distance between two points. I used to try to convince myself only the pleasant and the beautiful have positive value. The truth of the matter is life is, at times, a bittersweet reality and is its essence and also its glory. So, I have had a tendency to focus more on the sweet and try to avoid the bitter. Especially is it true if someone "ticks" me or says things that are injurious or is cocky and arrogant.

Going to the altar without spending time with God would be just as foolish. He's not tied to the altar. And with God around, I don't dare to mistreat anybody. When I make things right with someone I tried to avoid or who may have attempted to "tick" me off, God shows up, and His altar is at my elbow.

Take a detour to God by way of somebody you clobbered. You'll be in church faster than you think!

P.S.: I re-read last night's "sermon" after I received your response. In addition to the typos I pointed out, I read, again, the content of the P.S. and was somewhat chided for the rather caustic way I described a former student. Even though he was a "pain in the neck," and I was irritated by his brashness, he was thoughtful to introduce me as his teacher. I was too upset with him to appreciate anything he said. If part of his problem was my failure to be a more cognizant and interactive teacher, then I should be blaming myself more than him. Even though in teaching, one can only sharpen the axe brought to the classroom, there is a sense I was not effective in sharpening his axe. So, I have asked the Lord to forgive me. The next time I see him, I will seek to be more open to listening and perhaps have the opportunity to be a helpful friend. But maybe not! Rigid habits of personality are tough to change and can't be if not recognized by the individual. I have some work to do on "me" and in my relationship with him and others.

Hymn: "Lord, make me an instrument of Your peace; / Where there is hatred, let me sow love; / Where there is injury, let there be pardon; / Where there is doubt, let there be faith; / Where there is despair, let there be hope; / Where there is darkness, let there be light / And where there is sadness, let there be joy. / O Divine Master, grant that I may not so much seek / To be consoled as to console; / To be understood, as to understand; / To be loved, as to love; / For it is in giving that we receive, / It is in pardoning that we are pardoned, / And it is in dying that we are born to Eternal Life. Amen" (Francis of Assisi).

Meditation: Dear Father, Your servant Francis of Assisi said it best, "O Divine Master, grant that I may not so much seek to be understood as to understand; to be loved, as to love…" Teach us how to grow in our acceptance of You and of each other. Amen.

Devotional One Hundred Twenty-Five:

Time for a Poem and Not a Sermon

Vases

Two vases stood on the Shelf of Life
As Love came by to look,
One was of priceless cloisonné,
The other of solid common clay.
Which do you think Love took?

He took them both from the Shelf of Life,
He took them both with a smile;
He clasped them both with his fingertips,
And touched them both with caressing lips,
And held them both for a while

From tired hands Love let them fall,
And never a word was spoken.
One was of priceless cloisonné.
The other of solid common clay.
Which do you think was broken?

—Nan Terrell Reed

Grace, obviously, this poem speaks to our phone conversation about how far love reaches, especially the difficult and challenging decisions. Maybe the cloisonné was not broken because it was hard and tempered. You may remember my first "50-Second Sermon" had to do with broken cloisonné vases. But, it is also possible, in this poem, that both could have broken. To make a good point, the poet is emphasizing the fact the harder the vase, the less it shatters. But, sometimes, in the bittersweet of life, both vases are shattered. The important thing is *love* always stretches to understand. Either of us, or both of us, may break a vase, but *love* will try to put the pieces back together or consider the loss not as important as the *love* that took them to look and hold. That is the kind of *love* I am confident we share.

Hymn: "Take my life, and let it be consecrated, / Lord, to Thee' take my hands, / and let them move at the impulse of Thy love, / at the impulse of Thy love. / Take my will and make it Thine / it shall be no longer mine; / take my heart, it is Thine own, / it shall flow in ceaseless praise, / let them flow I ceaseless praise. / Take my love, my Lord, / I pour at thy feet in treasure store. / Take myself and I will be ever, / only, all for Thee, ever, / only, all for Thee" (Frances R. Havergal, "Take My Life, and Let It Be Consecrated").

Meditation: Dear Father, when life and the things of life get broken, may we not lean on our own understanding but place our trust in the "solid rock" of Your love and forgiveness. Amen.

Devotional One Hundred Twenty-Six:

Ecstasy and Good Sense

In 1 Corinthians 14:8 (NIV), we read, "If the trumpet does not sound a clear call, who will get ready for battle"?

The church at Corinth had a strong, charismatic flavor. Many in the congregation spoke in unknown tongues. To them, speaking in "tongues" was ecstasy no human words could express.

Since people couldn't understand unknown tongues, Paul insisted this experience ought to be in private. Speaking publicly in tongues was like a trumpeter sounding "charge!" to the cavalry by playing everything at once. As has been said, it is like a soldier mounted and riding off rapidly in all directions.

It is okay to hit every note on the trumpet to warm it up. But you warm up so you can play a tune. The gospel of Christ says a lot and means a lot at the same time. The story of the cross puts me in the ranks of the committed, not because I am mystified, but because I get the message.

P.S.: This sermon did not grow out of tonight's phone visit, as you can tell. However, just as you took a nap in the midst of reading, I went to sleep while watching a religious broadcast. Following a rousing hymn, some began to give off spiritual utterances.

But our phone conversation took on much more meaningful content affecting us, such as your check, the fur coat, cemetery flowers, your supper menu, etc. Obviously, our tongues were busy sharing information about the day but also remembering all the good things that have come into our lives from last August till now. No single tongue, certainly not mine, could ever put into words what a mountainous and joyous reconnection with you means to me. As we said, it is in the realm of the indescribable and miraculous. And I do love you for the way you have poured so much of your life into mine and done so in such a caring, tender way. I am overwhelmed by the togetherness we now feel for each other. Let me repeat the last line of the "sermon." It is not because I am mystified but because I have received the clear, understandable message of a God-sized love growing day by day. A part of the "trumpet sound" I would make is this. True love, among everything else, puts you in the ranks of the committed. So *blast* the trumpets!

Hymn: "Before the throne of God above / I have a strong and perfect plea; / a great High Priest whose name is Love, / whoever lives and pleads for me. / My name is graven on His hands, / my name is written on His heart. / I know that while in heaven He stands / no tongue can bid me thence depart, / no tongue can bid me thence depart" (Vikki Cook and Charlie Lee Bancroft, "Before the Throne of God Above").

Meditation: Great High Priest, we rejoice in the knowledge that You know us, care for us, and have redeemed us by faith in Your Son. Let that good news ring forth from our lips all day long. May our life flow on in endless song as we join in praise for eternal redemption. Amen.

Devotional One Hundred Twenty-Seven:

The Authority of Knowing

In Mark 1:22, we read that Jesus taught people as one who had authority.

In high school, I had a biology teacher who lacked authority. The class was in a constant uproar. Unlike my chemistry class, taught by Mr. Hoover, an outstandingly gifted and organized teacher, the learning in biology was at a standstill. The teacher was handsome, congenial, young, and muscular. He was a fine football coach, but he obviously didn't know much about biology. One day, a retired teacher took over. Never had he been an athlete; apparently, he was physically over the hill. On his first day in class with us, he began quietly, "This is a class in biology." That day, the class settled down. He knew his subject, and he knew how to relate it to students.

Jesus absorbed life's curriculum in the presence of God. He knew how things were. He knew people. He had authority for the winds and waves, and the hearts of men obeyed him. Most of all, He understood the growth tasks of His students and gave them the most cogent, clear understanding of how to "live and learn the lesson."

P.S.: I did not know where to begin tonight's "sermon." It has happened other times, as you know. I have usually picked up on some ideas from our phone conversations. Tonight, we ended up talking about your job and my teaching role. We have spent long years of productive service in Christian ministry organizations. A huge part of our identity is wrapped up in those roles. I am certainly grateful for God's goodness in providing opportunities for such service. It has not been toil but effective and rewarding work. Work, after all, is one of God's best gifts to the human race. It is toil that is a curse, work without purpose or meaning. Though I will continue teaching at Dallas Baptist University, you will be leaving forty-seven years of service in Southern Baptist entities. For thirteen of those years, we worked together. As we join together in marriage, let us resolve to keep learning and serving together. With such resolve, I believe God will open up appropriate and meaningful opportunities for continued usefulness. Who knows what it represents? Perhaps there are "surprises" that will open to us. In fact, they could provide fulfillment, emotional support, and financial reward. I believe DBU will let me teach as long as I am physically and intellectually able. Whatever we do, whether in your role or mine, we will do it together. We have been somewhat independent for a long time and will necessarily become more interdependent. The challenge is to let up without letting go of personal identity as we discover new and fulfilling opportunities.

Hymn: "This is my Father's world, / And to my list'ning ears, / All nature sings, and round me rings / The music of the spheres. / This is my Father's world, I rest me in the thought / Of rocks and trees, of skies and seas; / His hand the wonders wrought. / This is my Father's world / The birds their carols raise; / The morning light, the lily white / Declare their Maker's praise. / This is my Father's world, / He shines in all that's fair; / In the rustling grass I hear Him pass, / He speaks to me ev'rywhere" (Maltbie D. Babcock, "This Is My Father's World").

Meditation: Dear Lord, You have promised in Your Word that You will be with us to the end. Use our gifts and talents to serve as You intend, empowered by Your Spirit for the work to which we are called. Amen.

Devotional One Hundred Twenty-Eight:

The Sin of Presumption

In Matthew's Gospel, we read: "Therefore keep watch, because you do not know what day your Lord will come" (Matthew 24:42, NIV). In addition to this statement by Jesus, James provided the most beautiful illustration of the brevity of life when he said that each day "appears for a little while and then vanishes" (James 4:14, NIV).

The two verbs James used were used by Aristotle to refer to the appearance and disappearance of a flock of birds as they swept across the sky. We don't see them. Then we do. Then we see them no more. They are here one moment and gone the next. So is life. Life passes quickly. As the poet put it:

> When as a child I laughed and wept.
>
> Time crept.
>
> When as a youth, I dreamed and talked,
>
> Time walked.
>
> When I became a full-grown man,
>
> Time ran.
>
> While older still I grew,

Time flew.

Soon I shall find in traveling on,

Time gone!

—Anonymous Swiss Poem

If life is brief, we need to live each day to the fullest. As Proverbs reminds us, "For you do not know what a day may bring forth" (Proverbs 27:1b, NIV).

P.S.: Grace, I have no intention of dwelling on the brevity of life since we both are aware of it. However, the more I thought about it, the more I am aware we must make each day count. I have noticed in the last few days my mind has been moving to the least romantic things like "moving, packing, selling a house, choosing items for Memphis and also Fort Worth." (It makes me aware I have never had two "home locations.") So, there are all kinds of decisions awaiting us. Obviously, I do request help from you. For instance, help me think of the detail and logistics required for both of us, but especially for me, since I have the big job of closing the house. It will not happen on its own. So, this sermon tonight is primarily for me, but I am also requesting you to lend me your organizational skills. I wish we could do this together, with you here to help me. There will be "sentiment" to deal with, being separated from my kids for part of the year, and most of all, just plain old hard work. It has to be done. It is part of the required discipline and personal accountability transition requires. It is true, as is said, "Yesterday is but a memory and tomorrow a longed-for dream." But all I (or we) really have is today. I am struggling to deal with it. (Get it done, Jim.) I have made some progress, but I have a long way to go before it can be pronounced "done." So, I am "sketching out a roadmap." It should keep me motivated. I am praying God helps me waste not a single day for the moment we will be sharing life together.

Hymn: "O Christ, our hope, our heart's desire, / Redemption's only spring, / Creator of the world art Thou, / Its Savior and its King. / How vast the mercy and the love / Which laid our sins on Thee, / And led Thee to a cruel death / To set Thy people free. / But now the bonds of death are burst, / The ransom has been paid; / And Thou art on Thy Father's throne, / In glorious robes arrayed. / O Christ, be Thou our lasting joy, / Our ever great reward; / Our only glory may it be / To glory in the Lord!" (John Chandler, "O Christ, Our Hope, Our Heart's Desire").

Meditation: God of all time and eternity, let each day of our lives reflect the reality that from the past, the future will appear. It is a mystery revealed in season, something You alone can see. Let us, therefore, redeem the time given each day by Your sovereign hand. Amen.

Devotional One Hundred Twenty-Nine:

No Glitter, Glamour, or Gossip

A contemporary temptation in popular theology, and the rage in Christian publishing, is to put Jesus into a coat and tie to teach a leadership seminar. The Sermon on the Mount may be replaced by the Sermon from the Top Floor Corner Office. Jesus's disciples become His management team. The Bible becomes the strategic plan. Jesus the Savior remains but now meets Jesus, the *mentor*.

It is very easy to re-clothe Jesus in contemporary images to meet current needs rather than let Jesus be Jesus. The temptation is to impose our own agenda on the biblical text instead of being challenged by it. Jesus is certainly interested in the corporate office but is not interested in glitter, glamour, and gossip; He is interested in grace, giving, goodness, and God-like service. John, in Chapter 10, reminds us, "For the son of man did not come to be served, but to serve, and to give his life to be a ransom for many" (Mark 10:45, NIV).

P.S.: This "sermon" is based on two ideas from the text, now that I think about it. Part of it grows from your friend's "inside information source." Obviously, we all like to be the bearers of knowledge, and some delight in being the "town crier." But the real reason for this message is based on why I began to care for you. We talked at length about those common attractions. For me, it has to do with your spirit of servanthood. In simple terms, it is one of your strongest gifts. For me, servanthood means using your life to help others meet their goals. *That is who you are.* I have never known anyone more committed to the small details that make it possible for others to serve. You are a servant's servant. And that is the driving attraction of your life and the reason I was attracted to you. Of course, it all began in those years we worked side by side. I saw this gift of yours applied to every level of administrative responsibility. Now, it is reinforced by the power of mutual love. After many years of leadership opportunities, I know fully we lead by serving, and we serve by leading. Servanthood and servitude are often confused, but they are not the same. Servitude may be imposed. Servanthood is embraced. Servitude could enslave others, but servanthood emancipates. Servitude can denigrate, but servanthood always uplifts. Servitude can crush, but servanthood fulfills. Servitude can cause despair, but servanthood rejoices!

So, before this strong attraction emerged, our relationship was and is based on a common understanding of and commitment to servanthood. And what's more, I can't think of a better way to start a marriage. The essential goodness of Jesus was His capacity to serve, even giving His own life, unparalleled by anyone before Him or after Him. That testifies to the life to which we, too, are called, and I now look forward to being a "team" with you in serving each other, our extended family, and others.

Hymn: "For All the saints, who from their labors rest, / who

Thee by faith before the world confessed, / Thy name, O Jesus, be forever blest. Alleluia! Alleluia! / O blest communion, fellowship divine! / We feebly struggle, they in glory shine, / yet all are one in Thee, for all are thine. Alleluia! Alleluia! / From earth's wide bounds, from ocean's farthest coast, / through gates of pearl streams in the countless host, / singing to Father, Son and Holy Ghost. Alleluia! Alleluia!" (William Walsham How, "For All the Saints").

Meditation: Dear God, thanks that Your creation deserves our best in thoughtful service. Loving puts us on our knees, needing Your empowering strength. So help us serve. Amen.

Devotional One Hundred Thirty:

Makeover Madness

Chances are, if you flip the channels far enough, a TV show with a makeover contest will show up. Shows like *Ambush Makeover*, *Trading Spaces*, or *Fixer Upper* are fascinating and cover many aspects of human life, not just housing, dress, and the like. *Naked and Afraid* pits man against nature. Some of these shows are personal and deal with dress and appearance. The truth is that external makeovers have a short shelf life.

Eventually, hair grows out, makeup runs out, wrinkles and bellies pop out, and trendy furniture gets thrown out. At the end of it all, we're still looking at ourselves in the mirror, and it's what we can't see that really matters.

Want a makeover that lasts? Put away the eyeliner and pick up on the advice Paul gives to the Corinthians. He says, "So from now on we regard no one from a worldly point of view. Though we once regarded Christ in this way, we do so no longer. Therefore, if anyone is in Christ, he is a new creation; the old has gone, the new has come" (2 Corinthians 5:16–17, NIV). Because of what Christ has done through His death and resurrection, the outward man eventually declines, but the inner man is being strengthened day by day. A Christ makeover is a "redo" that works and never goes out of style.

P.S.: I am glad the two of us like reality shows. With this common interest, we can keep up to date in current style, architecture, vacation plots, furniture, physical makeover, dress, etc. Also, I was knocked off my feet to see the picture of you wearing your new fur coat. Obviously, I am taken away by your physical beauty and our need to keep ourselves fit and strong. I work on that, more so now, because I want to keep my body in the best shape for the future of our time together. We both take great delight in our physical abilities. I hope we can keep it that way for a long time. Of course, the real lesson for us is a Christ makeover; it is the one that guarantees a life beyond the camera lens and the bathroom mirror. Let us resolve to keep doing makeovers as long as we can, but also be prepared to see personal identity based on what is in the heart. That will see us to the end regardless of the wrinkles.

Hymn: "Teach me your way, O Lord, teach me your way! / Your guiding grace afford, teach me Your way! / Help me to walk aright, more by faith, less by sight; / lead me with heavenly light, teach me Your way! / When doubts and fears arise, teach me Your Way! / When storm clouds fill the skies, teach me Your way! / Shine through the wind and rain, through sorrow, grief, and pain; / make now my pathway plain, teach me Your way!" (B. Mansell Ramsey, "Teach Me Your Way").

Meditation: Heavenly Father, help us grasp the truth that life is more than the epidermal or the anatomical. We are made in Your image, and though the earthly physical appearance may change, You have ordered, for those who trust You, an eternal life that knows no physical bounds. Give us the courage to live by this truth. Amen.

Devotional One Hundred Thirty-One:

What Not to Wear

A hot show that had its origin on British BBC made its way into the U.S. It makes ugly ducklings—fashion-impaired persons—into stylish swans. But a very different transformation occurs when Jesus takes off His robe and begins to wash the disciples' feet. On the last night of His life, Jesus was dressed in a loose-fitting outer garment. It was functional but dressy enough for the dinner portion of the evening, including broken bread and shared wine. But when it came time to teach and serve, He took off His outer garment, then wrapped a towel around His waist and washed the feet of His disciples.

His servant lesson was designed to help His followers know what clothes should be worn by Christians bent on serving others and each other. You may ask, "What clothes are ill-suited for Christians bent on serving?" The classic text is found in Colossians 3. One might paraphrase what Paul says: "As God's chosen ones, clothe yourselves with compassion, kindness, humility, meekness, and patience," a five-point sartorial splendor. But in order to put those things on, He says you must take off the clothes of "anger, wrath, malice, slander, abusive language from your mouth, and most of all do not lie to one another, seeing that you have stripped off the old self with its practices and have clothed yourselves with the new self, which is being renewed in knowledge according to the image of its creator" (Colossians 3:5, 8–10, NIV). We are all naked before God, and He sees through the illusion of looking good while not actually being good. What matters to Him is how we treat each other when we think no one else is looking.

P.S.: This "sermon" is a continuation of the previous one, in a sense. But it does pick up on one of your favorite shows. *Say Yes to the Dress* is one of them. Also, I was interested in your description of the wedding scenes. These shows result in a delighted person and a growing audience because we like to see how sometimes tough love is never about dressing like a supermodel. It is about ordinary Janes and Joes avoiding "what not to wear" and dressing instead with the best fitting, best-looking clothes possible. That means clothes that are perfectly suitable for the bodies of the participants. That all brings me to one additional reason why I love you. You care about your appearance, but you never have to spend huge sums to make you look like a "supermodel." Rather, you spend time finding the best prices for apparel that enhance your beauty. We will do many things together and have lots of fun living out our days. One of the things I look forward to is sharing in your adventure to find clothes at the least costly price!

Hymn: "For the beauty of the earth, / for the glory of the skies, / for the love which from our birth / over and around us lies; / Lord of all, to Thee we raise / this our hymn of grateful praise. / For the joy of human love, brother, sister, / parent, child, friends on earth, and friends above, / for all gentle thoughts and mild; / Lord of all, to Thee we raise this / our hymn of grateful praise" (Folliott S. Pierpoint, "For the Beauty of the Earth").

Meditation: Dear craftsman of earth's treasures, we give thanks for all created order and mankind as the highest. Teach us how to care for ourselves in mind, body, and spirit. In all we say and do, may it honor You. Amen.

Devotional One Hundred Thirty-Two:

Sitting in Judgment

In Colossians 2:16 (KJV), Paul writes, "Let no man therefore judge you in meat, nor in drink, nor in respect of an holy day, for the new moon, or the Sabbath days." Paul uses a present negative command in this verse: "Stop, therefore, allowing anyone to sit in judgment upon you."

Barclay says, "The whole New Testament rejoices in the glorious fact that, once a man knows Jesus Christ, there is nothing between him and God, that the door is wide open for every man." As Paul did, we, too, must regard with the gravest suspicion any teaching or interpretation that would put any being back into the bondage of legal requirements.

God's normal, healthy child is concerned with fellowship with the Father and knowing Jesus Christ. When man concentrates on these two things, his life will be pleasing to the Lord. In the next verse, Paul is inferring from Old Testament scripture that legalistic regulations are just a shadow of things to come. The reality is in Jesus Christ. As the shadow foretells the coming presence, so the law itself points us to Christ. So Paul says not to chase after the "shadow" when you already have the reality of Christ.

P.S.: This "sermon" is in response to the person in your nominating committee meeting today who wanted to make a peripheral matter into a major test of fellowship. Every denominational group can determine standards of faith and practice. I understand. Many Protestant denominations have a creed or covenant. But sometimes, even in our own Baptist family, it becomes a test of fellowship. As Dr. Jack McGauran, my Southwestern colleague and professor of the Greek New Testament, said, "I will sign every page of Holy Scripture, but not a creedal statement. For me, it is the *kerygma* that should be our test of Christian fellowship. Our earlier confessions of faith are general enough to reflect the diversity of interpretation on various issues of Scripture."

But historically, the bedrock foundation of our faith is based on belief in the virgin birth of Christ, His sinless life, His vicarious death on the cross for the sins of mankind, His bodily resurrection, and His victorious return to the Father's house to be the propitiation for man's sins. I do wish this kind of spirit of confessional faith would be the primary way of determining fellowship in the body of Christ. In verse 18, which follows the above passage, in The Message Bible, Paul says, "Don't tolerate people who try to run your life, ordering you to bow and scrape, insisting that you join their obsession with angels and that you seek their visions. They're a lot of hot hair; that's all they are. They're completely out of touch with the source of life, Christ" (Colossians 2:18, MSG). Of course, if you quoted verse 18 to legalistic types, you would be disqualified. In the Metropolitan Baptist Church in London, there is a tremendous plague—quoting its beloved former pastor, Dr. Charles Spurgeon, who asks, "How much of external religion is fiction, fluff, form, or foam?" I am so glad that you and I share a common commitment to the essence of the gospel. Living in the negative will never result in a positive.

Hymn: "Break Thou the bread of life, / Dear Lord, to me, / As Thou didst break the loaves / Beside the sea, / Beyond the sacred page I seek Thee, Lord, / My spirit pants for Thee, O living Word. / Bless Thou the truth, dear Lord, / To me, to me. / As Thou didst bless the bread By Galilee; / Then shall all bondage cease, All fetters fail; / And I shall find my peace, / My All in all / Thou art the bread of life, / O Lord, to me. Thy holy Word the truth / That saveth me; / Give me to eat and live With Thee above; / Teach me to love Thy truth, / for Thou art love" (Mary A. Lathbury and Alexander Groves, "Break Thou the Bread of Life").

Meditation: God of the living Word and the written Word, we pray each one, wise and simple, may discover Your truth of ageless worth until all lands receive the witness and Your knowledge fills the earth. We pray this in the name of the living Word. Amen.

Devotional One Hundred Thirty-Three:

Your Voice Was Worth a Million

There is no "sermon" tonight because we could never talk. I rang and rang and rang. No answer. I was worried something was wrong. I kept calling, and finally, you answered. I do ask your forgiveness for waking you late in the night. Let me also say, "I was worried sick something bad had happened." I was anxious to know you were okay. Finally, at last, the sound of your voice was worth a million. For 45 minutes or more, I fretted about what to do. I thought about calling you on your landline should you not answer the cell. Obviously, you needed sleep, and I should have eased my mind. (Somebody else you know has been prone to go to sleep in the recliner.) But I let my anxiety win out. My feelings of concern made me more aware of just how very much I need you, and I don't know what I would do if something happened to you. You have become such a part of me that for 45 minutes, I had a strong reminder our lives have truly become one.

Furthermore, this sense of togetherness has become so strong it causes me, at times, to respond with more emotion than reason. In my mind, I knew you were more likely asleep, but my emotions needed to verify nothing was wrong. Morning, afternoon, evening, and night, my thoughts turn to you. It is mystifying how

I have been *surprised by Grace*.

Hymn: "Give to the winds your fears, / hope, and be undismayed; / God hears your sighs and counts your tears, / God shall lift up your head. / Through waves and clouds and storms, / He gently clears the way; / wait for His time, / so shall the night soon end in joyous day" (Translator John Wesley; Author Paul Gerhardt, "Give to the Winds Your Fears").

Meditation: Sovereign God, help us fully trust Your strong hand. In times of needless fear, strengthen our reason and resolve. The prison of fear becomes a nightmare. You alone can bring hope and confidence to minds and hearts. Help us to live, day or night. Amen.

Devotional One Hundred Thirty-Four:

Time for a Poem

The languid, pensive, and intimate phone visit left me with a deep longing to be with you. So, it is obvious I need to dwell on these deep, thoughtful emotions that flood over me like hurricane waves pounding the seashore. After we hung up, I came back to the bedroom, pulled out my volume of *Poems That Live Forever*, and read, again, "Of Love" (from *The Prophet*) by Kahlil Gibran. Perhaps you have read it before, but it is one of the most poignant expressions of human love I know. I can't send the first part of the poem because of the very personal, rich-in-detail prelude that sets the context for the strong message of passionate love so described. If you do not have access to the poem, I will read the first several verses to you tomorrow night. So, after a graphic portrayal of love's reality, he closes with the following powerful summation of the gift and reality of abiding love:

> Love gives naught but itself and takes naught from itself.
>
> Love possess' not, nor would it be possessed;
>
> For love is sufficient unto love.

When you love you should not say, "God is in my heart" but rather, "I am in the heart of God."

And think not you can direct the course of love, for love, if it finds you worthy, will direct your course.

Love has no other desire but to fulfill itself.

But if you love and must needs have desires, let these be your desires:

To melt and be like a running brook that sings its melody in the night.

To be wounded by your own understanding of love;

And, to bleed willingly and joyfully.

To wake at dawn with a winged heart and give thanks for another day of loving;

To rest at the noon hour and meditate love's ecstasy;

To return home at eventide with gratitude:

And then to sleep, with a prayer for the beloved in your heart, and a song of praise upon your lips.

P.S.: These prayerful words from Gibran capture the plucking of my heartstrings. They summarize the strong passions that linger deep inside me. As we have shared on other occasions, this love of ours transcends physical understanding. But it is real, and I bless the Lord every day for this gift of love that now is ours. I am sure our capacity to love anew is built on the foundation of spousal love shared many years with your LeRoy and my Jo. I am thrilled we can celebrate the lives of our first spouses. We have experienced it before and have a greater capacity to know its reality. It is now part of meaningful stewardship with each other. Why, then, should we be "surprised"?

Hymn: Bryan Jeffery Leach wrote a hymn entitled "All Things Are Yours." The hymn speaks of our need to heed the compassion of Christ. If we do, Christ says to us that we become His head, His hands, and His heart. If we give out of true love and compassion, then the gifts we share with others become gifts to us as well.

Meditation: Great God, we give thanks, for Your giving has no ending. Let divine love permeate our love for others, all home and kindred, too. Thank You that in Your divine plan for human life, You provided the choice of a "significant other" to be partner and wife. Bless Grace and Jim as we enter into that sacred realm. Amen.

Devotional One Hundred Thirty-Five:

"Life Calculator"

Are you dying to know when you'll die? Probably not! But there is one person I know, among many others, who has researched qualities of life that enhance longevity. Beyond modern gerontologists, Jesus's sobering parable about Dives, recorded in Luke 16, is the best place to start. Lazarus was tormented by hunger, and Dives was feasting on his wealth and was too preoccupied with his selfish life to be of help. Dives, who presumably had every choice available to him and the power to shape his lifestyle any way he wanted, is sent to suffer the torments of hell.

In a sense, the problem with any narcissistic culture like ours is you don't see people when you are totally focused on yourself. We don't see the blind, the lame, the ill, the suffering, the dirty, the imprisoned, the child, the poor. They're outside our field of vision.

There is no indication that Dives mistreated or abused poor Lazarus, only that he lived his life in such a way Lazarus, along with all the other afflicted hungry people at the gates of the rich, were rendered invisible. Only after he died and felt the consequences of his lifestyle, one of ignoring the prophet's summons to care for the poor and the hungry and Moses's call to love God and neighbor, did he want to make a change in his living. Then it was too late. Father Abraham reminds Dives that, even though he will not get a chance to warn them personally, his five living brothers still have time to heed the call of Moses and the prophets. So do we.

P.S.: It is obvious that intellectually, we understand the stewardship of life. As I mentioned in the above "sermon," modern-day gerontologists have researched qualities of life, given other uncontrollable factors that enhance longevity. Dr. David Demo is a well-known gerontologist in Boca Raton, Florida. He developed a death calculator. It received support from the United States Administration on Aging. His calculator is actually a simple quiz that includes, as I remember, about twenty-two questions like, "Do you have an annual physical exam?" If so, add three years to your score. If not, subtract three years. "Do you volunteer on a personal conviction basis?" If so, add two years to your score. If not, subtract one year. "Are you able to laugh at and learn from your mistakes?" If not, subtract three years. "Do you smoke a pack of cigarettes daily?" If so, subtract four years. "Do you own a pet?" Add two years for an interactive pet. If you are left-handed, subtract one. "Are you a religious person, and do you practice your faith?" If so, add two years. Most of the lifestyle patterns he identified are obvious, both those to be avoided and those to be adopted.

On his website, he wrote, "Long life isn't just a result of smart genes and dumb luck. Most of the time, it's due to moderate eating, sleeping, diet, exercise, work, and leisure. In fact, 80 percent of the factors that control how long you live are related to your lifestyle, not your genes." I tell myself and my students that Dr.

Demo's quiz may predict with some accuracy the qualities that enhance longevity. But, it is not really the point of his death calculator. The point is to live in the healthiest way possible before you're dead and not like Dives, with no choices at all. From most indications, you and I are choosing to do the things that make for a long life. I want it, not just because we want as much time together as possible but also so that God can use our lives to help others know the differences between quantity and quality of life. Surely, we must pay attention to the lives of others but also to our own. That was the motivation that led Henry David Thoreau in 1854 to the radical decision to live alone for a time. He did not want to let life pass him by—he wanted to live it with full attention. I love what he writes in *Walden*: "I went to the woods deliberately to confront only the essential facts of life and see if I could not learn what it had to teach, and not, when I came to die, discover I had not lived." We need to stay focused on living, not reasons why living is difficult, and therefore withdraw. But by doing all the right things with diet, exercise, moderation, etc., we can expect God to honor good decisions about life and therefore bless us with many good years. I do hope so!

Hymn: "Christ be near at either hand, / Christ behind, before me stand; / Christ with me where-e're I go, / Christ around, above, below. / Christ be in my heart and mind, / Christ within my soul enshrined; / Christ control my wayward heart; / Christ abide and ne'er depart. / Christ my life and only way, / Christ my lantern night and day; / Christ be my unchanging friend, / guide and shepherd to the end" (Traditional Irish Text, the Lorica of St. Patrick,

"Christ Be Near at Either Hand").

Meditation: Dear Father of time and eternity, we are aware that physical life is but a vapor, here today and gone tomorrow. Help us to live eternally by trusting in Your salvation and being good stewards of the physical life given as stewardship for worshiping Your hand of blessing. Amen.

Devotional One Hundred Thirty-Six:

Support in the Household of Faith

In writing to the Galatians, Paul says, "As we have therefore opportunity, let us do good to all men, especially to them who are of the household of faith" (Galatians 6:10, KJV). This verse, like verse 2 of the chapter, is an encouragement to believers to love others as Christ did: "Carry each other's burden and in this way you will fulfill the law of Christ" (Galatian 6:2 NIV).

Paul challenges us to be constructively involved in working that which is helpful, good, and encouraging to others, especially those who face difficulties. This is compassion in action! We show our love for others by taking action and helping them bear their load or burdens.

I was asked on one occasion, "Why does God allow difficult people in my life?" I could not answer immediately but then said, "What other kinds are there?" No one is exempt from difficulties. But the great people in life are ordinary people with extraordinary amounts of determination not to be sidetracked by difficulty.

P.S.: I don't need to tell you what prompted this "sermon." I truly regret some of our friends are not happy. After we talked, it hit me pretty forcefully. Should God get rid of all the people having difficulties or who were difficult people—if he were to remove everybody with quirks, flaws, ugliness, and sin—we would get awfully lonely. We typically wish God would give us a life without difficult people in it. But how many characters in Holy Scripture had to face difficulty or had difficult people to deal with? Moses had Pharaoh, Elijah had Jezebel, and Esther had Haman. Jacob had Laban. David had Saul, and John the Baptist had Herod. Even Jesus had Judas. If God loves you and wants to shape you, He will send some difficult people your way. But I realize I must take heart because I am the difficult person He is sending to shape somebody else. If I could only learn to have rivers of living water still flowing through me in these relationships, I might become unstoppable as Christ's helper. As we pray for our dear friends, may we find ways to help them rise above the seemingly unacceptable they face and learn to love and laugh again. I thought of the verse from "Higher Ground" we sang in our youth.

"My heart has no desire to stay / where doubts arise and fears dismay. / Tho' some may dwell where these abound, / my prayer, my aim, is higher ground." Pray that as a helper and friend, I won't let the problems of others get any bigger than my desire to help and serve. In the meantime, thanks for letting me share this burden with you.

Hymn: "I'm pressing on the upward way, / new heights I'm gaining every day; / still praying as I onward bound, / 'Lord plant my feet on higher ground.' / Lord, lift me up and let me stand, / by faith, on heaven's table land. / A higher plane than I have found; / Lord, plant my feet on higher ground" (Johnson Oatman, "Higher Ground").

Meditation: Dear God, we pray the prayer written by William Law, who wrote, "There is nothing that makes us love a man so much as praying for him. By considering yourself as an advocate with God for your neighbors, you would never find it hard to be at peace with them yourself." Help us so pray. Amen.

Devotional One Hundred Thirty-Seven:

Salute to a Star Employee

It is always a good thing when a faithful and competent employee is recognized. Paul, in his brief letter to Titus 2:9–10 (NIV), urges, "Teach slaves to be subject to their masters in everything, to try to please them, not to talk back to them, and not to steal from them, but to show they can be fully trusted, so that in every way they will make the teaching about God our Savior attractive." Earlier, he includes attributes worthy of any person, master or workman. He encourages training in love, being a good example, honoring the word, exercising discipline, being careful with the tongue, and finally, godliness on the job.

In these two verses, Paul states five things in response to the question, "What does godliness look like for an employee or a servant?" First, there must be a submissive spirit. Next, the person should be well-pleasing or sincere, like "Joseph found favor in his eyes and became his attendant. Potiphar put him in charge of his household and he entrusted to his care everything he owned" (Genesis 39:6, NIV). Also, he or she is admonished to be supportive, not argumentative. Again, Paul admonishes the person not to pilfer or be dishonest and not to steal from the master. Finally, he says a good employee will show good faith or loyalty so that he or she is trustworthy. The ultimate purpose behind Paul's instructions to bondslaves (employees) is seen in the phrase, "that they may adorn the Doctrine of God our Saviour in all things" (Titus 2:10, KJV).

P.S.: I do wish I could have been with you today when you received a well-deserved recognition of ten years of service with the Mid-South Baptist Association. First of all, I know how important this job opportunity was for you ten years ago. But I also know you have poured your life and soul into your work. Much of your identity is wrapped up in the joyful rewards that come from faithfully serving in God's work through the churches. Having served with you for thirteen years, I know how you have demonstrated Christian professionalism in your relationship with pastors and church leaders. You have been, as I have known you to be, prudent, prompt, creative, effective, and very loyal to the mission of the association. You have been blessed to have competent leaders like Mike Day and now Mitch Martin.

As a former "boss" and now husband-to-be, let me tell you how very proud I am of you, of your life and loyalty to God's work. As Paul states in his letter to young Titus, "You have adorned and beautified the teachings of the Word and lifted up the doctrine of God our Savior in every respect" (Titus 2:10, KJV). In these last months, busy though you will be, take time to reap the rewards of faithful service. Delight in the commendations of those who surround you, love you, and care for you. Receive with gratitude all the fruits of your transforming grace, like obedience to the task, cheerfulness, willingness, and integrity. These and many other gifts and talents represent your godliness in relationships. And the joy for me, in keeping with God's will for our lives, I will be immeasurably blessed to have you as a partner in life. How good God is to bring us together and give us the opportunity to love and serve each other but also all those in the "household of faith."

Hymn: "Let all things now living a song of thanksgiving / To God the Creator triumphantly raise, / Who fashioned and made us, protected and stayed us, / Who guideth us on to the end of our days. / His banners are o'er us, His light goes before us, / a pillar of fire shining forth in the night, / 'Til shadows have vanished and darkness is banished, / As forward we travel from light into light. / His law He enforces, the stars in their courses, / The sun in orbit, obediently shine. / The hills and the mountains, the rivers and fountains, / The deeps of the ocean proclaim Him Divine. / We too, should be voicing our love and rejoicing / With glad adoration a song let us raise. / 'Til all things now living unite in thanksgiving / To God in the highest, hosanna and praise!" (John S. B. Monsell, "Sing to the Lord of Harvest").

Meditation: Dear God, You have given to mankind the privilege of work. It is a special gift. Sometimes, we are tempted to think of work as toil, but toil is the result of work without purpose or meaning. Help us find meaning in our work and see it as an opportunity to serve others, just as Jesus set for us the best example of servanthood. Help us be like Him. Amen.

Devotional One Hundred Thirty-Eight:

A Poem Not a Sermon

In the classic homiletic tradition, a poem should follow a sermon. Last night, my heartstrings were expressing praise and gratitude for your queenly gifts. Obviously, I am very proud of your accomplishments in life, not just the ten years of outstanding service with the Mid-South Baptist Association. But, beyond that, there is thanksgiving in my heart for your many years of service in Baptist life. Beyond all the merits of servant leadership that characterize your work, there is deep gratitude in my heart for you. Qualities of character, like altruistic, believable, compassionate, dependable, efficient, faithful, gracious, humble, intelligent, joyous, kind, loving, motivated, nice, officious, personable, qualified, responsible, sure, trustworthy, unusual, vivacious, Williams (to-be), youthful, and zestful. I could go back through the alphabet several times, listing qualities of character that reflect your queenly traits. So, while we are still "celebrating" your happy day on Monday and receiving thanks for a job well done, let me come back to a poem I could have included in last night's "50-Second Sermon." Better than I could do, Justin Huntly McCarthy summarizes my feelings of gratitude for you in the following verses.

If I Were King

If I were king ah love, if I were king!

What tributary nations would I bring

To stop before your scepter and to swear

Allegiance to your lips and eyes and hair.

Beneath your feet what treasure I would fling:

The stars should be your pearls upon a string,

The world a ruby for your finger ring,

And you should have the sun and moon to wear,

If I were king.

Let these wild dreams and wilder words take wing,

Deep in the woods I hear a shepherd sing

A simple ballad to a sylvan air,

Of love that ever finds your face more fair,

If I could not give you any godlier thing,

If I were king.

—Justin Huntly McCarthy

You may find all of this a bit "heavy," but I want to be affirming of your qualities of life and express gratitude for the way you bring blessing to me. Of course, there is the spark of godlikeness in the human spirit, and we can ignore or squelch such image and regretfully judge on the basis of external appearance or circumstances. Too often, we judge people on their cultural image, not their ultimate worth. Part of our ministry as believers is to summon up in people the strong image of God within them. And, especially for those of family we love, it is incumbent on us to affirm the image of godlikeness that is reflected in their lives. Sometimes, we may be more compassionate with others than with our very own family. Many ministers deal with the issues and problems of others, and sometimes spouses and children get leftovers. Obviously, ministry begins at home. Let me once more tell you how very proud I am of you, your life, and your commitment to join me in starting anew.

Meditation: Dear Loving Father, Your creation of mankind began within the context of family. Help each of us do all we can to make our own family strong and healthy. It happens when the godly character is demonstrated by parental influence. So help us grow in Your knowledge, forgiveness, and grace. Amen.

Devotional One Hundred Thirty-Nine:

Lessons for Dad and Lad

Last night, my son and I had an enjoyable evening together, discussing his work and the changes taking place in my life. He has recently been through the challenges and decisions related to several different job offers. Of course, he knows there are many changes coming to my life thanks to God's gift of new love. My loving son, always seeking to be an encourager, said, "Dad, you amaze me with your energy for life. What is the secret?"

In a moment of reflection, abundant life requires you to "keep on plowing." In Matthew 13:44, Jesus describes what life is like for kingdom participants. He says, "The Kingdom of heaven is like treasure hidden in a field when a man found it, he hid it again, and then in his joy went out and sold all he had and bought that field" (Matthew 13:44, KJV). There may be fields to plow, but what a treasure when you can own the field.

The lesson for Dad and lad is "plowing may give you blisters, but keep on plowing." Jesus calls it as it is. He says in words like these, "If you plow along with Me, you will feel the blade turn down, and at times, in disgust, you may want to stop plowing. You might even feel tempted to curse your luck, but after catching your breath, plan to dig out the large rock that's stopping the plow. But it will not be a rock. It will be a treasure so vast you will go home and sell everything you have to buy the fields and own the treasure." So, son, I have learned in life if you keep on plowing, there are "surprises" and treasures beyond compare.

P.S.: Last night's conversation with Jeff kind of "circled the wagons." But it was good. You can tell by my visit in last night's phone conversation it gave us the opportunity to explore the realities of change before us. Then, in reflecting on the meaning of this lesson for Dad and lad, I have thought about the two of us and the challenges it represents. So, it caused me to think, *Have you ever seen anything in life you wanted so badly you would sell everything you had to own it? Something that nothing else you have ever owned could stand in the way of purchasing?* The truth is for those really seeking to live in God's kingdom, life should be lived with excitement and risk. It is in the kingdom and its possibilities we have a true adventure. Jesus is saying to His followers, "If you start this plowing, don't try to do it alone. If you will let Me share your plowing, I'll put treasures in front of your blade." Neither of us is aware of what is out there in the future. We know from already experiencing love for each other that it is multiplying, and our common interests and values are the foundation for a happy, productive marriage. Last night's conversation with Jeff reinforced my firm belief that you and I need to keep on plowing.

Hymn: "Savior, Thy dying love / Thou gavest me, Nor should I aught withhold, / Dear Lord, from Thee: / In love my soul would bow, / My heart fulfill its vow, / Some of-f'ring bring Thee now, / Something for Thee. / At the blest mercy seat, / Pleading for me,

/ My feeble faith looks up, / Jesus to Thee: / Help me the cross to bear, / Thy wondrous love declare, / Some song to raise, or pray'r, / Something for Thee. / Give me a faithful heart, / Likeness to Thee, / That each departing day / Henceforth may see some work of love begun, / Some deed of kindness done. / Some wand'rer sought and won. / Something for Thee" (Sylvanus D. Phelps, "Something for Thee").

Meditation: Dear Father, You have created us to be servants of all. You long for captives set free, sick to be healed, hungry to receive food, homeless needing family, burdens of mankind lifted. Deepen our compassion for all in need. Remind us daily there is much work to be done. May Your mercy and grace flow through us as we keep our hands on the plow. Amen.

Devotional One Hundred Forty:

But Lord, We Could Die Someday

In John 11:1–26, the writer gives the account of Jesus raising Lazarus from the dead. Jesus's miracle was two-fold. He wanted His followers to understand physical death is real, but for believers, His miracle gave Him the moment in eternal time to state one of His greatest eternal truths, "I am the resurrection and the life. He who believes in me will live, even though he dies; and whoever lives and believes in me will never die" (John 11:25, NIV).

Certainly, physical death, real as it is, changes my relationship with others and the world. But according to the Lazarus story and the rest of the New Testament, death is simply another one of God's territories, a point through which I move into something else. As a believer, I will still know life. I still communicate, teach, and learn. Death does not end me. And, even though in my finiteness, the physical fact of death may continue to be frightening, any large change is frightening. The reality is death does not stop growth or relationships any more than Lazarus's death or Jesus's death did. Lazarus did, of course, eventually die (*but he never ended.*) That is the ultimate promise of God's great revelation in Christ given to believers. Every experience in physical life can be deposited in the empty tomb of Christ's triumphant resurrection. His resurrection will be ours, also.

Anyone who believes in Jesus can know time is not relentlessly stalking every life step. Sure, I will die and will cease existing in this earthly dimension. But His promise is new dreams, new visions, and new rooms open before me. All I have built and done here that is worthy will not be wasted.

P.S.: Grace, a part of tonight's phone visit was my earnest plea to have at least twenty more years for us to blend our lives. That is a strong hope, and of course, calendar time is not in our hands. There is much we can do to enhance and redeem time. So, in light of our yearning to really know and experience each other for as long as possible, it might be well to underscore the real reason for our faith. Having already experienced the death of spouses, we know there is a limit to physical relationships. But it is helpful to me as I think of this new relationship with you to look at Jesus's concept of time. There was no narrow limit to His future and, therefore, none to His present. He just lived day after day in the light of His endless future. Time was not His enemy; it was His friend, just as it can be for us, however long that may be.

Moving forward, our understanding of death affects our ability to live daily with a sense of freedom. What I believe He wants is to set us free from the tyranny of believing life and the events of the world have the greatest power. They don't. Even the heartbeat can stop, and still, we continue in His hands, living and growing, conscious of His work going on in us. So, death does not place a limit upon us. We could think that in your eighties, life is about over. Jesus simply extends our vision to see death as powerless to affect our present potential or His plan for our today and tomorrow. I do agree that at eighty, it makes sense to reassess our lives. It is true most of the time, we do need to change, risk, and dare, but not because the clock is ticking away. Rather, because of our sense of belonging to each other and to *Him*, we discover how to avoid wasting time and learn how to be the best stewards of time and opportunity. It is interesting to me that Jesus didn't go around asking people if they believed in death. He went around asking them if they knew anything about resurrection. It is a fact of life that only as I die to something, to some security, to some plan, will resurrection and newness take place. To be alive with each other in marriage, we experience "deaths" that already have and will take place, but the result will be a new life with each other. Truly, it is in that context we can celebrate what we learned with Jo and LeRoy and build strength upon strength, sharing our lives together.

Hymn: "When I can read my title clear to mansions in the skies, / I'll bid farewell to every fear, and wipe my weeping eyes. / Should earth against my soul engage and fiery darts be hurled, / then I can smile at Satan's rage, and face a frowning world. / Let cares, like a wild deluge come, and storms of sorrow fall! / May I but safely reach my home, my God, my heaven, my all" (Isaac Watts, "When I Can Read My Title Clear").

Meditation: Eternal Father, You have sounded the transformation trumpet by preparing an eternal home for believers. May we learn to die to self and receive Your eternal life through belief in the resurrection life of the Lord Christ. We rejoice in His promise He prepared a place for us where life has no end. In His resurrected power, we pray, amen.

Devotional One Hundred Forty-One:

"Opening Up," Giving and Receiving Love

According to the Holy Scripture, also borne out by psychological research, is love at the very center of life. Some may call it the "need for meaning." In a larger scriptural sense, God's plan of redemption flows from His great and creative love for each person. That is what Bethlehem is all about. His overarching love is best exemplified in the "incarnation" when God, through His Son, "emptied Himself," took on the form of a servant, lived a sinless life, and ultimately gave His life a ransom for man's sins.

So, the first step in defining love lies in accepting the premise the love we need is larger than romantic love. Love that satisfies is much more than emotion or adrenalin. It is the choice of a style of living, a willingness to be "open" to love in all areas of life. Loving is "giving and receiving" raised to the level of intentionality. Giving love is easier than receiving love. Why is it that most find it difficult to receive and accept love? It is difficult because if we receive help, we lose control. To receive love admits we are needy, and for most of us, it is the ultimate hurdle.

"Opening up" is not an event that happens only once but a day-by-day process. One of the central blocks to receiving love is the fear of showing weakness and need. But we can't receive until we admit we need love. When we do, we become a channel through which love can flow. One of the chief paradoxes of life is "Only as I lose life can I find it; only as I lay it down will I be able to pick it up. Only as I empty myself will I ever be filled."

P.S.: We have been on this theme in recent conversations, including tonight. "Incarnation" means wherever I am, I choose to be a person for others. So, God, in His wisdom, placed me in a world where I have contacts, like my DBU students, and a world of friends. If I choose to allow "incarnation" to work through me, then His love fills my life as it flows through. No other form of love will do that. To love is to live out God's love. It means carrying the pain of others and acting on their behalf. It means others will know I am present and available, seeking to be tangible evidence of God's love. It means I am open, vulnerable, and ready to receive help from any source. Real love is not an illusion. I need not be cynical about love fulfilling my life. We have already discovered, in this first year of our reconnection, that love is not an illusion. But it can only be fulfilling if I allow it to take the shape it took in Bethlehem. The incarnate life was God's plan for redeeming love. If I allow Him to live through me, channeling His love into His world, I am portraying what happened in Bethlehem. So, even now, let us walk the road to Bethlehem.

Hymn: "Comfort, comfort, ye my people, / speak ye peace, thus saith our God, / comfort those who sit in darkness, / mourning 'neath their sorrows' load. / Speak ye to Jerusalem of the peace that waits for them; / tell her that her sins I cover, / and her warfare now is over. / Hark, the voice of one that crieth in the desert far and near, / bidding all to true repentance since the kingdom now is here. / O that warning cry obey! / Now prepare for God a way; / let the valleys rise to meet Him and the hills bow down to greet Him. / Make ye straight what long was crooked, make the rougher places plain; / let your hearts be true and humble as befits His holy reign. / For the glory of the Lord now o'er earth is shed abroad; / and all flesh shall see the token that His word is never broken" (Johannes Olearius, "Comfort, Comfort Ye My People").

Meditation: Dear Father, You sent Your Son, born in Bethlehem, as Savior for all mankind. His sinless life, sacrificial death, and bodily resurrection validate the reality of incarnational love. May we receive His eternal love and let it be lived in us, day by day. Amen.

Devotional One Hundred Forty-Two:

Surrounded by Change

One may paraphrase Isaiah 43:18–19 when the prophet says of God's guidance, "Behold, I will do a new thing; now it shall spring forth; shall ye not know it?" (Isaiah 43:17a, KJV). Change is hard. It is a part of human nature to resist anything that forces us out of our comfort zone. The prophet reminds us sometimes God does a "new thing." He did so often with the Old Testament patriarchs. In a recent Sunday school lesson, the focus was on Abraham and Sarah. Think of it. The first recorded change in their lives took place when Abraham was seventy-five years old. For some, the more "mature in years we are," the harder it is to embrace change. Not so for Abraham and Sarah.

During more than sixty-five years of vocational Christian work for me and forty-seven years of service for you, there have been many changes in our ministry. Each change involved a different set of circumstances, but every time, it was difficult to say goodbye. One of the changes for me was influenced by the forced resignation of my boss, but as it turned out, it brought rewarding and challenging leadership opportunities I would not have missed for the world. Joyfully, it brought us together in service and ministry at the Brotherhood Commission, SBC. To put it bluntly, I might not ever have met you. During each transition I have made, I have had increasing reasons to appreciate the lives of Abraham and Sarah. When they left the Ur as God commanded, He did not reveal their destination. They left in obedience, following God to an unknown place and uncertain future. Two phrases from Deuteronomy 31 can be a comfort as we face an uncertain future: "For the Lord himself goes before you; he will never leave you or forsake you" (Deuteronomy 31:6a, NIV). Because our Lord God is eternal and not bound by time, He not only walks beside us, but He also goes before us to prepare the way. Also, in Isaiah 52:12 (NIV), the prophet adds untold security for us when he writes, "For the Lord will go before you, and the God of Israel will be your rear guard." The obedience of faith brings change, but we don't have to handle these changes alone.

P.S.: This "sermon" is a bit longer than 50 seconds. In light of the panoply of emotions we shared tonight on the subject of "oneness," it made me aware of how the obedience of faith brings unspeakable reward and blessing. As we enter into a second marriage covenant, it brings major change. Let's remember the Lord is our "rear guard." As our kids would say, "He has our back." God surrounds His children. Therefore, we can lift our hands and future in faithful obedience to God's call. There will be both tough and tender moments on the journey, but I, for one, am confident He will go with us, ahead of us, and be our "rear guard." Let us promise to help each other handle the adjustments that change requires.

Given our age, it may be both easier and harder. I remember

reading in *Reader's Digest* it may have been Pearl S. Buck who said, "You can judge your age by the amount of pain you feel when you come in contact with a new idea." I promise to be your helper while you adjust to your current work role. And I am counting on you to help me handle the role adjustments of marriage. Having experienced so much of the very best of each other's gifts, we can grow from "strength to strength," knowing we do not walk alone, but we walk with Him.

Hymn: "We walk by faith and not by sight, / No gracious words we hear / from Him who spoke as none e'er spoke / but we believe Him near. / We may not touch His hands and side, / nor follow where He trod; / but in His promise we rejoice, / and cry, "My Lord and God!" / And when our life of faith is done, / in realms of clearer light / we may behold You as You are, / with full and endless sight" (Henry Alford, "We Walk by Faith").

Meditation: Great Sustaining God of the Universe, we thank You for faithful servants like Abraham, who provided worthy examples of handling change. May we have courage and strength for the living of our day and a future You may give us. Amen.

Devotional One Hundred Forty-Three:

The Love of Family

It did my heart a world of good to hear the report of your bridal luncheon with your family. Families are like Christmas trees—the closer the ornaments are to the star, the closer they are to each other. The closer we are to each other as marriage partners, the closer family members will be to us. Jesus said, "A new command I give you: love one another, as I have loved you, so you must love one another. By this all men will know that you are my disciples, if you love one another" (John 13:34, NIV). I know you join with me in letting our new home be a proving ground, not only for our faith but also a laboratory of growing love for each other and for our new blended family. A good formula we can adopt is summarized in a rephrasing of the "Fruits of the Spirit" (Galatians 5:22–26):

- Joy is love's consciousness.
- Peace is love's confidence.
- Patience is love's habit.
- Kindness is love's vitality.
- Goodness is love's activity.
- Faithfulness is love's quantity.
- Meekness is love's tone.
- Temperance is love's victory.

May these eternal truths be the theme of our lives and the environment in our home and with our extended family.

P.S.: Tell Cindy not only did her thoughtful wish for you prompt tears for you but also for me and, I'm sure, for others. I was overwhelmed when you read to me her prepared statement. It was a vivid reminder I am receiving a life partner who has spent her whole life serving others and certainly her family. I am so happy you heard such commendation from your beloved daughter, but also that the rest of your assembled family members could hear and affirm such truth. We will not be or could be "perfect in love," but it can be the goal of our marriage. I am confident we will grow in our love for each other, and when God is in control of our lives, love will flow in unlimited supply. I love you more each day.

Hymn: "Glorious things of thee are spoken, / Zion, city of our God; / He, whose word cannot be broken, / Formed thee for His own abode: / On the Rock of Ages founded, / What can shake thy sure repose? / With salvation's walls surrounded, / Thou may smile at all they foes. / See, the streams of living waters, / Springing from eternal love, / Well supply thy sons and daughters, / And all fear of want remove: / Who can faint, while such a river / Ever does their thirst assuage? / Grace which, like the Lord, the giver, / Never fails from age to age. / Round each habitation hovering, / See the cloud and fire appear / For a glory and a covering, / Showing that the Lord is near! / Glorious things of thee are spoken, / Zion, city of our God; / He whose word cannot be broken, / Formed thee for His own abode" (John Newton, "Glorious Things of Thee Are Spoken").

Meditation: Dear Father, thank You for children who reflect parental values and demonstrate wisdom and grace in response to parental change. Even though it is difficult for children from first marriages to adjust to new parental relationships, help both children and parents "live out the fruits of the Spirit" as enshrined in Holy Scripture. Amen.

Devotional One Hundred Forty-Four:

Reflections on Dreams

Here goes. I will try to repeat last night's late, late sermon based on Paul's reference to the fruits of the Spirit found in Galatians 5:22–26. I took a nap in my favorite chair, and when I awoke, I remembered I had missed sending a "sermon." During my nap, I dreamed we were together at a concert of orchestra and choir. But the choir never appeared. But we enjoyed sitting and having a delightful conversation. The night before, I also dreamed about us, so it was two in a row. There is a very familiar song that reminds me you are always on my mind. Wide awake, I began to think about our dreams, not the subconscious ones during sleep, which may be strange, but the real ones that set the path for the future.

In reflection, my mind went back to a lecture given by my philosophy professor at King's College London. He said, "God knew what He was doing when He established a belief system and gave man the powers of rational choice and affection." He stressed, "If you strip away all mystery, leave all truth naked and mathematically exposed, then something as real as the sweet and the romantic will be removed, as well as scientific endeavor emerging from a studied hypothesis." He emphasized, and I have quoted him in my own lectures and manuscripts, "It is our ability to dream that makes us unique." We have been created in the image of God. Therefore, we have powers of rational thought and affection not known by other animals. So, faith in every dimension of life is discovering the unknown. There will always be new things unknown to the explorer. It is faith or belief in the unknown that confronts those frontiers with a thrilling leap. Then, life becomes vibrant with new discoveries.

Faith is dreaming God's dream since He is the source of all knowledge and truth. Thank God we have the ability to dream and plan. Success is not an accident. It comes from a life focused on where it is going and how it plans to get there. One may dream dreams that never come true. But enough of them do, thank God, to make you want to dream on. I will never forget my professor saying, "Don't let the past drag you down; you can change it, and don't let the future frighten you; you can control it by visions, dreams, and hopes that are fulfilled through belief and faith." So, moving forward, one must learn from the past, plan for the future, and then live life to the fullest in the present.

P.S.: Grace, I am sure God has brought us together. How else do you explain the unbelievable discovery of each other and the powerful dynamic of oneness we have experienced? Human love can never be perfect, for it belongs to the divine. But it is close enough for me. I am absolutely thrilled our hopes and dreams have brought us to the prelude of marriage. It is only natural we are preoccupied with the anticipation of a ceremony, receptions, honeymoon, and the first walk as married partners. But in it all, it is time to order our lives through new dreams and plans that help guarantee our future lives. God does have a plan for us. That is obvious. Let us go forward with dreams and visions, some seemingly impossible, seeking God's will. That will guarantee a secure future. It will not be an accident. Rather, it will be the result of our collective mind seeking what is best within the informed will of God.

Hymn: "Jesus, Thou joy of loving hearts, / Thou fount of life, Thou light of all, / from the best bliss that each imparts, / we turn unfilled to hear Thy call. / Thy truth unchanged hath ever stood; / Thou savest those who on Thee call; / to them who seek Thee, / Thou art good, to them who find Thee, all in all. / O Jesus, ever with us stay, / make all our moments calm and bright; / chase the dark night of sin away, / shed o'er the world Thy holy light" (Latin Hymn, Translator Ray Palmer, "Jesus, Thou Joy of Loving Hearts").

Meditation: Dear God, the Creator of all things, in all the seasons of life, You give a song. Thanks for the new melodies of praise You have granted to us. May it be so now and always. Amen.

Devotional One Hundred Forty-Five:

The Merciful Are Shown Mercy

In the remarkable Sermon on the Mount, Jesus makes it very plain: "Blessed are the merciful, for they will be shown mercy" (Matthew 5:7, NIV). They are blessed because they point to a greater goodness found in the character of God. When we forgive others, we can't help but comprehend how God has forgiven us. In forgiving others, we experience His matchless grace and begin to feel what He feels.

To strengthen His point, Jesus tells the story of a king who decided to close his accounts for those who worked for him. After notifying his debtors it was time to pay, one person owed a huge amount. It was a debt so large it could never be repaid. The king was compassionate and, on hearing the reason for the person's situation, forgave the debt. But as the man was leaving the palace grounds, he met a man who owed him a small debt, grabbed the debtor, choked him, and demanded repayment immediately. In spite of a plea for mercy, none was given. As the story goes, the one just forgiven by the king had his debtor thrown in jail. When the word got to the king, he was furious, and as Jesus says, "In anger his master turned him over to the jailers to be tortured, until he should pay back all he owed" (Matthew 18:34, NIV).

Consider this question. Could a person be set free and then imprison another for the same neglect? Do you want to be a conduit of God's grace? Or have the reputation as a bottleneck? You don't have to be a genius to figure that one out! Jesus says, "This is how my heavenly Father will treat each of you unless you forgive your brother from your heart" (John 18:35, NIV).

P.S.: Grace, forgiveness is necessary for healthy living. Anger and resentment are like cocaine for an addict. The desire when overdosed kills. Anger can do the same for the angry. Physical illness often is the result of anger, high blood pressure, elevated cholesterol, and damage to the arterial system. It robs one of good emotional health, leading to depression. It, likewise, is spiritually damaging, shriveling the soul. God's mercy and grace is the one thing that sets people free. We are at a time in life when every day is even more of a special blessing. It is too late for either of us to "stir up a storm of anger." I do not ever remember a time when I saw anger displayed by you. It may have happened away from my presence, but if it did, you handled it discretely. I may have said this in other ways, but one of the most important "surprises by grace" has been your merciful and forgiving spirit. I want the same for myself and for us.

Hymn: "O Love that wilt not let me go, / I rest my weary soul I Thee; / I give Thee back the life I owe, / That in Thine ocean depths its flow / May riches, fuller be. / O Light that fol-l'west all my way, / I yield my flick'ring torch to Thee; / My heart restores its borrowed ray, / That in Thy sunshine's glow its day May brighter, fairer be. / O Joy that sleekest me thro' pain, / I cannot close my heart to Thee; / I trace the rainbow thro' the rain, / And feel the promise is not vain That morn shall tearless be. / O Cross that liftest up my head, / I dare not ask to hide from Thee; / I lay in dust life's glory dead, / And from the ground there blossoms red, / Life that shall endless be" (Cecil Frances Alexander, "O Love That Wilt Not Let Me Go").

Meditation: Dear Father of all mankind, we have learned through life's experiences what it means to receive forgiveness. First, it was receiving Your salvation. Then, through challenging life decisions, we learned it is better to forgive than regret. How closeness and trust increase when actions are loving and just. May we grow in our capacity to love as You love, even in times when tough love is necessary. May forgiveness abound as the ground and source for happy living. Amen.

Devotional One Hundred Forty-Six:

Thacker's Gap Saint

This sermon is a recasting of one by Roger Carstensen. Thacker's Gap is a place near Herod in Pope County, Illinois, where my maternal grandparents lived. According to most, Hank, a longtime villager, was by consensus the nearest to a saint in Thacker's Gap. He was the terror of sinners and the scourge of the lukewarm. He'd had a vision. They say an angel with a golden crown and silver feathers showed up as clear as the movies over Hank's head during a camp meeting and brushed a cherub's smile across his face. He went to work on the less fortunate, "Where is your smile? Where is your angel?" If you couldn't ante up a molted silver feather or flash a cherub's smile, He would tell you where you should go…smiling!

In 1 Corinthians 12, we read the apostle Paul had vision trouble. His trip to the third heaven was too bright to live with. So God gave him a "thorn in the flesh" to keep him real. I guess it takes a thorn to keep somebody close to God enrolled in the human race. Why did not Hank have one? Maybe Thacker's Gap needed a pain, and Hank was it.

P.S.: Ever know somebody who seemed called of God to be a pain? Typically, they have a "kickative" mentality and enjoy being fault-finders rather than fact-finders. If I wanted to know something about a land of beauty and poetry with verdant valleys and cascading streams, I would not send a vulture out to provide a portrait of the terrain. In all probability, he would come back to report, "I found a dead carcass beneath a tree."

We see what we want to see. Persons who have a low self-image and little appreciation for their own talent typically find fault with someone else. It is compensation for their personal neglect. They try to build themselves up by tearing somebody else down. After all, we do have the power of choice and self-determination. Most of all, as Jesus did, choose to forgive rather than curse.

As we join our lives together, I never want to be a fault-finder. But rather seek always to let God be the judge of other people's behavior. Most of all, I want to be a peacemaker inside our own home, family, the church, our society, and a world that needs peace. Though this sermon was shared with my students many years ago, it is a current lesson for me, as the ticking of today's clock. I need to practice what I preach, so help me.

Hymn: "Sing praise to God who reigns above, / the God of all creation, the God of power, / the God of love, the God of our salvation; / with healing balm my soul He fills, and every faithless murmur stills: / to God all praise and glory. / What God's almighty power has made in mercy He is keeping; / by morning glow or evening shade His eye is never sleeping; / within the kingdom of His might, lo! / All is just and all is right: to God all praise and glory. / The Lord is never far away, / but through all grief distressing, / an ever present help and stay, / our peace and joy and blessing; / as with a mother's tender hand He leads His own, His chosen band: / to God all praise and glory. / Thus all my toil-some way along I sing aloud His praises, / that all may hear the grateful song my voice unwearied raises; / be joyful in the Lord, my heart! / Both soul and body bear your part: / to God all praise and glory" (Johann Jakob Schutz, "Sing Praise to God Who Reigns Above").

Meditation: Dear God of heaven and nature, we acknowledge the diversity of Your created order. Your people are diverse in culture, nation, and race. Each person is unique. By your Spirit, unify our desires to see each created being as a reflection of Your love, hope, joy, and peace. Amen.

Devotional One Hundred Forty-Seven:

The Thacker's Gap Invalid

(Another Thacker's Gap sermon reworked from one by Roger Carstensen.)

Uncle John was the worst patient the Pope County, Illinois, hospital ever had. He swore at the nurses, threw his breakfast tray across the room, and bit his thermometer in half. Why? Simple. He had never been sick a day of his life. He got up at 5 a.m. singing and jumping. Worked fourteen hours and danced in the evenings. Never had an ache in his bones, a cavity in his teeth, or glasses on his nose.

Uncle John understood God Almighty had made him special. He sympathized with poor fools who got sick. So he made a fool of himself at the hospital.

Jesus said in Matthew 9:12 that we'll have no need for a physician. He reserved His ministry for the sick. Uncle John didn't know he'd been sick when he was well. He had an overdose of good luck. May God grant us that Beloved Physician who, companion of our happy days and moments, sustains us when we write the bitter pages of our health bio.

P.S.: Grace, if and when either of us or one of us is hampered by physical or mental challenges, I want you to know such circumstances will be handled by trusting the Great Physician, regardless of any limitations imposed on us. The inspiration for these thoughts was triggered by the recent deaths of Susan McKnight, a dear friend in my Hudson Oaks Neighborhood Group, and Bill Souder, a longtime friend from Hurst, Texas. The rest is from the recall of a "Thacker's Gap sermon." We are at a time in life when the loss of friends is occurring too rapidly. In the meantime, let us resolve to make every day *His* day, but ours also!

Hymn: "We cannot measure how You heal / or answer every sufferer's prayer, / yet we believe Your grace responds / where faith and doubt unite to care. / Your hands, though bloodied on the cross, / survive to hold and heal and warn, / to carry all through death to life and cradle children yet unborn. / So some have come who need your help / and some have come to make amends, / as hands which shaped and saved the world, / are present in the touch of friends. / Lord, let your Spirit meet us here to mend the body, / mind, and soul, to disentangle peace from pain, / and make Your broken people whole" (John L Bell and Graham Maule, "We Cannot Measure How You Heal").

Meditation: Dear Father and Redeemer, grant us relief from damaging fear and give us rest with Thee in the life You give us, steep though the road at times may be. Amen.

Devotional One Hundred Forty-Eight:

Heart Power Is the Result of a Pure Heart

From reading these "50-Second Sermons," you are already aware Max Lucado is one of my favorite authors. The first book of his I read was *The Applause of Heaven*. Since then, he has published nearly a hundred. Max Lucado gives credit to Calvin Miller for introducing him to his own very crafty writing style. Calvin was my colleague at Southwestern Seminary for a time. Most everyone is familiar with Calvin's bestseller, *The Singer*. This "50-Second Sermon" idea flows from Matthew 5:8, a part of Jesus's Sermon on the Mount, the framework for Max's great book. Jesus says in this verse, "Blessed are the pure in heart, for they shall see God" (Matthew 5:8, NIV). Lucado comments, "To the Hebrew mind, the heart is a freeway cloverleaf where all emotions and prejudices and wisdom converge" (p. 120).

So the question for us, now and always, is, "What is the state of our hearts?" Moving closer to the wedding ceremony, we bring many gifts to the altar. Gifts of experience from first marriages, fabulous family ties with each beloved one of them, service in God's kingdom for many years, and friends too numerous to mention. But the most important gift we can bring is the resolve to offer each other purity of heart, mind, and soul. My resolve is David's prayer from Psalm 51:10a (NIV), "Create in me a pure heart, O God." That is a permanent joy!

P.S.: We have been talking about many things, like staying in my Texas house for fall semesters at DBU, selling it and renting a Fort Worth apartment for the autumn months, making your Memphis house our primary address, and relating to new family relationships for each of us. These are all exterior things, and we both know so-called "cosmetic changes" are only skin deep. A mountain of decisions will be thrust upon us as we put our lives together. Every exterior decision is important, but the most important thing for us to remember is that He, who made us, knows how to purify us on the inside and the outside.

Hymn: "Breathe on me, Breath of God, / fill me with life anew, / that I may love what Thou dost love, / and do what Thou wouldst do. / Breathe on me, Breath of God, / until my heart is pure, / until with Thee I will Thy will, / to do and to endure" (Edwin Hatch, "Breathe on Me, Breath of God").

Meditation: Father God, in order to please You and then others, we need to purify the heart. Though our hearts are not perfect, we are one with you through faith in Your Son. So breathe on us, breath of God, till we are wholly Thine. Amen.

Devotional One Hundred Forty-Nine:

Keep On Doing Good

In his Galatian letter, St. Paul wrote, "Therefore, as we have opportunity, let us do good to all people, especially to those who belong to the family of believers" (Galatians 6:10, NIV). As we move toward the ceremony of wedding vows, let "doing good" be our resolve. A bank slogan says it best, "Great people are ordinary people with extraordinary amounts of determination."

Even when exhausted, let us not grow weary in "doing good." Vince Lombardi said, "Fatigue makes cowards of us all." And Bud Williams said, "Real champions are not always perfect in all they do but have learned those who are tough get going when the going gets tough."

How is that done? The only way to adventure in life, with all its danger, unpredictability, and high stakes, is an intimate faith relationship with God, whose ways may not be understood at the time. The great apostle not only believed it but practiced it. He kept on "doing good"! What waits for us? There is not one thing that enduring faith in God cannot achieve.

P.S.: I am aware some people question a second marriage decision, especially "for those in their eighties." What are the driving forces behind our marriage decision? We have agreed these include companionship, security, trusting friendship, and physical attraction as common denominators. But one driving motivation for me is the need for an understanding partner to help me "finish my calling." The full-time expression of my call involved teaching others in seminary and other academic institutions, leading denomination entities whose stated mission, Christian publishing, is to respond to human needs. That calling was for life, but now, in the retirement years, it is expressed in a different arena. Now, the privilege of teaching college students enrolled at Dallas Baptist University has brought untold rewards. In my doing so, I feel like I am still "doing well." The privilege of parenting an extended family will help us in "doing good." You will be a "helpmeet," and together, we will succeed in God's calling if we do not faint. I promise to help you. And with your help, we can climb new mountains. Sir Edmund Hillary failed in his first effort to climb Mt. Everest, even losing one team member in the attempt. The British Empire tried to give him a hero's welcome, but at a banquet, he told an assembled banquet audience, "Mt. Everest, you have defeated me. But I will return. So much for that! I'll defeat you because you can't get any bigger than I can." May that spirit dominate our lives as we continue fulfilling God's call.

Hymn: "I'm pressing on the upward way, / new heights I'm gaining every day; / still praying as I onward bound, / "Lord plant my feet on higher ground." / My heart has no desire to stay / where doubts arise and fears dismay; / though some may dwell were these abound, / my prayer, my aim is higher ground. / I want to scale the utmost height / and catch a gleam of glory bright; / but still I pray till heaven I've found, / "Lord, lead me on to higher ground" (Johnson Oatman, Jr., "Higher Ground").

Meditation: Faithful Father God, by Your guiding hand, help us continue being constructively involved in working in that which is helpful, good, and encouraging to others. May we welcome new mountains! Even though it may mean dealing with difficulty or feeling fatigued, by Your power, help us climb the "new mountains." Amen.

Devotional One Hundred Fifty:

Moving Toward Excellence

This year of engagement with you in Tennessee and me in Texas has been full of surprises. There are too many to count, but many are described in the one hundred and fifty "50-Second Sermons." We have learned a lot about each other.

As we eagerly await the wedding ceremony, what is an appropriate last "sermon" for us? The apostle Paul provides one answer. He was always on the move to achieve "excellence" in his service to Christ. In Philippians 3:13–14 (NIV), he says, "Brothers, I do not consider myself to have taken hold of it yet. But one thing I do: forgetting what is behind and straining toward what is ahead, I press on toward the goal to win the prize for which God has called me heavenward in Christ Jesus." The faithful apostle asserts his mission for Christ is to run to win. He understood discipline produces reward, finding the goal and hitting the mark, and extra "stretching" effort produces excellence. Notice he kept striving. In my quoted reference to last night's sermon, Vince Lombardi said, "Fatigue makes cowards of us all."

As we begin life together, we would do well to remember failure is not fatal; success is not permanent, but it is courage that counts. The runner who puts the last ounce of effort into the race feels the glorious satisfaction of having given everything to the moment. Let's resolve to be Olympians.

P.S: The byline of *Surprised by Grace* is titled *A Journey toward Unexpected Reconnection*. There is no doubt God put our lives together. We start this earthly journey confident of an eternal connection. I do not know how this came to my desk, but I have had it for a long time. It is a quote from Bobby Richardson. He was a famous New York Yankee baseball player and Christ-follower, summarizes it best. What better words to close these one hundred and fifty "sermons"? Let his words be ours as we journey together.

Your name may not appear down here in this world's hall of fame,

In fact, you may be so unknown that no one knows your name,

The Oscars here may pass you by, and neon lights of blue,

But if you love and serve the Lord, then I have news for you.

This hall of fame is only good as long as time shall be,

Keep in mind God's hall of fame is for eternity,

To have your name inscribed up there is greater yet by far,

Than all the halls of fame down here, and every man-made star.

This crowd on earth may soon forget the heroes of the past,

They cheer like mad until you fall, and that's how long you last.

But God, He never does forget, and in His hall of fame.

By just believing in His Son, inscribed, you'll find your name.

I tell you, friend, I wouldn't trade my name, however small,

That's written there beyond the stars in that celestial hall.

For any famous name on earth or glory that they share.

I'd rather be an unknown here and have my name up there.

Hymn: "O God, our help in ages past, / our hope for years to come, / our shelter from the stormy blast, / and our eternal home. / Under the shadow of Thy throne, / Thy saints have dwelt secure, / sufficient is Thine arm alone / and our defense is sure. / Before the hills in order stood, / or earth received her frame, / from everlasting Thou art God, / to endless years the same. / A thousand ages in Thy sight / are like an evening gone, / short as the watch that ends / the night before the rising sun. / O God, our help in ages past, / our hope for years to come / be thou our guide while life shall last, / and our eternal home" (Isaac Watts, "O God, Our Help in Ages Past").

Meditation: Loving Father, You have guided us under Your wing. We pray as we seal our marriage vows You would please guide us day by day and through all eternity. Amen.

CONCLUSION

This book contains a description of the "engagement year" before Grace and I married. That happy event occurred at First Baptist Church in Nashville, Tennessee, on January 2, 2016. It was a "formal event" with six at the wedding party. Dr. and Mrs. Lloyd Elder, Mr. and Mrs. Jack Knox, and Grace and me!

Dr. Elder performed the ceremony. His wife, Sue, read scripture, and Jack and Ann Knox stood as witnesses. It goes without saying Lloyd and Sue Elder are eternal friends. We have served together in God's calling since 1971. That included my role as interim Minister of Education at Gambrell Street Baptist Church, Fort Worth, Texas, where Lloyd served as pastor from 1969 to 1975. Though we knew each other as doctoral students at Southwestern Seminary, we became "brothers in ministry" during those years. After he served as assistant to the executive director at the Baptist General Convention of Texas, he returned to Southwestern Seminary as the executive vice president. My years of service on the Southwestern Seminary faculty began in 1962, so we were back together in a wonderful partnership. In 1983, he was elected president of the Baptist Sunday School Board (now LifeWay). In 1984, he asked me to serve as his assistant, and I was elected unanimously by the board of trustees. Later, in a corporate reorganization, I was appointed executive vice president. Though circumstances brought changes in our work roles, Lloyd and Sue Elder are and have been dear friends, and hardly a week goes by that we do not converse.

When Grace and I talked about the wedding, I insisted she choose the minister. She could have chosen her pastor or her beloved former pastor, Dr. Ken Story, but she said, "Since we want it to be a private wedding, how about Lloyd Elder?" In good faith, we wanted a private wedding, not having to expect a host of family and friends from Fort Worth and Memphis to attend. We wanted a church wedding, so we chose First Baptist, Nashville, because it was where Jo and I were members during my service at LifeWay. It is also where the elders continue in membership.

Jack and Ann Knox were chosen as witnesses for several reasons. First of all, Jack and Ann were close friends to Grace. Also, he had served as chairman of trustees at the Brotherhood Commission Southern Baptist Convention and knew Grace in that relationship. Jack, for years, operated a moving company, and his firm moved me from Nashville to Memphis when I was elected president of the Brotherhood Commission. When I retired and moved back to Fort Worth, again, Jack's firm provided moving services. Lastly, when Grace and I married, Jack was Grace's Sunday school teacher, and since that time until now, we have delighted to "sit under the feet" of a competent Bible teacher.

You may be wondering about a formal wedding in a large sanctuary with only six in attendance. It was formal. Grace's wedding gown was beautiful, as is she, and the men were in black. With thanks to Michael Valentine, music was "performed" by CDs; it included a wedding march, Josh Groban and Sarah Brightman's

"The Prayer," and Andrea Bocelli, supported by the Mormon Tabernacle Choir singing "The Lord's Prayer." Grace and I read our own vows, me with trembling hands. Sue read from 1 Corinthians 13, and Lloyd, as ever, was masterful in delivering the chosen ceremonial charge. Connie Bushy photographed, and Michael Vallentine videotaped the wedding. Lastly, we owe a great debt to Tom Crowe, who at the time was the executive pastor of the church. Tom arranged for the ceremony.

Following the wedding, we had a lovely dinner with the wedding party at the Opryland Hotel in Nashville. Grace and I spent our first night together in this beautiful facility. It was the end of the Christmas season, so the millions of lights and décor added much to the excitement of our "grand beginning."

After the days in Nashville, we returned to Memphis for a wedding reception for Memphis family and friends held at Germantown Baptist Church on January 10, 2016. A week later, we went to Fort Worth for a reception for my family, friends, and colleagues held at Gambrell Street Baptist Church. Each event was delightfully done, with guests able to watch the wedding video.

Our honeymoon, following the receptions, was a trip to a resort in St. Lucia. January was a good time to be on a warm Caribbean island in a fantastic resort with a private beach, nine restaurants, all-inclusive food, entertainment, and much more. A highlight was a two-mile zip-line excursion over the rainforest. (I'm not sure we could now handle all the steep stair-climbing.) It was a great week, and regardless of age or financial circumstances, a honeymoon is a must!

That was seven years ago, and in this our eighth year of life together, I am still being *surprised by grace*. It would require volumes to share the joys and delights of these years. That is one of the reasons we share our experiences in this book.

What We Learned

What kind of advice would we offer to those contemplating marriage, especially for those considering a second marriage? Much of what is recorded in this book is from two people in their eighties. It is never too late!

First of all, we would implore you to seek a godly partnership, with both partners committed to such a mission. You should be making emotional and spiritual investments in your relationship during the engagement and certainly in your marriage. That means maintaining open communication lines, providing mutual support, and practicing love for each other in all your actions and words. Mutual love grows from one to the other. Expect to love each other more and more. Most of all, immerse yourself in seeking to follow God's plan for marriage, found in Holy Scripture. Marriage is never perfect, but it is more so when behaving as those who keep searching for God's direction for marriage. If marriage flourishes through God-erected walls, what can you expect?

Secondly, there will be security for each if complete openness prevails. It begins with shared conversation. Grace and I can say anything to each other because we trust each other. We are secure in each other's love. We understand intercourse for marriage partners includes physical intercourse, and the tender and vibrant sex relationship is an essential part of it. But, a godly marriage also includes emotional, intellectual, and spiritual intercourse. When that is true, marriage partners are enmeshed in each other. Their hearts do safely trust in each other. I would also say the physical garden should be walled in. It is a sacred place, full of pleasure and fulfillment, and is like what one has called "the courtyard of the kingdom." This private kingdom is possible regardless of age.

Thirdly, in a God-sized marriage, there should be stability. It happens best when God is in control and rules. Grace and I each are committed to the New Testament concept of mutual submission as unto the Lord. That means that marriage is not a patriarchy. The husband is not a dictator. Rather, he is a spiritual leader (1 Corinthians 11:3). Neither should marriage be a matriarchy. Some wives want to exercise awesome power. A happy marriage is characterized by mutual consent. Then, marriage becomes a kingdom of peace.

In the material realm, stability is achieved when husband and wife demonstrate, through respectful dialogue, a consensus in every aspect of the decision-making process. Again, this requires discipline and shared responsibility. For example, we each have our own bank accounts but have a complete understanding of who pays what. God has given us adequate resources to meet our needs. This has happened because we never overspend our income. That means saving accounts and investments grow. At death, her saved resources go to her heirs, and mine likewise to my heirs. This is a principle we agreed to prior to marriage. And, thank God, we are financially secure, and our assets continue to increase in value.

This stability in marriage is strengthened because we have given ourselves the freedom to maintain individual identity. That answers the question, "Who is in charge?" It is not, "I am in charge," or the spouse says, "I am in charge." Our marriage is growing because we say truthfully, "We are in charge!" That provides the best context for decision-making. Ultimately, we joyfully say, "God is in charge."

The last piece of advice we offer is this: recognize that if God is in control, there develops a harmony of beliefs. Out of that richness of fidelity, serenity occurs. It means this harmony of beliefs produces a peaceful serenity—oneness of goals. When God enables marriage partners to mutually participate in all that is important, confusion is eliminated, and serenity exists, you may ask, "How is that achieved?"

First of all, our marriage exists within the reality of Christ's Lordship. As believers, we worship corporately with our church congregation. That experience of worship is enhanced by regular attendance in a Bible study group. Then, each day, following breakfast, we have a special time of worship. Typically, that includes reading a chapter from the Bible, a book at a time. Next, we read a printed devotional, like the ones in this book. Each major denomination and respected spiritual leaders market these materials. They are numerous and are readily available in bookstores and the internet, both dated and undated. Finally, our family worship includes a prayer time. Always, we thank God for His attributes and especially His redemption plan for mankind. For Christian believers, it is a joy each day to renew our allegiance to Jesus Christ and give thanks for His eternal salvation provided for each believer. Lastly, the prayer time ends with intercessory prayer for family, friends, the church, our nation, and its leaders. Finally, we pray for our world and its need for peace.

Is it possible for you to take this advice? Some of you may long to start over and rebuild your marriage. You can if you really want to reshape your marriage nearer to your heart's desire. Those choosing a second marriage can have a fresh start. In this book, you have read how we prepared for a new union. It did not happen on its own. Much dialogue occurred. The building of our friendship occurred first. Next, we began to search for answers to the question, "What does this friendship mean?" It did not take long for us to think about a deeper friendship. Then, we believe a "spiritual connection" was made in our lives, which raised the question of a "permanent friendship." If marriage is to last, it must be based on meaningful and mutually desired bonding. When that happened for us, marriage began to be considered. The rest of the story is in this book.

As this friendship leading to marriage grows, each partner must act on the basis of their responsibilities rather than clinging to their rights. Then, a stronger welding of the relationship develops and grows. For us, we believe our personal relationship with Jesus enables us to love and give, to forgive and ask forgiveness, to forget ourselves, and, in so doing, to receive joyfully from our beloved. That means "each one" is on the "other team." Sometimes, in weakness, these actions are difficult. But, not so if each partner seeks to find those qualities and traits admirable in the other, never focusing on faults or failures. If these actions are made real, day by day, God will make your marriage ever more intimate and harmonious. Your marriage will be full of delight. That is true serenity.

One last word! Grace and I truly believe our marriage is a private "little kingdom." That kingdom is built on King Jesus. He can empower you to make it a reality. If you do not know the kingdom of our Lord Jesus, who is God's Son and our personal Savior and friend, we ask you to receive Him as your own personal Savior. Repent of your sins, trust Him by faith in His power of redemption, and follow Him as Lord of your life. One simple way to do that is to read Romans 3:23, Romans 6:23, and Romans 10:8–10. Ask God through His Spirit to help you believe in Him as you consent to these bedrock salvation realities. This "Roman Road" to eternal salvation provides a direct path to receive God's eternal grace and forgiveness. Both Grace and I received this eternal pardon in our earlier years. We want you to experience that same gift of eternal salvation if you have not done so. We promise you that if you do, you are in for amazing, incredible, indescribable *surprises of grace*!

BIBLIOGRAPHY

Barclay, William. *Barclay's Commentary.* Westminster John Knox Press, 1999

Browning, Elizabeth Barrett. *Sonnets from the Portuguese.* Hanover House, 1954

Chapman, Gary. *The Four Seasons of Marriage.* Tyndale House Publisher, 2012

Chapman, Gary. *The Marriage I've Always Wanted.* Moody Publisher, 2005

Croft, Roy. *I Love You.* Blue Mountain, 1979

Eggerich, Emerson, Dr. *Love and Respect.* Thomas Nelson, 2005

Evans, Tony. *Kingdom Marriage.* Focus on the Family, 2018

Gibran, Kihal. *The Complete Works of Kihal Gibran.* General Press, 2018

Grabe, Chris and Jenni. *The Rhythm of Us.* Nav Press, 2021

Harley, Wilard E. Jr. *His Needs, Her Needs.* Revell, 2013

Keller, Timothy and Inazu, John. *Uncommon Ground.* Thomas Nelson Publishers, 2021

Lucado, Max. *No Wonder They Call Him Savior.* Thomas Nelson Publishers, 2011

Lucado, Max. *Applause of Heaven.* Thomas Nelson Publishers, 2013

McCarty, Justin H. *If I Were King*. Good Press, 2012

Miller, Calvin. *The Singer: A Classic Retelling of Cosmic Conflict*. IVP Publisher, 2020

Perkins, Gloria. *The Immense Journey*. Vintage Publisher, 1959

Redding, David. A., *A Rose Will Grow Anywhere*. B and H Publishing Group, 1996

Richardson, Bobby. *The Bobby Richardson Story*. Revell, 1965

Robichaux, Chad. *Fight for Us: Win Back the Marriage God Intends for You*. Thomas Nelson, 2022

Thomas, Gary. *Sacred Marriage*. Zondervan, 2015

Tozer, A. W. *No Greater Love*. Bethany House Publisher, 2020

Wheat, Ed, and Gaye. *Intended for Pleasure*. Fleming H. Revell Company, 1981

Whittier, John G. *Eternal Goodness, One Hundred and One Famous Poems*. McGraw-Hill/Contemporary, 1958

Wilson, Dave, and Ann. *Vertical Marriage*. Zondervan, 2021

Wilcox, Ella Wheeler. *Poems of Passion*. Family Friends Poems, 1883

Printed in the USA
CPSIA information can be obtained
at www.ICGtesting.com
LVHW011658060424
776589LV00001B/3